Savoring India

WILLIAMS-SONOMA

Savoring India

Recipes and Reflections on Indian Cooking

Recipes and Text
JULIE SAHNI

General Editor
CHUCK WILLIAMS

Recipe Photography
ANDRE MARTIN

Food Stylist
SALLY PARKER

Travel Photography
MICHAEL FREEMAN

Illustrations
MARLENE McLOUGHLIN

Oxmoor
HOUSE®

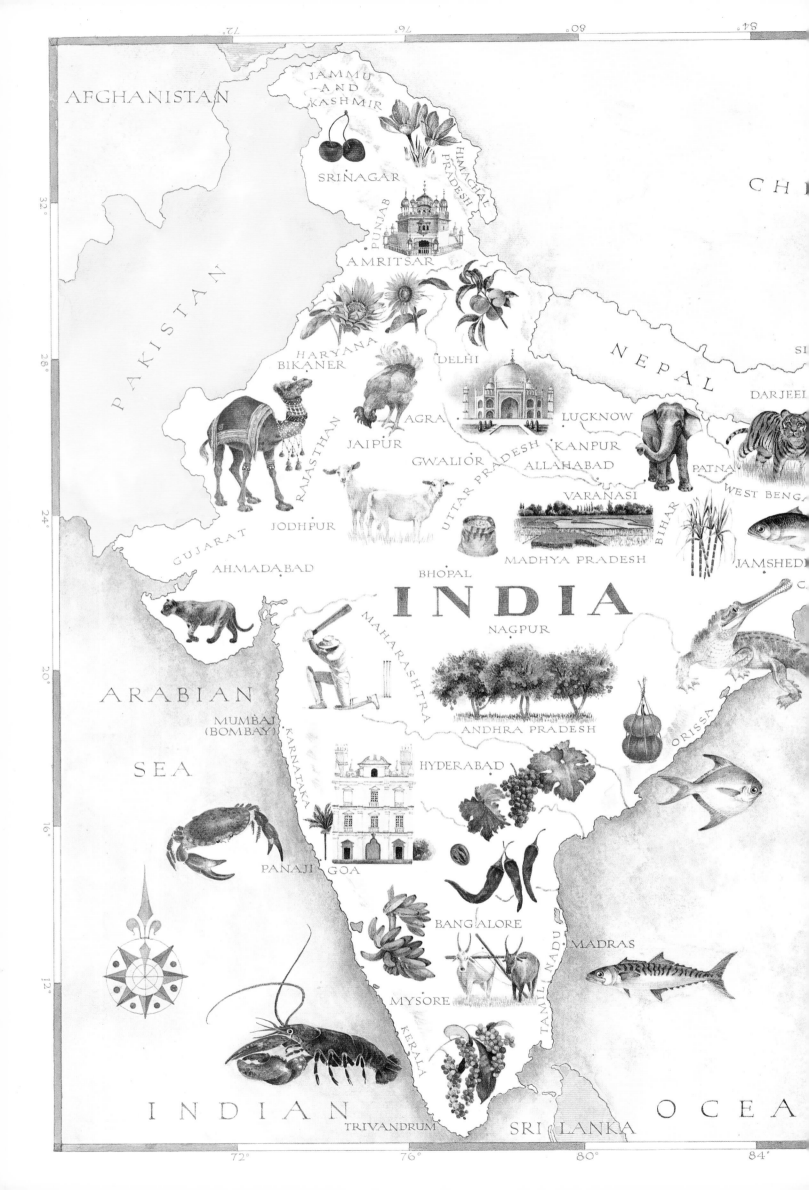

AFGHANISTAN

PAKISTAN

JAMMU -AND KASHMIR

SRINAGAR

HIMACHAL PRADESH

PUNJAB

AMRITSAR

HARYANA
BIKANER

DELHI

AGRA

NEPAL

SI

DARJEEL

LUCKNOW

JAIPUR

RAJASTHAN

GWALIOR

KANPUR

UTTAR PRADESH

ALLAHABAD

PATNA

WEST BENG

JODHPUR

GUJARAT

AHMADABAD

VARANASI

BIHAR

JAMSHED

BHOPAL

MADHYA PRADESH

INDIA

C

NAGPUR

ARABIAN

MAHARASHTRA

MUMBAI
(BOMBAY)

KARNATAKA

SEA

ANDHRA PRADESH

ORISSA

HYDERABAD

PANAJI

GOA

BANGALORE

MADRAS

TAMIL NADU

KERALA

MYSORE

INDIAN

TRIVANDRUM

SRI LANKA

OCEA

Contents

INTRODUCTION

The Indian Table

SOMEONE ONCE ASKED ME to explain a strange phenomenon: Whenever she went a week without Indian food, she developed cravings for the flavor of roasted cumin and cilantro, fried mustard seeds and ginger, green chiles and coconut. I told her that this was both natural and unavoidable. Spices, the cornerstone of Indian cooking, are seductive, and once the palate has become accustomed to them, their absence will be noticed.

It is the skillful blending of spices that gives Indian food its subtly magical flavors, aromas, and textures. Yet this is a cuisine that is often, initially, thought to be monotonous in its spiciness, one in which "spicy" is a byword for fiery, mouth-blistering heat. This perception reminds me of something the late connoisseur M. F. K. Fisher said during one of my visits to her home in Sonoma, California. "In many ways," she observed, "Indian food is like a grain of rice. Consider basmati, for instance." And she held out a few grains in her palm—Mary Frances, as I knew her, had a fondness for basmati, which I had the privilege of cooking for her a few times. "At its simplest," she continued, "it is like a plain old starch, but imagine the choices when you consider all the varieties of rice [some six thousand are grown worldwide], cooked using different cuisine styles and recipes!"

Indian food could indeed be equated with a grain of rice. On the surface it may seem homogeneous, all chile and heat,

Left: In Jaipur, Rajasthan, a dancer celebrates Holi, the elephant festival. **Above top:** India boasts a diverse array of edible plants that is drawn upon by its many vegetarians. **Above:** Buddhist prayer flags flutter at Mahakala Shrine on Observatory Hill in Darjeeling, Assam.

Above top: A bullock cart laden with brilliantly colored cotton cloth makes its way to market. Indians ascribe particular significance to some colors: red brings good fortune, black is bad luck (because it is associated with widowhood), and yellow signifies spring. **Above:** *Kolam*, or "painted prayers"—designs made out of rice or colored rice flour—are used to decorate the entrances and ritual altars of South Indian Brahmin houses. They are a form of worship of the elements, and are rendered in various designs, each with a specific meaning. **Right:** In a market, a cart displays various types of legumes. Inexpensive and rich in protein, these dried peas and beans are a vital part of the Indian diet.

but closer examination reveals a remarkable assemblage of many different ingredients, culinary techniques, and traditions. This is a truly diverse cuisine, its common feature being the imaginative—and judicious—layering of spices. An Indian restaurant might offer lamb roasted with cumin, garlic, and pomegranate; steamed dumplings of bamboo shoots, lemongrass, and soy; or fish braised in coconut, chiles, and ginger. Flat breads, sweet dinner rolls, stir-fried rice noodles, and rice crêpes could appear side by side. Accompaniments ranging from a cheese platter to bowls of tomato and onion, dried fish *sambal* (relish) with tamarind, or chile oil might be set down. A diner unfamiliar with Indian food might well wonder if this varied table were eastern Mediterranean, Middle Eastern, Central Asian, Southeast Asian, or Asian in origin. In fact, it is all of these and more. This is because the food of India has evolved to reflect the many and varied influences of its geography, its history, and the cultural and religious heritage of its people.

India comprises three distinctly different geographical land masses. The Himalayas, the long sweep of snow-covered mountain ranges, form the northern border. The cool, dry Indo-Gangetic plain (or Himalayan foothills) stretches from Punjab and the deserts of Rajasthan in the west through India's populous and fertile heartland, fed by the water and silt deposits of the mighty Brahmaputra and Ganges Rivers, to West Bengal and the Ganges delta in the east. The main (southern) peninsula, known as the Deccan plateau, is volcanic, humid, and fertile, flanked by the Arabian Sea to the west and the Bay of Bengal to the east. The moisture-laden winds that rise from these two bodies of water react with the protective barrier of the Himalayas, producing the famous monsoonal rains upon which India's harvests depend.

These fertile lands, replenished by the annual monsoon, have been farmed continuously for centuries, so that as early as 3000 BC, India had the fresh produce with which to develop a fairly sophisticated cuisine that included wheat and millet phulkas (puffed bread), fried breads, cooked vegetables such as eggplant, jackfruit, squashes, yams, beans, and greens,

and fruits such as berries and mangoes. Rice was cultivated on the Indo-Gangetic plain and in deepwater beds in southern India.

Meat, poultry, and fish were flavored with ghee, kari leaves, cardamom, black pepper, turmeric, cinnamon, mustard, coconut, ginger, tamarind, and citrus. But only a handful of these spices—such as kari leaf, cardamom, and pepper—were native to India. Some were introduced by traders. Contact with the Persians from the 2nd millenium BC brought saffron, as well as onions, garlic, pomegranates, dates, black mulberries, and the craft of cheese making. Many other spices, culinary techniques and cooking vessels were introduced by the steady waves of immigrants that have moved across the country since the Aryans of Central Asia first arrived, in 2000 BC. Some of these people came to rule and make fortunes; some offered an olive branch and assimilated, seeking spiritual enlightenment; while still others came to escape religious persecution.

Above top: Haridwar, in Uttar Pradesh, is the goal of countless Brahmin pilgrims. From *ghats* (steps) built on the banks of the Ganges, the faithful bathe in this most sacred of India's rivers. **Above:** Adobe houses are typical of Rajasthan. One house is initially built, then more are added as the family grows, until a compound is formed of independent, but related, structures. **Right:** Indians love the cheerful yellow and orange of marigolds. Garlands of them are popular for wedding decorations and *puja* (offerings to the gods).

The armies of Alexander the Great entered India in 327 BC, bringing special cooking pots, whose shapes are still used in southern India. Then came the Romans, bearing Mediterranean wine and spices such as coriander, cumin, and fennel. The Muslim sultans who ruled much of northern India in the 13th to 16th centuries are credited with introducing breads such as *paratha, lucchi,* nan, and *kulcha.* But by far the strongest influence on the cooking of the north came from the Moghuls, who dominated northern India from 1526 to 1761. They introduced the most sophisticated and opulent of cuisines (known as Moghul cooking or classic Indian cooking)—dishes enriched with cream and fruit purées, nuts, raisins, onions, and garlic, known for their delicate flavor. The royal kitchens also created a new spice combination, garam masala, to season *biriyanis* (layered meat and rice pilafs) and *kormas* (dishes braised in rich sauces).

Spices lured Portuguese traders, the first of the European colonizers, to India in the late 15th century, and by 1510 they had captured and colonized Goa, on the west coast. These traders, also zealous missionaries, married the

local women and converted them to Christianity. They also introduced cashews, papaya, maize, avocados, tomatoes, peanuts, potatoes, cocoa, pork, and perhaps most importantly, chile. In time, they created a cuisine second only to that of the Moghuls, with pork and seafood dishes a specialty. The culinary influence of later colonizers—the English, French, and Dutch—was less pronounced, although without the English, India would not have its world-famous Assam and Darjeeling teas.

Perhaps the most profound influence on Indian cuisine, however, is religion. Of India's approximately 1 billion people, 80 percent are Hindus. Jains, Buddhists, and Sikhs—once part of the Hindu faith—today form distinct cultural and religious communities. Their cuisines reflect their differences and the dietary laws of their religions, which forbid them to eat beef; indeed, Jains, Buddhists, and many Hindus are strict vegetarians. Also, Hindus of different castes cook and spice their food in different ways. Similar variation is found among the Muslims, India's largest religious minority, who comprise some 13 percent of the population but are not, contrary to popular belief, a single homogeneous group. Rather, they have different ancestries—Arab, Delhi Sultanate, Afghan, Moghul, Gulf, and Persian—and live in different regions. All form distinct cultural communities with distinctive cuisines, though all share the Muslim prohibition of pork. The Parsis (Zoroastrians of Persian origin) and Jews who came to India to escape religious persecution settled in Calcutta, Cochin, and Bombay. Jews omit pork from their diet, while Parsis do not eat beef; their cuisines are a rich fusion of European and Persian influences.

There is one final influence: the individual cook. Indian food is an intensely personal expression that reflects each cook's creative flair. How someone chooses to use coconut, for example—be it in slices, shreds, paste, milk, fried, roasted, or steamed—will result in the same recipe being transformed into several quite different dishes. Such personal touches create a complex and mysterious layering of flavors, adding depth and dimension to a cuisine that is both pleasing to the palate and intriguing and enjoyable to prepare.

Left: During Holi, the elephant festival, processions are led by elephants that have been lavishly adorned and brightly painted with auspicious symbols. **Above top:** A cyclist with milk cans attached to his vehicle makes his way along a Calcutta street. **Above:** After a meal, Indians like to chew betel leaves, or *pan*, along with spices such as fennel, cardamom, and cloves, to freshen the breath and aid digestion.

APPETIZERS AND SNACKS

Savories and snacks
stimulate the senses and
linger in the memory.

Preceding pages: A smiling street vendor expertly makes roti in Delhi's Chandni Chowk, one of India's most labyrinthine bazaars. **Above top:** One-third of the population of Jaisalmer, in Rajasthan, lives within the imposing walls of the city's massive fort. **Above:** A village woman cups water for her son to drink. **Right:** Sadhus renounce all worldly possessions and family and social ties to pursue a spiritual quest through meditation, pilgrimage, and the study of sacred texts. They carry cans in which well-wishers place alms in the form of food.

LIKE MANY OTHER seven-year-olds growing up in India, I had my first taste of snacks during my school lunch breaks. Our family cook typically packed a lovely boxed lunch of two flaky *parathas* (whole-wheat/wholemeal flat breads) carefully wrapped around a spicy, smoky mixture of potatoes and okra (this early introduction to okra must be the reason I adore it today). The neatly diced vegetables had been pan-roasted with cumin, coriander, black pepper, mango powder, and turmeric. No cilantro, mint, or kari leaf had been added. The absence of herbs in all take-out food is a cautionary measure, because any moisture from herbs can, in India's high temperatures, cause food to spoil. Some spices, such as turmeric and black pepper, do exactly the opposite; they act as antioxidants, retarding spoilage and thus keeping food tasting fresh. Ajowan seeds do the same, as well as acting as an effective digestive, and our cook took the extra precaution of adding some to the *parathas*. I didn't need any help with digestion, since I was getting enough exercise on the school cricket team, but I did appreciate the care she took to ensure that my lunch

remained fresh. The ajowan seeds also made the *parathas* taste particularly wonderful.

Given these fond memories of boxed meals, you might well assume that I sat through my prelunch class salivating. While it is true that I always waited impatiently for the bell to ring so that I could dash out of the classroom, the place to which I ran was not the dining area, where we sat with our lunch boxes, but rather the school *chatwala*-canteen. *Chatwala* means "*chat* salesman" or "*chat* chef." *Chat* originally referred to a specific spice-and-herb-laced salad, but today the term includes every conceivable Indian snack, from fried dumplings to fritters, fruit and noodle salads to tandoori meat tidbits. Technically speaking, all street foods are snacks, so they all qualify as *chat*.

The *chat* at the *chatwala*-canteen were the food of every Indian child's dreams—flaky, tangy, and spicy morsels, some a little too hot for a child's tolerance, but always irresistible. They were cooked by the canteen owner, an elderly Sikh gentleman, with the help of his wife and daughter, and I often slipped out of class a few minutes early to watch their last-minute preparations. I gazed at doughnut-shaped bean snacks called *bare* as they puffed and sputtered, turning from ivory white to golden brown. I watched the snack maker bend forward to knead a small mountain of dough for the samosas (vegetable dumplings) and *mathari* (savory crackers). I inhaled the salty aroma of chickpeas (garbanzo beans) that stood to drain after being simmered in *samundar jhag* (literally "ocean's foam," a briny mixture used by professional cooks to soften and plump legumes). I admired the crisp, golden samosas, stuffed with a gingery potato concoction, as they were lifted out of the smoking-hot oil. Next to the fire, vegetable,

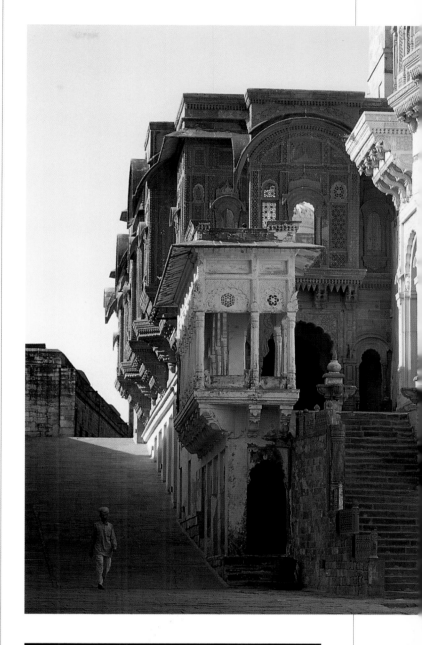

Left: According to a local saying, there are more coconut palms in southern India than there are stars in the sky. Coconut is an integral part of the region's cuisine, with coconut milk often replacing cow's milk. **Right top:** The desert state of Rajasthan—"Land of the Rajahs"—is dotted with the magnificent palaces and fortresses of its former rulers, such as Meherengarh Fort in Jodhpur. **Right:** An itinerant snack seller in Lucknow, Uttar Pradesh, carries his tray of wares expertly balanced atop his head.

Left: Roadside vendors cater to the Indian passion for snacks at any time of the day. **Below:** The markets on which most Indians rely may be large affairs, such as this one in Panjim, Goa, or simply a meeting of a few villagers at a rural crossroads. **Right:** The day's last light silhouettes *chhatri*s (temples) and bathers on the banks of the Betwa River in Orchha, Madhya Pradesh. **Below right:** A brightly decorated flask contains *usli ghee*, or clarified butter. A primary source of protein for India's vegetarians, it is also used to light lamps in temples.

cheese, and chile fritters laced with pomegranate and cumin were laid out, alongside a cool, tart, and tangy crispy noodle salad, the latter essential to balance the heat of the potato-and-pea patties piled nearby.

I never had my fill of snacks from the school *chatwala*-canteen except once, when I managed to buy four *samosas* and eat them all by myself at a single sitting. Usually, the canteen owner never sold anyone more than two pieces of a particular snack. He wanted to make sure every student got some because he made only a few of each type. Even today, the thought of those *samosas* and their seductive aromas makes me long for just a single bite.

This yearning for snacks is not mine alone. All Indians love snacking—almost as much as they love going to the cinema, or, as it is called in India, the *Desi* cinema (*desi* means "native" or "Indian"). More movie tickets are sold in India than in the rest of the world combined, and the moviegoing experience would not be complete without a hot, spicy, crispy treat, such as *masala kaju* (spiced cashews), *yera varuval* (spicy fried shrimp), *mathari,* or *pappadums* (lentil wafers), on which to nibble. So it is only natural that the street corners of Indian towns and cities, especially those around movie houses, are crowded with *chatwala* stalls.

My cinema snack of choice, the one on which my generation grew up, is *chipas,* the cayenne-laced potato chips that make the mouth burn with the same melodramatic intensity as the *Desi* cinema. With each betrayal of the heroine, I would take two quick bites of my *chipas* and join her as she cried her heart out. I never knew whether the tears

that cascaded down my cheeks were due to sympathy for her plight or the spicy heat let loose on my palate.

Chat do not always come in the form of appetizers and savories, however. For centuries, *chatwalas* at snack stalls in the mountainous areas of northern India have been serving steaming bowls of soup, to be enjoyed in place of a cup of tea. In recent years, soups have appeared alongside snacks at some urban stalls, where they are carefully paired and served as a soup-and-savory combination. A cup of piping-hot tomato or *mulligatawny* (curried chicken) soup with a crisp bean dumpling or corn puff makes a wonderfully warming combination on a cold wintry day. *Chatwalas* in many of the more humid regions of India actually specialize in soups, which help to activate the salivary glands and to aid in the vital replenishment of water lost through perspiration in the steamy climate. Soups are delicious with rice, bread, *pappadums,* or *mathari,* although I also serve them by themselves. In the south they are traditionally eaten from disposable *katori* (bowls) made of banana

leaves, and in the north from small metal *katori* on a *thali* (an individual platter).

Snacks such as *samosas,* kabobs, fritters of Bombay duck, potato, or eggplant, corn puffs, and yam and corn dumplings can be served all at once on a banana leaf or a *thali* in the traditional Indian style. Because these snacks are often fried, they are rich and quickly stimulate the taste buds. Take care to serve them in moderation, for they are intended only to tease and stimulate the palate, not to satisfy the appetite fully.

Many snacks, whether savories, appetizers, or soups, can be made ahead of time, then reheated at a moment's notice for an elegant beginning to a meal. Savories and appetizers are also delicious at room temperature, enjoyed between meals or eaten as finger food at a party. *Chat* are a treat not to be missed, stimulating the senses at the moment they are eaten, and then lingering in the memory just as those long-ago school lunch *samosas* remain fresh in my mind today.

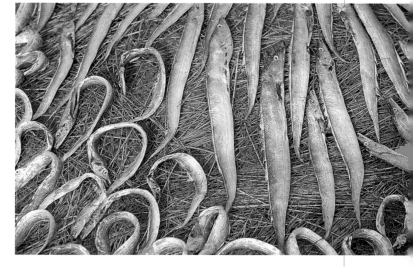

Left top: Some remnants of the British Raj, such as these bandsmen in Bikaner, Rajasthan, live on in modern India. **Left bottom:** The waters of the Arabian Sea, off India's southwestern coast, yield an abundance of shellfish, sardines, and mackerel, resulting in a local cuisine that is rich in seafood. **Above top:** The films produced by India's thriving movie industry are advertised on vivid billboards such as this one being wheeled across a street in Jaipur, Rajasthan. **Above:** Off the coast of Maharashtra, fishermen catch large quantities of Bombay duck, a fish that is then dried in the sun to make a popular, pungent snack.

Punjab

Aloo Samosa

savory pastries with vegetable stuffing

Anyone who has ever eaten at an Indian restaurant has most likely tried—and fallen in love with— samosas. Generally served as an appetizer, samosas are crisp, flaky-crusted, fried pastries with fragrant fillings. The most popular are filled with potatoes and peas, although it is not unusual to find others stuffed with lamb, chicken, lentils, or nuts.

In Punjab, Uttar Pradesh, and Delhi, samosas are the favorite nibble sold by street vendors and teashops. Their seductive shape and flavor make them perfect finger food for cocktail parties. For a simple family meal, I like to serve samosas with soup or a salad. Although they are traditionally served hot, straight out of the frying pan, they are equally delicious at room temperature and are therefore ideal for buffets or picnics. For variety, replace half the baking potatoes with sweet potatoes or yam.

FILLING

3–4 baking potatoes, about 1¼ lb (625 g) total weight, unpeeled and quartered

1 tablespoon ground coriander

1 teaspoon cayenne pepper

1 teaspoon ground pomegranate seeds (page 250) or 2 teaspoons fresh lemon juice

½ teaspoon ground turmeric

2 teaspoons salt, or to taste

2 tablespoons vegetable oil

1 cup (5 oz / 155 g) cooked fresh or thawed frozen green peas

1 teaspoon dried mint, crushed

PASTRY

2 cups (10 oz / 315 g) all-purpose (plain) flour, plus extra for dusting

1 teaspoon salt, or to taste

½ teaspoon baking powder

¼ cup (2 fl oz / 60 ml) vegetable oil

⅔ cup (5 fl oz / 160 ml) water

¼ cup (1 oz / 30 g) cornstarch (cornflour) dissolved in ½ cup (4 fl oz / 125 ml) water

vegetable oil for deep-frying

Tamarind Chutney (page 185) or Mint Chutney (page 210) (optional)

☙ To make the filling, boil the potatoes until very soft, about 15 minutes. Drain and, when cool enough to handle, peel and place in a bowl. Using a potato masher, mash until finely crushed. (Do not use a food processor, as this will make the potatoes gluey.) Add the ground coriander, cayenne pepper, pomegranate seeds or lemon juice, turmeric, salt, and oil. Mix well.

☙ Heat a large nonstick frying pan over high heat until very hot. Add the potato mixture, reduce the heat to low, and dry-fry, stirring, until the spices are fragrant and the potatoes are lightly fried, about 8 minutes. Return the potato mixture to the same bowl. Fold in the peas and mint and set aside to cool completely.

☙ To make the pastry, in a large bowl combine the flour, salt, and baking powder. In a measuring cup, stir the oil into the water. Add the liquid to the flour, a little a time, until the dough comes together in a mass that can be kneaded. (Do not add more liquid than necessary; you might have up to 2 table-spoons of oiled water left over.) Turn out onto a floured work surface and knead for 1 minute. Cover with a cloth or wrap in plastic wrap and let rest at room temperature for 30 minutes.

☙ On a floured surface, roll the dough into a rope about 18 inches (45 cm) long, and cut into 8 equal pieces. Form each piece into a ball and then flatten it into a patty. Working with 1 patty at a time, roll out into a 6-inch (15-cm) circle, dusting often with flour. Cut the circle in half. Brush half of the straight edge of 1 semicircle with the cornstarch mixture. Form a cone by bringing the halves of the straight edge together; pinch the seam to seal. Holding the cone with the open end toward you, stuff it with 3 heaping teaspoons of the filling. Brush the edges of the open end of the cone with the cornstarch mixture and pinch the edges together to enclose the filling. Repeat with the remaining semicircle and then with the patties.

☙ In a *karhai*, deep-fryer, or large, deep pan, pour in oil to a depth of 3 inches (7.5 cm) and heat to 350°F (180°C) on a deep-frying thermometer. When the oil is ready, gently slip the pastries, a few at a time, into the oil. Do not crowd the pan or the *samosas* will not fry evenly. Fry, turning often, until golden, about 5 minutes. Using a slotted spoon, transfer to paper towels to drain. Keep warm in a low oven while you fry the remaining pastries in the same way.

☙ Serve the *samosas* by themselves or with the chutneys, if desired.

makes 16; serves 8

Uttar Pradesh

Kakori Kabab

royal lucknow kabobs

Since the eighteenth century, Lucknow, the capital of Uttar Pradesh, has been the home of the great Nawabs, the last in the Moghul empire's line of succession. It was in their royal courts and households that the extraordinary Nawabi cuisine originated. After India achieved independence in 1947, the Nawabs' powers dwindled, and many royal chefs left to open their own food stalls. Of all the preparations sold at these stalls, none is more popular than the sausage-shaped kakori kababs.

For a real kakori kabab *experience, one must visit the Hazratganj district in the old section of the city. Here the air is scented with the sweet aromas of cardamom, nutmeg, cumin, and roasting meats emanating from the kabob stalls. Made with ground lamb, powdered cashew nuts, roasted split peas, and fragrant spices,* kakori kababs *have an indescribable, complex flavor. Although traditionally sausage-shaped, they can also be formed into patties or balls. They taste best when charcoal-grilled, but may also be pan-grilled.*

Roasted split peas are available in Indian and Middle Eastern grocery stores. Green papaya adds a unique floral aroma to the kabobs, but is not essential; if it is unavailable, potato, jicama, zucchini, or underripe pear may be substituted.

1 teaspoon poppy seeds

3 tablespoons chickpea (garbanzo bean) flour or roasted split peas

2 tablespoons usli ghee *(page 247)*

1 small yellow onion, finely chopped

¼ cup (1 oz/30 g) cashew nuts, ground to a coarse powder in a food processor or mortar

1 tablespoon garam masala (page 249)

1 teaspoon ground black pepper

½ teaspoon ground cardamom

¼ teaspoon ground nutmeg

1 lb (500 g) ground (minced) lamb, beef, or goat

¼ cup (1 oz/30 g) grated green papaya (optional)

1 teaspoon salt

¼ teaspoon saffron threads, crushed

Mint Chutney (page 210)

❧ In a small, dry frying pan over high heat, toast the poppy seeds until they are fragrant and turn darker, about 4 minutes. If you are using chickpea flour, add it now and toast for 2 minutes more.

❧ Transfer to a mortar, blender, or coffee grinder reserved solely for spices and pound or process until powdered. If you are using split peas, add them now and pound or process until finely powdered.

❧ In a medium frying pan over medium-high heat, warm the *usli ghee*. When it is very hot, add the onion and cook, stirring often, until it is caramel brown, about 7 minutes. Stir in the cashew powder, garam masala, pepper, cardamom, and nutmeg. Transfer the mixture to a large bowl. Add the meat, papaya (if using), salt, saffron, and poppy seed mixture. Mix well and set aside for 30 minutes at room temperature for the flavors to blend. Divide the mixture into 16 portions. Using your hands, shape each portion into a sausage-shaped cylinder.

❧ The kabobs can be grilled or broiled. If using a charcoal grill, prepare a fire for direct-heat cooking. Position the grill rack 5 inches (13 cm) from the fire. Allow the coals to burn until white ash covers them and the heat is moderate. If using a broiler (griller), preheat it to the maximum temperature, positioning the broiler pan 5 inches (13 cm) from the element. Place the kabobs on the rack of the grill or broiler pan and cook, turning them 3 times, until cooked through and nicely browned, 8–11 minutes. Serve hot with the chutney.

makes 16; serves 4

Delhi

Chat

peach salad with mint and smoked cumin

The term chat *is used both for snacks in general and for this saladlike preparation designed to pique the appetite. Its primary seasoning is* chat masala, *a spice blend that includes roasted cumin, asafetida, black salt, mango powder, cayenne pepper, and black pepper. For a spicier, more robust flavor, add more* chat masala.

6 medium-ripe peaches

2 teaspoons fresh lemon juice

½ teaspoon cumin seeds

lettuce leaves

1½ teaspoons chat masala *(page 244)*

½ teaspoon salt

½ teaspoon finely grated lemon zest

¼ cup (¼ oz / 7 g) loosely packed fresh mint leaves

8 blackberries or 16 raspberries (optional)

❦ Bring a large saucepan three-fourths full of water to a boil and fill a large bowl with ice and water. Using a sharp knife, cut an X in the bottom of each peach and immerse the peaches in the boiling water for 30 seconds. Using a slotted spoon, transfer to the bowl of ice water to cool, then peel off the skin. Thinly slice the peaches. Immediately place the peach slices and lemon juice in a bowl and toss to coat the slices with the juice. (This prevents them from discoloring.)

❦ In a small, dry frying pan over high heat, roast the cumin seeds, tossing and shaking the pan, until they turn very dark brown, almost black, about 5 minutes. Remove from the heat and let cool for a few minutes, then lightly bruise them. (You can do this with a mortar and pestle or by putting the seeds in a paper or plastic bag on a work surface and running a rolling pin over them.)

❦ Line a platter with lettuce leaves. Add the *chat masala,* salt, lemon zest, and half of the mint to the peaches, toss well, and transfer to the platter. Scatter the cumin seeds, berries (if using), and the remaining mint leaves over the top. Serve immediately.

serves 6

Bombay Duck

Bombay duck is a favorite delicacy of the people of Maharashtra, a state on the west-central coast of India. It is not poultry, as its name implies, but a variety of tropical fish, *Harpodon nehereus*, which is abundant in Bombay's coastal waters. Each fish is about 16 inches (40 cm) long, with a silver-white, semitranslucent body. To catch its prey, the Bombay duck swims near the surface of the water. In the opinion of the local people, the fish's shiny appearance creates the illusion of a diving duck, hence its name.

Also called *bombil* or *bomla,* Bombay duck is sometimes eaten fresh but is more often dried before cooking. Geometric rows of these fish, gutted, salted, and hung to dry, are a spectacular sight along the beaches of Bombay. Fresh or dried, Bombay duck has a strong, distinct flavor that is an acquired taste for most people. Parsis (followers of the Zoroastrian religion, most of whom live in Maharashtra) are particularly fond of Bombay duck. Parsis cook the fish in curries and fritters. To appreciate its unique flavor, crisp-fry the dried fish and serve it like bacon.

Maharashtra

Sookha Bomla nu Cutless

dried bombay duck fritters

These are delicious, and fairly easy to prepare once you have the Bombay duck. Look for it in Indian grocery stores specializing in dried fish.

4 dried Bombay ducks (see sidebar, left)
½ cup (½ oz/15 g) fresh cilantro (fresh coriander), leaves and tender stems
¼ cup (1 oz/30 g) unsweetened flaked coconut
4 fresh hot green chiles such as serrano
1 large clove garlic
½ teaspoon ground cumin
½ teaspoon ground coriander
½ teaspoon salt
1½ teaspoons white wine vinegar
vegetable oil for frying
1 egg
1 cup (4 oz/125 g) dried bread crumbs
Tamarind Chutney (optional; page 185)

❧ Soak the Bombay ducks in cold water to cover for 3 hours. Drain, squeezing out as much water as you can, and pat dry on kitchen towels. Remove the head and tail from the fish and cut in half crosswise. Using your fingers, carefully remove the center bone and discard. Place the fish in a shallow bowl.

❧ In a food processor, blender, mortar, or grinding stone, combine the cilantro, coconut, chiles, garlic, cumin, ground coriander, salt, and vinegar. Process or pound until finely puréed. Rub the herb paste into the fish. Set aside to marinate for 10 minutes.

❧ In a large frying pan over high heat, pour in oil to a depth of ½ inch (12 mm) and heat to 350°F (180°C) on a deep-frying thermometer. Meanwhile, lightly beat the egg in a shallow dish, and spread the bread crumbs on a shallow plate. Dip each piece of fish into the egg, letting the excess drain off, then in the bread crumbs, pressing firmly to ensure they stick. When the oil is ready, gently slip a few pieces into it. Do not crowd the pan. Fry until golden brown, about 3 minutes. Using a slotted spoon, transfer to paper towels to drain. Keep warm in a low oven while you make the remaining fritters in the same way. Serve with the chutney, if desired.

serves 4

Karnataka

Katrika Bajji

eggplant fritters

Eggplant is a popular vegetable in Karnataka, especially in the form of spicy, asafetida-laced fritters.

1 lb (500 g) small to medium-sized eggplants (aubergines), cut into slices ⅛ inch (3 mm) thick

BATTER
1½ cups (7½ oz/235 g) chickpea (garbanzo bean) flour

¼ cup (1 oz/30 g) rice flour

2 teaspoons salt, or to taste

1 teaspoon cayenne pepper

1 teaspoon ground turmeric

½ teaspoon powdered asafetida (see sidebar, page 144) or 2 teaspoons minced garlic

2 tablespoons vegetable oil

1½ cups (12 fl oz/375 ml) hot water

vegetable oil for deep-frying

❦ Place the eggplant slices in a bowl with salted water to cover (using ½ teaspoon salt for each 1 cup/ 8 fl oz/250 ml water). This will keep them from discoloring while you make the batter.

❦ To make the batter, in a bowl, combine the chickpea flour, rice flour, salt, cayenne pepper, turmeric, asafetida or garlic, and oil. Mix until combined, then gradually add the hot water, stirring, until you have a pancakelike batter. (Depending upon the humidity, you may not need all of the water.) Whisk the batter until smooth.

❦ In a *karhai*, deep-fryer, or large frying pan, pour in oil to a depth of 1½ inches (4 cm) and heat it to 375°F (190°C) on a deep-frying thermometer. Meanwhile, drain the eggplant slices and pat them dry on paper towels. When the oil is ready, dip a few slices in the batter, letting the excess drain off, then gently slip them into the oil. Do not crowd the pan. Fry, turning frequently with tongs, until golden, about 4 minutes. Using a slotted spoon, transfer to paper towels to drain. Keep warm in a low oven while you fry the remaining fritters in the same way. Serve immediately.

serves 6

Maharashtra

Dahi Shorva

chilled fruity yogurt soup

The influence of the British Raj on Bombay's cuisine is reflected in this soup. The contrast of sweet pineapple against the tart yogurt and pungent mustard seeds is deliciously bold on the palate.

1 cup (8 fl oz/250 ml) chicken stock, vegetable juice, tomato juice, or water

4 cups (2 lb/1 kg) plain yogurt

3 teaspoons finely chopped fresh mint

1 teaspoon salt, or to taste

ground black pepper to taste

1 cup (6 oz/185 g) finely diced pineapple, peach, or nectarine

1 tablespoon vegetable oil or usli ghee *(page 247)*

¾ teaspoon brown mustard seeds

1 tomato, seeded and finely diced

❦ If using homemade stock, boil it for 3 minutes to kill any bacteria, then allow to cool before using.

❦ In a bowl, combine the stock, juice, or water; yogurt; 1 teaspoon of the mint; and salt and pepper to taste. Beat with a whisk or a fork until well blended and smooth. Stir in the fruit.

❦ In a small frying pan over high heat, warm the oil or *usli ghee*. When very hot, add the mustard seeds and cover the pan. When the seeds stop sputtering, after about 30 seconds, uncover, add the tomato, and immediately remove from the heat. Toss to coat the tomato with the spices.

❦ Ladle the yogurt soup into bowls. Divide the tomato mixture evenly among the bowls, making sure to get every drop of the spice oil. Sprinkle with the remaining 2 teaspoons mint and chill for at least 2 hours before serving.

serves 4–6

Makka Poa

corn puffs

I was served these scrumptious corn fritters—studded with sweet bell peppers, green onion, and cilantro and scented with cumin and garam masala—at the Cricket Club of Bombay. An iced beer was the perfect accompaniment.

1¾ cups (9 oz / 280 g) all-purpose (plain) flour

2 teaspoons baking powder

1½ teaspoons salt

1 teaspoon cumin seeds, roasted (page 246)

1 teaspoon garam masala (page 249)

¾ cup (6 fl oz / 180 ml) milk

1 egg, beaten

1 tablespoon unsalted butter, melted

1 cup (6 oz / 185 g) fresh or thawed frozen corn kernels

½ cup (1½ oz / 45 g) thinly sliced green (spring) onions, including tender green tops

½ cup (2½ oz / 75 g) minced red bell pepper (capsicum)

½ cup (¾ oz / 20 g) chopped fresh cilantro (fresh coriander)

vegetable oil for deep-frying

Tamarind Chutney (optional; page 185)

In a bowl, combine the flour, baking powder, salt, cumin, and garam masala. In a small bowl, whisk the milk, egg, and butter. Pour over the flour mixture. Mix quickly to form a lump-free batter. Fold in the corn, green onion, bell pepper, and cilantro.

In a *karhai,* deep-fryer, or large frying pan, pour in oil to a depth of 1½ inches (4 cm) and heat to 375°F (190°C) on a deep-frying thermometer. Using a teaspoon or a melon baller, gently slip heaping spoonfuls of the batter, a few at a time, into the oil. Do not crowd the pan. Fry the puffs, turning occasionally, until they are golden, about 5 minutes. Using a slotted spoon, transfer to paper towels to drain. Keep warm in a low oven while you cook the remaining puffs in the same way.

Serve hot or at room temperature with the chutney, if desired.

serves 6

Andhra Pradesh

Aloo Bhajia

potato fritters

Every state in India has its distinct fritter recipe. This one, from Andhra Pradesh, is very spicy and quite delicious. The fritters are just as tasty when made with zucchini, pumpkin, or eggplant.

¾ lb (375 g) Yukon gold or new potatoes

BATTER

1½ cups (7½ oz/235 g) chickpea (garbanzo bean) flour

2 teaspoons ground cumin

1–2 teaspoons cayenne pepper

1 teaspoon nigella seeds (optional; page 250)

1 teaspoon salt

¾ teaspoon ground turmeric

1 cup (8 fl oz/250 ml) hot water

vegetable oil for deep-frying

☀ Slice the unpeeled potatoes ⅛ inch (3 mm) thick and place in a bowl. Add water to cover and set aside.

☀ To make the batter, in a bowl, combine the chickpea flour, cumin, cayenne pepper to taste, nigella (if using), salt, turmeric, and hot water. Whisk until smoothly blended.

☀ In a *karhai,* deep-fryer, or large frying pan, pour in oil to a depth of 1½ inches (4 cm) and heat to 375°F (190°C) on a deep-frying thermometer. Meanwhile, drain the potato slices and pat them dry on paper towels. When the oil is ready, dip a few slices in the batter, allowing the excess to drain off, then gently slip them into the oil. Do not crowd the pan. Fry, turning frequently, until golden, about 4 minutes. Using a slotted spoon, transfer to paper towels to drain. Keep warm in a low oven while you fry the remaining slices in the same way. Serve at once.

serves 6

Karnataka

Mulligatawny

curried chicken and vegetable soup

Mulligatawny *means "pepper-water," and this soup, from the Mangalore Christians of Karnataka, is traditionally spicy hot. If desired, half a duck may replace the chicken; the cooking times will be the same.*

1 chicken, about 3 lb (1.5 kg), cut into
8–10 serving pieces and skinned

1 small bunch fresh cilantro (fresh coriander)

2 black or 4 green cardamom pods, lightly bruised

2 cassia leaves (page 244), broken into bits

6 cups (48 fl oz/1.5 l) water

2 cups (10 oz/310 g) finely chopped yellow onion

2 carrots, peeled and chopped

2 boiling potatoes, peeled and chopped

1½ cups (9 oz/280 g) chopped tomato

2 tablespoons cornstarch (cornflour) dissolved in
¼ cup (2 fl oz/60 ml) water, if needed

1 cup (8 fl oz/250 ml) coconut milk, light
(single) cream, or milk

1½ teaspoons salt, or to taste

¼ cup (2 oz/60 g) usli ghee (page 247) or
unsalted butter

1 tablespoon minced garlic

2 teaspoons ground cumin, garam masala
(page 249), or curry powder (page 249)

ground black pepper to taste

1¼ cups (6½ oz/200 g) hot cooked long-grain
white rice (optional)

juice of 1 lemon

½ cup (2 oz/60 g) sliced (flaked) almonds, toasted

☸ Place the chicken pieces in a large, heavy pot and scatter the cilantro, cardamom, and cassia leaves on top. Add 2 cups (16 fl oz/500 ml) of the water and bring to a boil over high heat. Reduce the heat to low, cover, and cook, occasionally skimming off any foam that rises to the surface, until the chicken is opaque throughout and firm to the touch, about 30 minutes. Using tongs, transfer the chicken pieces to a plate. When cool enough to handle, pull the meat from the bones and return the bones to the pot. Shred the meat neatly, cover, and and set aside.

☸ Add the remaining 4 cups (32 fl oz/1 l) water to the cooking liquid and bring to a gentle boil over medium-high heat. Reduce the heat to low, cover,

and boil gently for 30 minutes. Remove from the heat, strain through a fine-mesh sieve, and return the stock to the pot. Discard the contents of the sieve.

☸ Add 1 cup (5 oz/155 g) of the onion along with the carrots, potatoes, and tomato and bring to a boil over high heat. Cover, reduce the heat to medium-low, and cook until the vegetables are very soft, about 25 minutes. Remove from the heat and, working in batches, purée the soup in a food processor or blender until smooth. Strain the soup, if necessary, to remove lumps, and return it to the pot. It should be the consistency of a cream soup. If it is not, stir in as much of the cornstarch solution as needed to thicken it. Heat the soup until it is piping hot. Add the coconut milk, cream, or milk and salt to taste. Simmer gently over very low heat while you make the garnish.

☸ In a small frying pan over medium-high heat, melt the *usli ghee* or butter. Add the remaining 1 cup (5 oz/155 g) onion, the garlic, and cumin, garam masala, or curry powder. Sauté, stirring, until the onion is nicely browned, about 5 minutes. Add the shredded chicken and salt and pepper to taste. Sauté, tossing the chicken, until lightly seared and well coated with spices, about 3 minutes.

☸ To serve, place about 2½ tablespoons rice (if using) in each warmed bowl and ladle in the piping hot soup. Place the chicken on top and sprinkle with the lemon juice and almonds. Serve at once.

serves 8

Assam and West Bengal
Masaledar Gurda

kidneys on toast

Long ago, during my first visit to Assam, I was served these wonderful Raj-style braised kidneys on toast. Organ meats are very popular with meat-eating Indians, and this recipe can be prepared with lamb liver, sweetbreads, or, for a different but delightful flavor, chicken liver.

6 lamb or goat kidneys

½ cup (4 fl oz/125 ml) milk

¼ cup (1½ oz/45 g) all-purpose (plain) flour

salt and ground black pepper to taste

¼ cup (2 oz/60 g) usli ghee (page 247) or unsalted butter

1 teaspoon fresh lemon juice

¼ cup (1½ oz/45 g) minced yellow onion

1 teaspoon minced garlic

1 teaspoon ground cumin

1 teaspoon ground coriander

½ teaspoon cayenne pepper

½ teaspoon ground turmeric

⅛ teaspoon ground cinnamon

2 tomatoes, cored and finely chopped

¾ cup (6 fl oz/180 ml) water

2 teaspoons tomato paste

4 slices white bread

2 tablespoons finely chopped fresh cilantro (fresh coriander)

❧ Carefully trim away the skin of the kidneys and remove the veins. Cut each kidney into quarters and soak in the milk for at least 15 minutes, or preferably 1 hour. Drain the kidneys, discard the soaking milk, and pat the kidneys thoroughly dry on paper towels. On a large plate, combine the flour, salt, and a generous amount of black pepper.

❧ In a large nonstick frying pan over medium-high heat, warm half of the *usli ghee* or butter until very hot. Dust the kidney pieces in the seasoned flour, shaking off any excess, and add them to the pan. Cook, tossing and turning, until the kidneys are lightly seared all over, about 3 minutes. Transfer to a plate and sprinkle with the lemon juice.

❧ Add the remaining ghee or butter and the onion and garlic to the pan. Cook over high heat, stirring, until the onion is glazed, about 3 minutes. Stir in the cumin, coriander, cayenne pepper, turmeric, and cinnamon and mix well.

❧ Add the tomatoes and cook over medium-high heat until they are soft and begin to caramelize, about 5 minutes. Stir in the water and tomato paste and bring to a boil.

❧ Drain the kidneys and add them to the sauce. Reduce the heat to low, cover, and cook, checking and stirring occasionally to ensure that the sauce is not sticking and burning, until it is reduced and thick enough to coat the kidneys, about 15 minutes. Meanwhile, toast the bread and trim off the crusts.

❧ Check and correct the seasonings. Fold in the cilantro and serve the kidneys and sauce spooned over the warm toast.

serves 6

Uttar Pradesh
Masala Kheera

chilled spiced cucumbers

A common sight in India during the summer are pushcarts selling refreshing iced slices of watermelon, coconut, and cucumber. Spiked with taste-tingling spices such as chat masala *and black salt, they momentarily make you forget the scorching heat.*

2 very small, tender cucumbers, preferably Kirby variety, peeled and quartered lengthwise

juice of 1 lime

1 teaspoon chat masala (page 244) or cumin seeds, roasted and ground (page 246)

salt to taste

¼ teaspoon cayenne pepper (optional)

¼ teaspoon ground black salt (optional; see sidebar, page 167)

❧ Arrange the cucumbers on a chilled plate. Sprinkle with the lime juice, *chat masala* or cumin, salt, and cayenne pepper (if using) and serve at once. If you are using the black salt, sprinkle it over the cucumbers, then wait for 3 minutes before serving to let the aromas settle.

serves 4

Maharashtra

Shakkaravellikayangu Bonda

yam dumpling with roasted corn and cinnamon

Bondas—*spicy balls of mashed vegetables, dipped in chickpea batter and deep-fried—are classic snack-time treats that are traditionally served with a beverage such as coffee or tea. In many southwestern and southern states, they are often on the menu in restaurants and coffee shops. The filling is left entirely up to the discretion of the cook. Although the most common are plain potato* bondas, *those made with sweet potatoes, pumpkin, cauliflower, cabbage, or any combination thereof are becoming very popular.*

Depending on how much you mash the filling, its texture can be varied—from smooth and creamy, like mashed potatoes, to coarse and chunky, like hash browns. For best results, let the filling chill in the refrigerator for at least an hour. This will allow the filling to firm up and the nuts to absorb any excess moisture from the sweet potatoes or yams.

2 sweet potatoes or yams, about 1 lb (500 g) total weight

½ teaspoon ground cinnamon

½ teaspoon salt, or to taste

2 teaspoons fresh lemon juice

1 ear of corn, husks and silk removed

1 tablespoon vegetable oil

½ teaspoon brown mustard seeds

1 yellow onion, finely chopped

¼ cup (1 oz/30 g) finely chopped pecans or cashew nuts

BATTER

1¾ cups (8½ oz/265 g) chickpea (garbanzo bean) flour

¾ teaspoon baking powder

¾ teaspoon cracked black pepper

¾ teaspoon salt, or to taste

1¼ cups (10 fl oz/310 ml) hot water

1 tablespoon vegetable oil

vegetable oil for deep-frying

☙ Preheat an oven to 400°F (200°C). Place the sweet potatoes or yams on a baking sheet and bake until they are tender when pierced with a knife, about 45 minutes. Remove from the oven and, when cool enough to handle, peel and place in a bowl. Add the cinnamon, salt, and lemon juice and mash together with a fork or potato masher. Set aside.

☙ While the potatoes or yams are baking, use tongs to hold the ear of corn directly over the gas flame on the stove top, turning as needed to color evenly. Roast until evenly covered with several brown spots, about 5 minutes. Watch carefully, as the corn can burn and char easily. (Light charring is acceptable as it will enhance the overall flavor.) If you do not have a gas burner, place the corn on a wire rack over an electric burner and roast, turning, until it is evenly covered with brown spots, about 5 minutes.

☙ Hold the roasted ear stem end down on a cutting board and, using a sharp knife, cut down the length of the ear to remove the kernels in a layer about ⅛ inch (3 mm) thick. Rotate the ear with each cut until it is fully stripped. Add the corn kernels to the potato or yam and stir to combine.

☙ In a small frying pan over medium-high heat, warm the oil. When hot, add the mustard seeds and cover the pan. When the seeds stop sputtering, after about 30 seconds, uncover and add the onion. Cook, stirring occasionally, until the onion is brown and caramelized, about 6 minutes. Pour the contents of the pan over the yam mixture. Add the nuts and mix until thoroughly combined. Cover and refrigerate for 1 hour to allow the mixture to firm up.

☙ Divide the mixture into 16–20 portions. Lightly oil your hands and roll each portion into a ball. If making the balls ahead of time, arrange them on a baking tray in a single layer, cover, and refrigerate until you are ready to cook them. (The chilled balls hold their shape better and are easier to fry.)

☙ In a *karhai,* deep-fryer, or large frying pan, pour in oil to a depth of 1½ inches (4 cm) and heat to 375°F (190°C) on a deep-frying thermometer. Meanwhile, make the batter: In a bowl, combine the chickpea flour, baking powder, pepper, salt, hot water, and oil. Whisk until smooth. Dip a few of the balls into the batter, allowing the excess to drip off, and slip them into the hot oil. Do not crowd the pan. Fry, turning frequently with tongs, until the balls are nicely browned, about 4 minutes. Using a slotted spoon, transfer to paper towels to drain. Keep warm in a low oven while you fry the remaining balls the same way. Serve hot or at room temperature.

makes 16–20; serves 4–6

The Market

Every community, from such large, cosmopolitan cities as Bombay to the smallest rural villages that dot the coasts and deserts, boasts about its central open-air market. Indian cooks, who like to buy their groceries fresh at least every few days, if not every day, visit these traditional shopping places that are known by everyone simply as "the market."

Everything for the kitchen is available here; farm-fresh *gobhi* (cauliflower), *baigan* (eggplant/aubergine), *bhindi* (okra), and other vegetables; leafy green herbs; fragrant mangoes and perfectly ripe bananas; fish such as pomfret; shellfish; meat; and live poultry. Stalls sell special salts, local palm sugar, freshly pressed cooking oils, pickles and chutneys typical of the area, and the spice blends, or *masalas,* that play such an important role in the cooking of each region. Cooks can also buy clay pots (*chetti*) for cooking, iron griddles (*tava*) for baking breads, grinding stones (*sil-batta*) for making spice pastes, and cooking fuels such as wood charcoal, haycakes, and types of woodchips.

A place that dazzles the senses with its vibrant colors, sounds, and heady aromas, the market reflects the strength, variety, and vitality of Indian regional life.

Uttaranchal

Kaddoo ka Shorva

cream of pumpkin soup

Indian pumpkins, intensely orange and aromatic, are available in specialty stores and Indian grocery stores. Mexican calabash, sugar pumpkins, butternut squash, and buttercup squash may be substituted. For a spicier soup, double the amount of curry powder.

2 lb (1 kg) pumpkin or butternut or acorn squash

2 tablespoons usli ghee (page 247) or butter

2 yellow onions, chopped

1 teaspoon curry powder (page 249)

¼ teaspoon ground ginger

¼ teaspoon ground cinnamon

2 teaspoons sugar

3 cups (24 fl oz/750 ml) chicken stock or water

1½ cups (12 fl oz/375 ml) milk

1½ teaspoons salt, or to taste

2 teaspoons lemon juice

½ cup (4 fl oz/125 ml) heavy (double) cream (optional)

2 tablespoons sliced pistachios (optional)

❦ If using a piece of pumpkin or squash, peel it, scrape out the seeds, and cut the flesh into 1-inch (2.5-cm) pieces. If using a whole squash, first cut it in half. (Use a kitchen mallet to drive the knife through the tough skin.) Proceed as above.

❦ In a deep saucepan over medium–high heat, warm the *usli ghee* or butter. When hot, add the onions, curry powder, ginger, and cinnamon and cook, stirring occasionally, until the onions begin to brown, about 8 minutes. Sprinkle with the sugar and cook for 1 minute longer. Add the pumpkin or squash and chicken stock or water and bring to a boil. Reduce the heat to low, cover, and simmer until the pumpkin or squash is tender, about 20 minutes.

❦ Remove from the heat and, working in batches, purée in a food processor or a blender until smooth. Return the soup to the pan and stir in the milk and salt. Heat until the soup is piping hot, then stir in the lemon juice. Check and correct the seasonings and consistency; it should be the consistency of a cream soup. If it is too thick, add a little water. Ladle the soup into warmed bowls. Garnish with the cream and pistachios, if desired, and serve at once.

serves 6–8

Uttar Pradesh

Kabab

cocktail kabobs

This kabob recipe comes from the Muslim community in Agra, the home of the beautiful Taj Mahal. The kabobs may be made larger and served as a main dish.

2 tablespoons vegetable oil

1 cup (5 oz/155 g) finely chopped yellow onion

1 lb (500 g) ground (minced) beef, lamb, or goat

1½ teaspoons garam masala (page 249) or ground cumin

1 teaspoon salt, or to taste

⅛ teaspoon ground cloves

¼ cup (⅓ oz/10 g) finely chopped fresh cilantro (fresh coriander)

4 fresh mild green chiles such as Anaheim, minced

1 egg

1 slice white bread, crusts removed

2 tablespoons milk

Tamarind Chutney (page 185) or Mint Chutney (page 210)

❦ In a large nonstick frying pan over medium–high heat, warm the oil. When hot, add the onion and cook, stirring often, until it turns caramel brown, about 9 minutes. Transfer to a bowl and add the meat, garam masala or cumin, salt, cloves, cilantro, chiles, and egg.

❦ In a small bowl, soak the bread in the milk for 1 minute, mash it to a pulp, and add it to the meat mixture. Mix thoroughly, preferably with your hands, kneading the mixture until it is uniformly smooth and silky. Divide the mixture into 4 equal portions, then make 8 balls with each portion. (If necessary, dip your fingers in water to prevent the meat from sticking to them while you make the kabobs.)

❦ Heat 2 large nonstick frying pans over high heat until hot. Place 16 kabobs in each pan. Reduce the heat to medium–high and fry, shaking and turning, until they are cooked through and browned all over, about 8 minutes. If necessary, reduce the heat to medium during the last few minutes of cooking.

❦ Serve hot, warm, or at room temperature with the chutneys.

makes 32; serves 8

Diwali Festival

Celebrated during the month of Kartik, which corresponds to late October through early November on the Western calendar, Diwali is India's great festival of lights. Held in honor of Lakshmi, the goddess of wealth and prosperity, the holiday combines spectacular fireworks, pageants, decorative lights, feasting, drinking, merrymaking, and even some gambling. It also celebrates a significant event in Hindu folklore.

Diwali (also known as the feast of indulgence) inspires cooks to create imaginative preparations to please the palates of honored guests. Expensive food and elaborate garnishes reflect the host's hope for abundance in the coming year. Fragrant pilafs, almond-braised *badami* dishes, creamy *kormas, paneer* curries, and herbed *pooris* and *kulchas* are traditional holiday mainstays as are special sweets, candies, and savories called *mithai aur namkeen*. Until a generation ago, these latter treats were made at home, but today they are commercially produced by sweet makers, or *halwai*, and attractively displayed in shops. They are beautifully gift boxed and sent to friends and family worldwide along with Diwali greetings.

The legend that accompanies Diwali is of Rama, the god who freed his beautiful wife, Sita (who was an incarnation of Lakshmi), from Ravana, the demon king. Ravana had abducted Sita and imprisoned her in Sri Lanka for fourteen years. When Rama finally brought Sita back to India, the people rejoiced at their homecoming and welcomed them by lighting small oil lamps, *diya,* to illuminate a path along which they could travel from the southern tip of the country to Ayodhya, Rama's kingdom, in the north.

Today, during Diwali, houses, churches, temples, and other buildings are ablaze with both electric lights and the more traditional oil lamps in an unmistakable sign of welcome that echoes that earlier path. Fireworks ward off evil spirits so Lakshmi may enter people's homes.

In many ways the festival displays elements of such large Western celebrations as Christmas and New Year's Eve in a single, grand event. Indians of all religions and sects join in. For the trading communities, or *marvaris,* of India, it marks the beginning of the new financial year.

Madhya Pradesh

Bhutte ka Shorva

sweet corn soup with chile oil

The use of chile oil in this modern recipe shows a Chinese influence. For a vegetarian version, replace the chicken stock with vegetable stock or water.

3 cups (18 oz/560 g) fresh or thawed frozen corn kernels

1 small boiling potato, peeled and chopped

1 small yellow onion, chopped

2 slices fresh ginger

4 cups (32 fl oz/1 l) chicken stock

1¼ cups (10 fl oz/310 ml) milk

1 tablespoon cornstarch (cornflour) dissolved in 2 tablespoons milk

1¼ teaspoons salt, or to taste

2 teaspoons chile oil

1 teaspoon sesame oil

¼ cup (¾ oz/20 g) thinly sliced green (spring) onion, including tender green tops

In a deep pot, combine 2 cups (12 oz/375 g) of the corn with the potato, onion, ginger, and chicken stock and bring to a boil over medium-high heat. Reduce the heat to low and cook until the potatoes are soft, about 15 minutes. Remove from the heat and remove and discard the ginger slices.

Working in batches, process in a food processor or blender until coarsely puréed. Return the soup to the pot and add the remaining 1 cup (6 oz/185 g) corn and the milk. Bring to a boil over medium heat, add the cornstarch mixture, and cook, stirring, until thickened, 4–5 minutes. Stir in the salt.

To serve, ladle the soup into warmed bowls and top with a little of each of the chile and sesame oils and a sprinkle of the green onion.

serves 6

Delhi

Palak Shorva

fragrant spinach soup with cumin-scented potato croutons

This soup can be made with many types of greens, including Swiss chard, purslane, and regular or red spinach. Rinse them thoroughly to remove any grit. For a creamy texture, remove the stems and hard veins. To ensure a bright color, do not overcook the greens.

2 lb (1 kg) fresh spinach or other leafy greens (see note) or 2 packages (10 oz/310 g each) frozen spinach

1 boiling potato, peeled and chopped

1 yellow onion, chopped

1 large clove garlic, chopped

2 teaspoons ground coriander

5 cups (40 fl oz/1.25 l) chicken stock

¾ teaspoon ground black pepper

salt to taste

POTATO CROUTONS

3 tablespoons usli ghee (page 247) or olive oil

1½ cups (7½ oz/235 g) finely diced potato

1½ teaspoons ground cumin

salt to taste

lemon wedges (optional)

❧ Remove the stems from the spinach and discard. If you are using frozen spinach, thaw it thoroughly, then separate the leaves and remove and discard the stems. Set the spinach aside.

❧ In a large saucepan, combine the potato, onion, garlic, ground coriander, and stock and bring to a boil over high heat. Reduce the heat to low, cover, and simmer until the vegetables are very soft, about 30 minutes.

❧ Stir in the spinach, a portion at a time, so that the leaves quickly come in contact with the hot liquid and wilt. Cook until the spinach is heated through, about 2 minutes. Remove from the heat and, working in batches, purée in a food processor or blender until smooth. Return the soup to the pan. Stir in the pepper and salt and heat the soup until piping hot. Simmer gently while you make the potato croutons.

❧ To make the potato croutons, in a large frying pan over medium-high heat, warm the *usli ghee* or oil. Add the potatoes and sauté, tossing, until cooked through and brown, about 15 minutes. Sprinkle with the cumin and salt and continue sautéing, tossing, for 2 more minutes.

❧ To serve, ladle the piping hot soup into warmed bowls. Top with the croutons and drizzle with the seasoned butter from the frying pan. Serve lemon wedges on the side, if desired.

serves 6

Uttar Pradesh

Chipas

movie theater chips

Indian moviegoers make their own chips, which have a superior flavor to commercial types. For a hot treat, increase the cayenne pepper to 1½ teaspoons.

2 baking potatoes

¼ cup (2 fl oz/60 ml) cider vinegar

2 teaspoons chat masala (page 244)

1 teaspoon dried mint, crushed

1 teaspoon fine salt

½ teaspoon cayenne pepper

vegetable oil for deep-frying

❧ Using a mandoline, cut the potatoes into very thin waffled slices. Alternatively, using a sharp knife, slice them as thinly as possible. Place the slices in a bowl with cold water to cover. Stir in the vinegar and let soak for 1 hour. In a small bowl, combine the *chat masala,* mint, salt, and cayenne pepper. Set aside.

❧ In a *karhai,* deep-fryer, or large saucepan, pour in oil to a depth of 3 inches (7.5 cm) and heat it to 400° F (200°C) on a deep-frying thermometer. Meanwhile, drain the potato slices and pat them dry on paper towels. When the oil is ready, gently slip a handful of slices, one by one, into the oil. Do not crowd the pan. Fry the chips, turning, until they turn gold and crisp and the edges begin to brown, about 5 minutes. Using a slotted spoon, transfer to paper towels to drain. While the chips are still hot, sprinkle them with the spice mixture. Fry the remaining slices in the same way. When completely cool, store in an airtight container for up to 3 days.

serves 4

Punjab

Mathari

savory crackers with black pepper

These rich, filling pastry-dough crackers are a favorite after-school treat in northern India, where they are enjoyed alone or with a hot pickle or sweet chutney. Stored in an airtight container in a cool place, they will keep for up to four months.

1½ cups (7½ oz/235 g) all-purpose (plain) flour, plus extra for dusting

1 teaspoon salt

pinch of baking powder

¼ cup (2 oz/60 g) usli ghee (page 247) or vegetable shortening, melted

1 tablespoon cracked black peppercorns, preferably Tellicherry peppercorns

¼ teaspoon ajowan seeds (page 244) or 1 teaspoon dried thyme

⅓ cup (3 fl oz/80 ml) cold water, or as needed

vegetable oil for deep-frying

☙ In a bowl, mix together the flour, salt, baking powder, *usli ghee,* pepper, and ajowan or thyme. Gradually add the water and mix until a stiff dough forms. (You may not need all of the water). Turn out onto a floured work surface and knead lightly, dusting with extra flour as needed, until smooth, about 3 minutes. Divide the dough into 4 portions. Cover each with plastic wrap until you are ready to use it.

☙ On a floured surface, roll out 1 portion at a time, dusting often with flour, until it is ⅛ inch (3 mm) thick. Cut out plain rounds using a 2-inch or 4-inch (5-cm or 10-cm) cookie cutter. With a fork, prick each circle in several places to prevent it from puffing too much during frying.

☙ In a *karhai,* deep-fryer, or large saucepan, pour in oil to a depth of 1½ inches (4 cm) and heat to 375°F (180°C) on a deep-frying thermometer. When the oil is ready, gently slip a few rounds of cracker dough into it. Do not crowd the pan. Fry over medium heat, turning occasionally, until both sides are golden, about 3 minutes. Remove with a slotted spoon and drain on paper towels. Make the remaining crackers in the same way. Serve hot or at room temperature.

makes about 50 small or 24 large crackers

Kerala

Vayakai Bhajjia

plantain fritters

Popular in southern India, the plantain, a variety of banana, is prized for its slightly chewy texture. Vegetarians are particularly fond of it. Plantains are available in most grocery stores. When unavailable, firm, underripe bananas may be substituted.

1 large or 2 medium unripe green plantains

1 cup (8 fl oz/250 ml) water

½ cup (4 oz/125 g) plain yogurt

BATTER

1 cup (5 oz/155 g) chickpea (garbanzo bean) flour

2 tablespoons rice flour

1½ teaspoons salt

1 teaspoon cayenne pepper

¾ teaspoon ground turmeric

24 fresh or 48 dried kari leaves, finely shredded (page 248)

1 tablespoon vegetable oil, plus oil for deep-frying

½ cup (4 fl oz/125 ml) hot water

❈ Peel the plantain and cut on the diagonal into slices ⅛ inch (3 mm) thick. In a bowl, whisk the water and yogurt until smooth. Add the plantain slices and mix to coat them with the yogurt. (This will keep the plantain from turning dark.)

❈ To make the batter, in a bowl, combine the chickpea flour, rice flour, salt, cayenne pepper, turmeric, and kari leaves. Add the 1 tablespoon oil and mix well. Gradually add the water, stirring constantly, until you have a pancakelike batter. (Depending upon the humidity, you may not need all the water.) Whisk until the batter is smooth.

❈ In a *karhai,* deep-fryer, or large frying pan, pour in oil to a depth of 1½ inches (4 cm) and heat to 375°F (190°C) on a deep-frying thermometer. Meanwhile, drain the plantain slices and pat dry on paper towels. When the oil is ready, dip a few slices in the batter and gently slip them into the oil. Do not crowd the pan. Fry, turning often, until the fritters are golden, about 4 minutes. Remove with a slotted spoon and drain on paper towels. Keep warm in a low oven while you make the remaining fritters in the same way. Serve immediately.

serves 6

The Karhai

The *karhai* is the most important and versatile cooking utensil in India. This round-bottomed metal pan is similar in shape to the better-known Chinese wok, but is much heavier. It is used for everything from deep-frying *pakoras* (fritters) and *pooris* (balloon breads) to stir-frying vegetables and other ingredients, steaming dumplings, and making sweets and candies.

Within the last few decades, before melamine *thali* plates and plastic *ghara* (water jugs) infiltrated the village life of India, *karhais* were also used as babies' bathtubs. Or, painted with prayers, they housed the family's sacred *tulsi* (holy basil) plant.

The pans come in a wide range of sizes. Tiny five-inch (13-cm) *karhais* are just right for roasting spices. The mammoth forty-inch (1-m) versions are used in catering. *Karhais* are made of iron, aluminum, silver, stainless steel, or tin-lined brass or copper. My favorite is the hand-hammered iron *karhai,* about twelve inches (30 cm) in diameter.

After an initial scrub with soap and water, *karhais* are virtually maintenance free. Their weight makes them stable, but a wok ring can be used as a support, if desired.

Punjab

Murghi ke Pakore

chicken fritters

These fritters have a thick, spongy chickpea-batter crust laced with mango powder, ajowan seeds, garam masala, and green chiles. A popular appetizer in Indian restaurants serving Moghul fare, they are just as delicious made with shrimps, scallops, fish, or paneer.

BATTER

1¾ cups (8½ oz/265 g) chickpea (garbanzo bean) flour

¼ cup (1½ oz/45 g) rice flour or all-purpose (plain) flour

1½ teaspoons garam masala (page 249)

1 teaspoon mango powder (page 248) or 1 tablespoon fresh lemon juice

1 teaspoon baking powder

½ teaspoon ground turmeric

½ teaspoon ground black pepper

¼ teaspoon ajowan seeds (page 244)

4 fresh hot green chiles such as serrano, coarsely chopped

1 teaspoon salt, or to taste

1⅓ cups (11 fl oz/340 ml) hot water

½ cup (¾ oz/20 g) fresh cilantro (fresh coriander), leaves and tender stems

vegetable oil for deep-frying

1 skinless, boneless whole chicken breast, about 1 lb (500 g), cut into strips 3 inches (7.5 cm) long by 1 inch (2.5 cm) wide by ¼ inch (6 mm) thick

Mint Chutney (page 210) or Tamarind Chutney (page 185)

☙ To make the batter, in a food processor or blender, combine the chickpea flour, rice or all-purpose flour, garam masala, mango powder or lemon juice, baking powder, turmeric, pepper, ajowan seeds, chiles, salt, and water. Process until smooth. Add the cilantro and process only until it is finely chopped; a little texture in the cilantro will add to the appeal of the fritters. (If mixing the batter by hand, mince the chiles and chop the cilantro before combining them in a bowl with the other ingredients.)

☙ In a *karhai*, deep-fryer, or large frying pan, pour in oil to a depth of 1½ inches (4 cm) and heat it to 375°F (190°C) on a deep-frying thermometer.

☙ Meanwhile, pat the chicken pieces dry on paper towels. When the oil is ready, dip a few pieces of the chicken into the batter, letting the excess drain off, then gently slip them into the hot oil. Do not crowd the pan. Fry, turning frequently, until the coating is golden brown, about 6 minutes. Using a slotted spoon, transfer to paper towels to drain. Keep warm in a low oven while you fry the remaining chicken pieces in the same way. Serve the fritters at once with the chutney.

serves 8

Uttar Pradesh

Bhona Bhutta

fire-roasted corn with cayenne salt

During the winter months in northern India, when corn appears in the market, the air is perpetually scented with the lingering, smoky aroma of grilling corn. Indians eat the ears on the spot, slathered with the juice of lemons dipped in salt and cayenne pepper.

1 teaspoon cayenne pepper

½ teaspoon salt, or to taste

¼ teaspoon ground black pepper

2 very fresh, tender ears of corn, husks and silk removed

1 lemon, halved

☙ Combine the cayenne pepper, salt, and black pepper on a plate. Set aside until needed.

☙ Turn on 2 gas burners with the flame on high. Using tongs, hold an ear of corn directly over the gas flame and roast, turning as needed, until evenly covered with several brown spots, about 5 minutes. Watch carefully, as the corn can burn and char easily. (Light charring is acceptable as it will enhance the overall flavor.) If you do not have a gas burner, place the corn on a wire rack over the electric burner and roast, turning, until evenly covered with brown spots, about 5 minutes.

☙ To serve, place a roasted ear on each individual serving plate. Dip the cut side of each lemon half into the cayenne salt and place next to the corn. Each diner squeezes the lemon over the corn before eating. Pass any remaining cayenne salt in a small dish.

serves 2

Punjab

Bare

fried bean puffs with ginger and raisins

These delicious, protein-rich snacks have a crisp coating and soft, spongy interior. The flavoring varies from region to region; cumin, ginger, and chiles mark this version as coming from Punjab.

1 cup (7 oz/220 g) white split gram beans (page 246)
3 cups (24 fl oz/750 ml) hot water
½ cup (4 fl oz/125 ml) cold water
¼ cup (1 oz/30 g) finely chopped walnuts
⅓ cup (2 oz/60 g) raisins
1 tablespoon peeled and finely chopped fresh ginger
2 fresh hot green chiles, thinly sliced
1 teaspoon salt, or to taste
¾ teaspoon cumin seeds
vegetable oil for deep-frying
Coconut Chutney (optional; page 202)

Pick over the beans, removing any stones or misshapen or discolored beans. Rinse thoroughly and place in a bowl. Add the hot water and soak for 8 hours or overnight.

Drain the beans and transfer them to a food processor or blender. Process, gradually adding the cold water and stopping the machine often to scrape down the bowl until smoothly puréed. (This will take a few minutes, as the mixture contains very little liquid.) Transfer the purée to a bowl and stir in the walnuts, raisins, ginger, chiles, salt, and cumin.

In a *karhai,* deep-fryer, or large frying pan, pour in oil to a depth of 1½ inches (4 cm) and heat to 375°F (190°C) on a deep-frying thermometer. Using a small ice-cream scoop or melon baller, scoop out balls of the batter and slip them gently into the oil, a few at a time. Do not crowd the pan. Fry, turning frequently, until nicely browned on all sides, about 3 minutes. Using a slotted spoon, transfer to paper towels to drain. Keep warm in a low oven while you cook the remaining balls in the same way. Serve hot or at room temperature with the chutney, if desired.

makes 16–24; serves 8

Food and Good Fortune

An ancient Indian myth tells of a peasant family that welcomed a starving beggar into their home to share a meager bowl of rice. Moved by the kindness of the peasants, the beggar revealed himself to be Ganesha, one of the many Hindu incarnations of God. Ganesha was checking on the generosity of his subjects, and blessed this family with great riches. Thus, the correlation between good deeds and good fortune is engrained in the Hindu psyche.

Today, of the many customs prevalent among Hindus, none is more revered and adhered to than *danam,* the offering of food, gifts, and charity. The manual of Hindu code, *Dharma Shashtra,* specifies that a percentage of one's income be set aside for *danam,* a concept similar to the Christian tradition of tithing.

The forty-five-hundred-year-old Hindu treatise, the *Rig Veda,* describes *danam* as a spiritual act expressing the giver's gratitude to the creator for bringing him to the *bhumiloka,* the human world, and for many blessings. Over time a "wish list" began to accompany *danam.* The great forces of Surya, the Sun God, and Indra, the Thunder God, were invoked to bless the land with an abundant harvest. It also became commonplace to request

safe passage and heavenly comforts for departed relatives or to wish for the birth of a male child.

In the past, a *danam* could be as extravagant as building a temple, giving an elephant, or offering a measure of gold equal to the weight of the donor. A humble man would present a coconut and a fistful of paddy (fresh rice, before it has been dried) soaked in turmeric. The deep yellow of the spice symbolized gold and the coconut a cow.

In contemporary India, a *danam* which, in addition to more lofty material elements, comprises flowers, milk, *usli ghee,* bananas, betel leaves, betel nuts, vermilion, sandalwood paste, and incense, is followed by various rituals. Offerings of elaborate sweets are integral to the practice, and are proffered to the temple and the gods for their blessings. Non-food *danams* such as jewelry and gold and silver statues of god figures are usually kept by the temples, but sweets and eatables are often returned to the worshippers. Once they have been blessed, these sweets—*peda, laddoo, barfi, jalebi, modakum*—now called *prasada,* are eaten by Hindu worshippers, an act that is considered similar to the Christian act of communion.

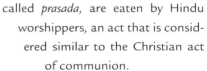

Himachal Pradesh

Dal Shorva

creamy lentil soup
with caramelized onion

*Indians have a way with seasoning lentils,
whether in a side dish of* dal *or in the form of soup.
In this soup, the sweet, caramelized onions
contrast with and round out the spicy flavors
of turmeric, cumin, and ginger.*

1½ cups (10½ oz/330g) red lentils

4 cups (32 fl oz/1 l) chicken stock or water

½ teaspoon ground turmeric

1-inch (2.5-cm) piece fresh ginger, peeled and
chopped

2 tomatoes, chopped

1 cup (8 fl oz/250 ml) milk

1½ teaspoons salt, or to taste

GARNISH

¼ cup (2 oz/60 g) unsalted butter

1 yellow onion, finely shredded

1 teaspoon cumin seeds

ground black pepper to taste

¼ cup (⅓ oz/10 g) chopped fresh cilantro
(fresh coriander) (optional)

❦ Pick over the lentils, removing any stones or mis-
shapen or discolored lentils. Rinse thoroughly and
place in a deep pot. Add the chicken stock or water,
turmeric, ginger, and tomatoes and bring to a boil.
Reduce the heat to low and simmer, uncovered, until
the lentils are soft, about 25 minutes.

❦ Remove from the heat and, working in batches,
purée in a food processor or blender until smooth.
Return the soup to the pot, stir in the milk and salt,
and heat until piping hot. Simmer gently over low
heat while you make the garnish.

❦ To make the garnish, in a frying pan over high
heat, melt the butter. Add the onion and cumin and
cook, stirring occasionally, until the onion is brown,
about 5 minutes.

❦ To serve, ladle the soup into warmed bowls and
sprinkle generously with black pepper. Divide the
onion–butter mixture among the bowls, sprinkle
with cilantro if desired, and serve at once.

serves 6

Maharashtra

Bhel Poori

crispy noodle salad
with hot and sweet chutneys

*Bhel poori, a specialty of Bombay, combines more
than two dozen individually prepared snacks, including
chickpea flour, grains, dried nuts and fruits, seeds,
herbs, and spices. Bhel mix is available in Indian
grocery stores and is used to prepare this palate-
tingling salad of the same name, which combines
a variety of ingredients, chutneys, and herbs.*

¾ cup (6 oz/180 g) plain yogurt

1 teaspoon minced fresh mint

pinch of salt, or to taste

2 cups crushed day-old crisp Pooris (page 191)
or plain corn chips

1 cup (3 oz/90 g) bhel mix (see note), Indian
savory snack mix, or party snack mix

2 cups (14 oz/440 g) cooked chickpeas
(garbanzo beans), home-cooked or canned

1 cup (5 oz/155 g) diced cooked boiling potatoes
(¼-inch/6-mm dice)

¼ cup (½ oz/15 g) alfalfa sprouts (optional)

½ cup (4 fl oz/125 ml) Tamarind Chutney
(page 185)

½ cup (4 fl oz/125 ml) purchased cilantro (fresh
coriander) chutney

¾ teaspoon cumin seeds, roasted and crushed

cayenne pepper or paprika to taste

¼ cup (⅓ oz/10 g) chopped fresh cilantro
(fresh coriander)

❦ In a bowl, combine the yogurt, mint, and salt. Set
aside until ready to serve.

❦ To assemble and serve individual *bhels,* divide the
pooris or corn chips and half of the *bhel* mix between
4 serving plates. If using canned chickpeas, drain
them and rinse thoroughly under cold water. Scatter
the chickpeas, potatoes, and sprouts (if using) on top.
Pour the yogurt mixture over the salad. Drizzle a little of each of the chutneys on top, then sprinkle with
cumin seeds and cayenne pepper or paprika.

❦ Sprinkle the remaining *bhel* mix and the cilantro
over the salads and serve immediately. The salads
must be eaten within 5 minutes, or the moisture
from the yogurt and chutneys will make them soggy.

serves 4

Dried Vegetables

Anyone who has visited India during the monsoon season (April to November, depending on the region) has witnessed the havoc wreaked by the torrential rains. Routine activities such as grocery shopping come to a halt as people retreat to their homes. As one waits for the deluge to end, which could be a few hours, or up to several days, dried vegetables, *sookhida,* replace their fresh counterparts on the menu.

All vegetables, even watery ones such as cucumbers, are dried. The drying begins in March, at the end of the winter harvest season. During this period it is almost impossible to find even the smallest space around a farmhouse that is not covered with slices of drying cauliflower, eggplant (aubergine), pumpkin, beet, or okra.

Dried vegetables are rehydrated by briefly soaking them in water just before use. Vegetarians have a particular fondness for *sookhida*—they have a slightly chewy composition similar to that of meat. Anyone who has breathed air still redolent with the aroma of drying cauliflower or green (spring) onions will know why we Indians helplessly crave a culinary tradition born of bad weather.

Rajasthan

Pappadums

lentil wafers

Pappadums, *or papads, are saucer-sized disks of dried beans, rice, or potato, which are fried or roasted before serving. Cumin, red pepper flakes, cracked black peppercorn, garlic, green chiles, and cilantro are some of the popular flavors. They are perfect with cocktails.*

4 *store-bought* pappadums
Peanut or corn oil for deep-frying

In a *karhai,* deep-fryer, or large frying pan, pour in oil to a depth of 2 inches (5 cm) and heat to 375°F (190°C) on a deep-frying thermometer.

When the oil is ready, use tongs to gently slip in 1 wafer, laying it flat in the oil. The wafer will puff, buckle, and turn creamy colored. It will also expand considerably. (All this will happen in 1–3 seconds, therefore one needs to move fast.) As soon as the whole wafer is evenly cream colored, use tongs to transfer it to paper towels to drain. Fry all the wafers in the same way. Serve hot or at room temperature.

serves 4

Snack sellers ply urban streets, singing songs to entice people to buy.

Tamil Nadu

Rasam

kari leaf–scented tomato broth

*Rasam, the spicy, curry-flavored lentil soup
of southern India, is the classic creation of Tamil Nadu
state. Tamilians like to add a little rice to the soup,
although it is delicious as is.*

1 cup (7 oz/220 g) red lentils

4 cups (1½ lb/750 g) chopped tomatoes

2 teaspoons curry powder (page 249)

6 cups (48 fl oz/1.5 l) water

24 fresh or 48 dried kari leaves (page 248)

1½ teaspoons salt, or to taste

2 tablespoons usli ghee (page 247)

1 teaspoon brown mustard seeds

1 teaspoon ground cumin

½ teaspoon powdered asafetida (see sidebar,
page 144) or 1 teaspoon minced garlic

juice of ½ lime

❦ Pick over the lentils, removing any stones or mis-shapen or discolored lentils. Rinse thoroughly and place in a deep pot. Add the tomatoes, curry powder, and 4 cups (32 fl oz/1 l) of the water. Bring to a boil over high heat, then reduce the heat to low and simmer, uncovered, until the lentils are soft, about 35 minutes.

❦ Remove from the heat and, working in batches, purée the mixture in a food processor or blender until smooth. Return the purée to the pot and add the kari leaves, the remaining 2 cups (16 fl oz/500 ml) water, and the salt.

❦ In a small frying pan over high heat, warm the *usli ghee* until very hot. Reduce the heat to medium-high, add the mustard seeds, and cover the pan. When the seeds stop sputtering, after about 30 seconds, uncover and add the cumin and asafetida or garlic. Let the mixture sizzle for 5 seconds, then pour the entire contents of the pan over the soup. Stir to combine. Bring the soup to a rolling boil. Stir in the lime juice and check and correct the seasonings. Ladle the soup into warmed bowls and serve immediately.

serves 6–8

Tamil Nadu

Meenakshi Vada

fragrant split pea fritters
with cashew nuts

*It is a constant challenge for India's millions
of vegetarians to create new recipes with vegetarian
ingredients. No vegetable holds greater potential than
the everyday pea. In this recipe, for example, split peas
are combined with cashew nuts, ginger, chiles, and
spices to produce the scrumptious and meaty-tasting
fritters that are called* vadas *in Tamil.*

1 cup (7 oz/220 g) yellow split peas (page 247)

3 cups (24 fl oz/750 ml) hot water

*1-inch (2.5-cm) piece fresh ginger, peeled and
roughly chopped*

*2 fresh hot green chiles such as serrano, roughly
chopped*

2 teaspoons all-purpose (plain) flour

1 teaspoon salt, or to taste

2 tablespoons water

½ cup (2½ oz/60 g) finely chopped shallots

*½ cup (2 oz/60 g) finely chopped toasted
cashew nuts*

*¼ cup (⅓ oz/10 g) finely chopped fresh cilantro
(fresh coriander)*

*12 fresh or 24 dried kari leaves, finely shredded
(page 248)*

vegetable oil for deep-frying

❀ Pick over the peas, removing any stones or mis-shapen or discolored peas. Place in a bowl and add the hot water. Soak for 3 hours, then drain. Transfer the peas to a food processor or blender. Add the ginger, chiles, flour, and salt and process until the peas are puréed, adding the 2 tablespoons of water during the processing. The mixture should be neither too coarse nor too smooth, with a texture similar to that of cooked hot breakfast cereal or cooked polenta.

❀ Transfer the batter to a bowl and fold in the shallots, cashew nuts, cilantro, and kari leaves, if using. Check the seasonings, adding more salt if necessary.

❀ In a *karhai,* deep-fryer, or large frying pan, pour in oil to a depth of 1½ inches (4 cm) and heat to 375°F (190°C). Meanwhile, spread a piece of plastic wrap about 10 inches (25 cm) long on a work surface. Scoop out heaping tablespoons of batter and place them on the plastic wrap 2 inches (5 cm) apart. Lightly press each portion of batter to form a patty.

❀ When the oil is ready, using a spatula, gently slip the patties, one at a time, into the oil. Cook only as many patties at one time as will fit comfortably in a single layer. Fry, turning frequently, until both sides are browned, about 5 minutes. Using a slotted spoon, transfer to paper towels to drain. If you are serving them hot, keep them warm in a low oven while you make the remaining fritters in the same way. Serve hot or at room temperature.

makes 16–20

Rajasthan

Boondi Shorva

buttermilk soup with
chickpea pearls

*The crisp, teardrop-shaped chickpea pearls called
boondi, available in Indian grocery stores, have
innumerable uses in Indian cooking. There are classic
as well as modern recipes in which the spicy* boondi
are combined with cool, spiced buttermilk or yogurt.

1 large cucumber

4 cups (32 fl oz/1 l) buttermilk

1 teaspoon salt

*1 teaspoon dried mint, crushed, or 2 teaspoons
finely chopped fresh mint*

*2 tablespoons chopped fresh cilantro (fresh
coriander)*

¼ cup (1 oz/30 g) finely chopped walnuts

¼ cup (1½ oz/45 g) raisins

1 teaspoon cumin seeds, roasted and bruised

*1 cup (5 oz/155 g) chickpea pearls or deep-fried
potato shreds*

❀ Peel, halve, and seed the cucumber, then grate it into a bowl, saving the juices. Add the buttermilk, salt, mint, cilantro, walnuts, raisins, and cumin. Using a wooden spoon or a fork, mix until smooth. Stir in ¾ cup (3½ oz/105 g) of the chickpea pearls or potato shreds. Cover and refrigerate for 30 minutes.

❀ To serve, ladle the soup into chilled bowls and top with the remaining chickpea pearls or potato shreds.

serves 4–6

Haryana

Aloo Tikki

potato patties with spicy pea filling

On Naisadak ("New Road" in Hindi) in the old section of Delhi, you will find one of the best stalls selling the quintessential Delhi treat aloo tikki or, as a Delhiite would simply say, tikki. On a 36-inch (100-cm) round iron griddle that sits over a smoking wood-fire stove, perfectly shaped potato patties are arranged along the rim. Just before serving, the tikkis are moved to the center to be crisped over higher heat. Then they are cut open to expose the spicy pea filling, served on a bargad leaf (the large, round, leathery leaf of a shady tree, which is used as a disposable plate), and drizzled with tamarind chutney.

Although I can't bring the Naisadak tikki-stall to you, this recipe will attempt to take you there. The secret of success lies in being very patient. The longer and more slowly you pan-fry the patties, the thicker and crisper the crust will be and the more delicious the potato will taste.

POTATO MIXTURE

¼ cup (2 oz/60 g) roasted split peas (page 247) or ¼ cup (1¼ oz/35 g) chickpea (garbanzo bean) flour

1 lb (500 g) baking potatoes, boiled, peeled, and mashed

1 tablespoon cornstarch (cornflour)

1¾ teaspoons salt

PEA FILLING

½ cup (4 fl oz/125 ml) vegetable oil

1 teaspoon cumin seeds

1 cup (5 oz/155 g) thawed frozen green peas

1 teaspoon peeled and grated fresh ginger

3 fresh hot green chiles such as serrano, minced, seeds included

½ teaspoon cayenne pepper

¾ teaspoon salt

½ cup finely chopped fresh cilantro (fresh coriander), leaves and tender stems

Mint Chutney (page 210)

Tamarind Chutney (page 185)

❧ First, make the potato mixture: If using split peas, place them in a mortar or a coffee grinder reserved solely for spices and pound or process them to a fine powder. If using chickpea flour, toast it in a dry frying pan until it is reddish brown, about 4 minutes. In a bowl, combine the split pea powder or chickpea flour, potato, cornstarch, and salt. Mix well and set aside until needed.

❧ To make the pea filling, in a small frying pan over high heat, warm 1 tablespoon of the oil. When very hot, add the cumin seeds and cook until they turn several shades darker, about 30 seconds. Add the green peas and cook, stirring occasionally, until they look dry and limp, about 5 minutes. Remove from the heat and stir in the ginger, chiles, cayenne pepper, salt, and cilantro.

❧ Transfer the pea filling to a bowl. Using a potato masher, crush it to make a coarse mixture.

❧ To make the patties, divide the potato mixture into 8 equal portions. Do the same with the pea mixture. Working with 1 portion of potato mixture at a time, roll it into a ball. With your thumb, make a wide depression in the center and place 1 portion of pea filling in it. Bring the sides together to cover the pea filling completely with the potato mixture. Flatten the ball and shape it into a pattie.

❧ In a large griddle or frying pan over high heat, warm 2 tablespoons of the oil. Add 4 of the patties, reduce the heat to medium-high, and cook, turning once or twice, until both sides of the patties are crisp and brown, at least 8 minutes total (a longer cooking time will produce a crisper, more flavorsome result). Drizzle more oil around the patties during cooking as needed. Remove with a spatula and keep warm in a low oven while you cook the remaining 4 patties the same way. Serve with the chutneys.

serves 4

Dumplings, fritters, and fruit and noodle salads are among the many delectable snacks that Indians love.

Gujarat

Masala Kaju

spiced cashews

These zesty cashew nuts are utterly irresistible. They pose a real threat as a meal spoiler if you don't pay careful attention to how many you consume.

¼ cup (2 fl oz/60 ml) vegetable oil

2 cups (10½ oz/330 g) raw cashew nuts, preferably large whole nuts

1½ teaspoons chat masala (page 244) or mango powder (page 248)

½ teaspoon salt

¼–½ teaspoon cayenne pepper

❧ In a *karhai* or large frying pan over medium-high heat, warm the oil. Add the nuts and fry, stirring and tossing, until they turn light brown, about 6 minutes. Using a slotted spoon, transfer to a baking sheet or a large plate so that the nuts are in a single layer. Before the cashews cool completely, combine the *chat masala* or mango powder, salt, and cayenne pepper to taste. Sprinkle over the nuts and mix lightly. (Do not over-mix, or the spices will slip away from the nuts.)

❧ The nuts can be served warm or at room temperature. Store in an airtight container for up to 3 weeks.

serves 8

Kerala

Yera Varuval

masala shrimp fry

Varuval literally means "pan-fried" or "crisped."
I first tasted this popular recipe, a classic example of
the Keralan heritage, at a friend's house. In Kerala,
the dish is made with succulent small shrimp that have
an oyster-like aroma and texture. First, the shrimp are
coated with a spice rub that includes turmeric, cayenne
pepper, garlic, and ginger. Then they are pan-seared
and topped with fried onion shreds, kari leaves, and a
cilantro mixture to produce a rich layering
of flavors and textures. For variety, bay and sea
scallops may be used in place of the shrimp.

1½ lb (750 g) medium-sized shrimp (prawns)

1 tablespoon fresh lime juice

2 teaspoons peeled and grated fresh ginger

1 teaspoon minced garlic

1 teaspoon ground cumin

½ teaspoon cayenne pepper

¼ teaspoon ground turmeric

pinch of ground cloves

3 tablespoons vegetable oil

1 small yellow onion, thinly sliced

¼ cup (¼ oz / 7 g) fresh kari leaves (page 248)
or a combination of fresh basil and fresh cilantro
(fresh coriander) leaves

❧ Peel the shrimp, leaving the last shell segment
with the tail fin intact, and devein. Rinse, pat dry on
paper towels, and place in a bowl. Add the lime juice,
ginger, garlic, cumin, cayenne pepper, turmeric, and
cloves. Toss to combine and set aside to marinate for
30 minutes at room temperature.

❧ In a shallow frying pan over high heat, warm
2 tablespoons of the oil. Add the onion and cook,
stirring occasionally, until it is light caramel brown,
about 5 minutes. Stir in the kari leaves or basil and
cilantro. Transfer the onion mixture to a plate.

❧ Add the remaining 1 tablespoon oil to the pan
over high heat. When it is smoking hot, add the
shrimp and cook, turning and tossing, until they turn
pink and curl, about 3 minutes. Transfer the shrimp
to a platter. Scatter the onion mixture on top and
serve immediately.

serves 6

Tiffin

Indians have a custom of greeting even
unexpected visitors with beverages and
food. This tradition began when sages (holy
Hindu Brahmin priests), who regularly trav-
eled long distances, stopped along the way
to ask for a little water and food. Today the
visitor is equated with the sage, and the
offering is more a courtesy than a duty.
Such snacks are known as tiffin. The gesture
of serving them is a literal one as well as
symbolic, and so the venerable snack-time
meal endures.

In southern India, tiffin can be a handful of
roasted peanuts or an elaborate fried dish
of rice noodles accompanied with sauces
and sambals. Most common are spicy
savories like *ompadi* (fried noodles), *masala
vada* (fried dumplings), and *bajjia* (fritters),
and sweets such as *laddoo* (sweet balls),
halwa (puddings), and *jangari* (candied
twists). Recently, cut-up fruits, sliced fresh
coconut, and legume salads have become
popular. The beverage of choice is coffee
prepared in the southern Indian style, with
milk and sugar, much like caffe latte.

MAIN DISHES

Local produce and religious traditions influence the dishes of every region.

Preceding pages: A family picnics beside one of the Sasbahu temples, which form part of the massive fortress of Gwalior, in Madhya Pradesh. The complex is built on a 300-foot (90-m) hill that rises above the town. **Above top:** Every morning at Amritsar's Golden Temple, the *Guru Granth Sahib,* a book sacred to the Sikh faith, is carried in a golden palanquin around the tank, or holy reservoir, before being installed in the temple. **Above:** A monsoonal mist wreathes ricefields near Quilon, Kerala. **Right:** Originating in Persia (now Iran), the tandoor, a type of clay oven, spread to neighboring regions, including areas of northern India. It can be used for baking, grilling, and roasting simultaneously, producing meltingly tender results.

ONE OF THE MOST memorable meals I have ever attended was a *wazwan,* a Kashmiri Muslim wedding feast, held aboard a houseboat on Dal Lake in Kashmir. Nestled among the snow-capped Himalayas in the northernmost part of India, the valley of Kashmir is a land of ferns and pines, almond and walnut orchards, and fields of saffron. It is also the home of the *wazas,* feast chefs of Persian and Afghan ancestry who are renowned for their expertise in the cooking of sheep. Working ceaselessly from dawn until dusk and using unique culinary techniques and secret spice combinations, they transform the meat, wasting no part, into an array of smoked, braised, caramelized, simmered, and crisp-fried dishes.

We ate in the traditional Kashmiri style, sitting on rugs and leaning against plump cushions. A comfortable position was essential, since what followed was nothing short of a dining orgy: a thirty-course, nonstop parade of dishes. After five hours, I was still working my way through courses twenty-two and twenty-three. The portions were moderate, thankfully, and the meal itself followed the traditional Indian concept of *thali*-style serving, with several dishes presented at once, accompanied

with rice, breads, and side dishes. In a sense, the *wazwan* is simply a much more extravagant, elaborate, and indulgent version of the typical Indian meal.

Kashmiri cooking is similar to the Persian-influenced Moghul cooking of northern India, both being enriched with cream, almonds, and saffron, but the latter uses the more popular and plentiful goat meat instead of lamb. Goats are tough and adaptable, making them better suited to the hot, dry northern plains where Moghul cooking predominates, while sheep prefer the cool slopes of the Himalayas. Lamb and goat are the most commonly consumed red meats in India, as Hindus, Buddhists, Jains, and Sikhs are forbidden to eat beef, while Muslims and Jews shun pork. So pork and beef are only found in predemininantly Christian areas, such as Goa and Kerala on the southwest coast. And while *mutton* technically refers to the meat of a mature sheep, in India it also denotes lamb and goat. (This confusion dates from the British Raj when, for the sake of convenience, the English *memsahibs* called all red meat "mutton.") The lamb available in the West is well suited to Indian dishes traditionally made with the meat of sheep or goats.

But the meat that Indians value most highly is neither lamb nor goat. It is chicken. Poultry is always prepared and cooked without the skin, which is considered unclean. The skin also prevents the wonderful flavor of the spices from penetrating the flesh. Northern Indians, particularly the Punjabis, are known for their superb chicken preparations, including *murgh masala* (chicken in tomato sauce), *murgh hariali* (chicken with green herbs), and *makkhani murgh* (butter chicken). For the latter, day-old tandoori chicken is slowly braised in a buttery, creamy, ginger-laced gravy until the chicken pieces soak up the sauce and are transformed into moist, perfumed morsels. Many Punjabis make tandoori chicken just so they can turn it into *makkhani murgh* the next day. I personally have a difficult time choosing, since I also adore tandoori chicken. This spice-imbued,

Far left: Ruined temples and ricefields flank the Betwa River, in Orchha, Madhya Pradesh. Crops such as rice are traditionally grown around temples to provide them with an income. **Left:** The Konkan women of Goa are renowned as astute businesspeople. They run, among other enterprises, the region's markets, such as this fish market in the capital, Panjim. **Above:** Tiny, oval-shaped pears are grown on the lower slopes of the Himalayas in Uttaranchal and Kashmir. Sweet, flavorful, and highly perfumed, they are prized in northern India.

yogurt-marinated bird makes a delectable main course or a fine appetizer. Similarly, many of the drier dishes in this chapter—grilled pieces of tandoori fish, Goan grilled prawns encrusted with spices, chicken kabobs, spicy chicken salad, cheese patties with coriander, or lamb kabobs with roasted chickpeas—can be served in small portions as a starter.

While tandoori chicken, *saag gosht* (lamb with spinach), and *matar paneer* (peas and cheese in fragrant gravy) are familiar names in the Indian food lexicon, the country's considerable seafood repertoire is less well known. Many Indians, such as those of West Bengal, Orissa and Tamil Nadu who live along the waterways of the east coast, prefer freshwater fish to saltwater varieties, even though India is bound by the sea on two sides. The fish are caught in local rivers and streams and used exclusively in local specialities. The people of the Konkan region and Kerala on the west coast traditionally fish in bays. Their most popular catches are pomfret, a delicate fish similar to Dover sole, and large, succulent, stripe-shelled tiger prawns. Although many

Indian fish species are unavailable fresh in the West, salmon, sea bass, flounder, sole, haddock, and monkfish make excellent substitutes.

Finally, there are vegetables, legumes, cheese, and eggs. Over 800 million Indians are practicing vegetarians, and Indian cuisine places a special emphasis on vegetarian preparations, ensuring that they are pleasing to the palate as well as healthful and wholesome. As a result, nonvegetarian Indians often cook vegetarian main dishes solely because they are delicious. Eggs in particular are held in high regard, and Indian cooks work hard at creating special preparations that are considered on a par with Moghul classics such as *korma* and kabobs. Although this fondness for eggs is partly due to their flavor, their primary appeal lies in their perceived resemblance, when halved, to the narcissus flower, the beauty of which has been extolled by Persian poets for centuries.

The basic philosophy that underlies every Indian meal is "mix-and-match." The idea of

Left top: Varanasi, in Uttar Pradesh, has been a religious center since 2000 BC. The city was blessed by Shiva and has always been the most venerated of Hindu pilgrimage sites. Each day, thousands of Hindus gather on the banks of the Ganges to bathe ritually and offer prayers and flowers. **Left bottom:** After visiting a temple, a family eats *prasada*, sweets that have been blessed. **Above top:** Elephants make light work of hauling brush on a road in Calicut, Kerala. **Above:** A henna hand painter in Delhi decorates a client with intricate temporary tattoos.

a main course is, culturally speaking, alien to Indian custom, where all dishes except sweets are served together, creating a variety and balance of color, flavor, texture, and nutrition. Dishes featuring meat, poultry, or seafood are, however, generally held in great esteem, so can be thought of as main dishes due to the cost of their ingredients. Other dishes gain main-dish status through the use of complex cooking methods or elaborate combinations of foods, such as vegetables roasted in a sealed clay pot, or stuffed with cheese and herbs and simmered in a sauce or baked in the tandoor.

As you travel from region to region in India, you will find that the same dish, be it of eggplant (aubergine) or chicken, eggs, goat, or chickpeas, travels with you, taking on the subtle differences that are the result of local spices and seasonings, ethnic cooking techniques, and religious food taboos. In the north, cumin, mango powder, and cilantro predominate, while fenugreek, coconut, and tamarind accent many southern foods. Chiles, mustard, and nigella perfume the sauces of eastern India, and black pepper, ajowan, and yogurt are much loved in the west. Thus, an infinite variety of tastes and textures is created to suit the palate of a complex and diverse society.

Above top: Whitewashed buildings and *ghat*s line Pushkar Lake, in Pushkar, Rajasthan. According to legend, the lake was created from one of three rose petals that fell from the hand of Brahma. **Above:** *Lal gajar,* or red carrots, are a speciality of India and Pakistan. Though more expensive than the orange variety familiar in the West (known in India as *vilayati,* or "foreign"), they are highly valued for their flavor and glorious color. The color is especially intense when they are cooked. **Right:** A guardian of the Golden Temple in Amritsar, Punjab, takes part in a procession marking the Ninth Guru's Day. This celebration is held by the Sikh community each November in remembrance of their martyr Guru Tegh Bahadur, who was beheaded in 1675 for his refusal to change his religion and accept Islam.

Maharashtra
Masalchi Mutton

meat braised with black pepper and fresh herbs

On India's tropical west coast, amid the Hindus and Christians, is a tiny community of Jews. Known as Bene Israel, they are believed to be the descendants of the original Jews in India who arrived at this region in the second century BC. The Bene Israel possess a cuisine that is a wonderful amalgam of Indo-Jewish flavors. One delectable example, masalchi mutton, *is traditionally made for the Passover Seder using only freshly harvested spices It tastes best when made with goat meat, called* mutton *in India, but lamb makes a fine substitute. For a hotter dish, increase the quantity of peppercorns.*

1½ cups (1½ oz/45 g) packed fresh cilantro (fresh coriander), leaves and tender stems

6–12 fresh hot green chiles such as serrano, stemmed

6 large cloves garlic

2-inch (5-cm) piece fresh ginger, peeled and roughly chopped

2–3 tablespoons water, if needed

8 green cardamom pods

1 cinnamon stick, broken into bits

6 whole cloves

1 tablespoon ground coriander

1 teaspoon ground turmeric

1 teaspoon cayenne pepper

2 teaspoons cracked black peppercorns

2 cassia leaves (page 244)

4 tablespoons (2 fl oz/60 ml) peanut oil

2 lb (1 kg) lamb or goat shoulder meat, trimmed of fat and sinew and cut into 1-inch (2.5-cm) pieces

3 yellow onions, finely chopped

3 tomatoes, chopped

2 teaspoons salt, or to taste

In a food processor or blender, combine 1 cup (1 oz/30 g) of the cilantro, the chiles, garlic, and ginger and process until finely puréed. If necessary, add the water to speed up the process. Set aside.

With the base of a heavy pan, lightly crush the cardamom pods to open them and release the seeds. Do not discard the skins. In a small, dry frying pan over medium-high heat, combine the cardamom seeds and skins, cinnamon, and cloves. Roast the spices, shaking and tossing constantly, until fragrant, about 4 minutes. Let cool, then transfer the spices to a grinding stone, mortar, blender, or a coffee grinder reserved solely for spices and pound or process them to a fine powder. Transfer to a small bowl and add the ground coriander, turmeric, cayenne pepper, peppercorns, and cassia leaves. Set aside.

In a large, shallow nonstick frying pan over high heat, warm 1 tablespoon of the oil. When hot, add a few pieces of the meat and cook, turning and tossing, until it loses its red color but is only lightly fried, about 3 minutes. (Do not overbrown the meat, as this will make the sauce very dark.) Using a slotted spoon, transfer the seared meat pieces to a bowl. Repeat in batches with the remaining meat.

To the same pan, add the remaining 3 tablespoons oil and the onions. Reduce the heat to medium-high and cook, stirring occasionally, until the onions are golden brown, about 10 minutes. Add the cilantro paste and cook, stirring, until it loses its raw aroma, about 2 minutes.

Add the tomatoes and cook, stirring occasionally, until they look soft, about 5 minutes. Return the meat with its juices to the pan. Add the spice mixture and salt and mix well. Reduce the heat to low, cover, and simmer gently until the meat is fully cooked and very tender, about 1½ hours. Check and stir often to ensure that the meat is not sticking and burning. Turn off the heat and let the dish rest for 5 minutes, covered, before serving. Check and correct the seasonings. Transfer to a warmed platter, sprinkle with the remaining cilantro, and serve.

serves 6

West Bengal and Haryana
Chenna and Paneer

homemade cheese

Cheese is expensive in India, and highly valued. Most families make their own. There are two types: chenna, *a curd cheese, and* paneer, *which is chenna that has been pressed to give it a firmer texture. Some Indians sprinkle* paneer *with garam masala as part of a main meal, and some restaurants now serve fried* paneer *cubes atop one of many regional salads. Some* chenna *or fried* paneer *with bread and a pickle makes a simple and delicious light lunch. These cheeses also form the basis of many other savory and sweet dishes.*

8 cups (2 qt/2 l) milk

3–4 tablespoons fresh lemon juice

all-purpose (plain) flour for dusting

vegetable oil for frying

❧ Line a sieve with a double layer of cheesecloth (muslin). Place the sieve over a large bowl and set aside until needed.

❧ In a deep enamel or other nonaluminum pot over medium-high heat, bring the milk to a boil. Reduce the heat to low, and once the milk is at a low simmer, add 3 tablespoons of the lemon juice. With a wooden spoon, stir the milk very slowly while the white curd (*chenna*) forms, leaving behind thin, yellowish whey. This should take about 1 minute. If the cheese does not form completely, add more lemon juice. Pour the cheese and whey into the sieve and allow to drain thoroughly. Discard the whey.

❧ To make *paneer*, loosely wrap the *chenna* in the same cheesecloth and set it in a baking dish. To compress the cheese and give it the right texture, weigh it down with a pot filled with water. When it feels firm, after about 1 hour, remove, unwrap, and cut it into neat ½-inch (12-mm) cubes. Dust the cheese with all-purpose flour. In a large frying pan over medium-high heat, warm enough oil to cover the bottom of the pan. When hot, add the cubes and fry until light golden, about 2 minutes.

❧ Serve at room temperature or chilled, or refrigerate, tightly wrapped in plastic, for up to 5 days.

makes 1¼ cups (10 oz/315 g) chenna *or 2 cups (10 oz/315 g)* paneer *cubes*

Milk and Milk Products

Of all foods, perhaps none is held in higher esteem by Indians than cow's milk. It is believed that milk and its many by-products were introduced into India by the invading Aryans during the second millennium BC. The ancient Holy Vedic scriptures sing the praises of milk as *amrita,* "nectar," and of clarified butter as a soul-purifying source.

For India's hundreds of millions of practicing vegetarians, milk is a near-perfect food. The milk of cows and water buffalo is considered superior to that of the goat, sheep, camel, horse, donkey, or yak, in that order. Indians prefer to drink milk warm, slightly sweetened, and scented with saffron, tea, or coffee. Milk is used in both savory and dessert sauces.

There are eight by-products of milk that are in frequent use in the Indian kitchen: *malai* (cream), *dahi* (yogurt), *khadi dahi* (yogurt cheese), *chenna* or *paneer* (farmer's cheese), *mattha* (buttermilk), *makkhan* (butter), *usli ghee* (clarified butter), and *khoya* (milk fudge). Most Indian homes, like that of my mother, still buy cow's or buffalo's milk twice a day and make these products on a regular basis. In general, Indian cooks do not like to purchase ready-made milk products for fear of adulteration or stale ingredients. They also dislike homogenized milk because the cream does not separate and settle at the top. It is this cream that cooks use when preparing the best butter and *usli ghee.*

Mattha—the buttermilk by-product that remains after separating out the butter—is called a yogurt drink, and is popular throughout India. In the north, where milk is plentiful, the yogurt drink is rich, thick, and sweet. In the south, it is thinner and often flavored with kari leaves, ginger, and coconut. The Indian cream *malai* is essentially clotted cream or crème fraîche. It is served on toast or chapatis (flat breads) and sprinkled with jaggery or fruits. For children in particular, it is regarded as a special treat. The milk fudge, *khoya,* has a taste similar to that of condensed milk. *Khoya* forms the basis for most Indian desserts and sweets. My mother has a creative and unique method of making *khoya* that calls for sour fruit. The result is a delicious milk fudge. I have yet to see it used in any desserts in my mother's house, however, since it is always devoured the moment it is removed from the *karhai!*

Uttar Pradesh

Anda Masala

eggs braised in fragrant gravy

*Since I first ate these Patna-style eggs in 1963,
I have become a staunch fan. I don't know whether
their appeal is due to the lovely flavor of the Indian
free-range eggs or the combination of them with the
spicy, garlicky-tomato gravy. But the formula
is magical. I like to serve them at brunch
or supper with bread.*

4 eggs, hard boiled and peeled

1 tablespoon vegetable oil

1 teaspoon cumin seeds

1 yellow onion, finely chopped

1 cinnamon stick

2 teaspoons ground coriander

½ teaspoon red pepper flakes

½ teaspoon ground turmeric

2 cloves garlic, thinly sliced

¾ teaspoon salt, or to taste

1 large tomato, puréed

1¼ cups (10 fl oz/310 ml) water

2 tablespoons chopped fresh cilantro (fresh
coriander)

⚜ Place the eggs in a bowl with water to cover. Set aside until needed.

⚜ In a wide, shallow pan over medium-high heat, warm the oil. When hot, add the cumin and cook, stirring, until it darkens, about 15 seconds. Add the onion and cinnamon and cook, stirring occasionally, until the onion is light brown, about 6 minutes. Stir in the coriander, red pepper flakes, turmeric, garlic, and salt. Cook, stirring, until the garlic is lightly fried, about 2 minutes. Add the tomato and cook, stirring, until it loses its raw aroma, about 5 minutes. Add the water and bring to a boil. Reduce the heat to low, cover, and simmer gently for 5 minutes to allow the flavors to blend.

⚜ Remove the eggs from the water and pat them dry on paper towels. Cut each egg lengthwise into neat halves, ensuring the yolk is still intact. Carefully slip the eggs, cut side up, into the sauce. Continue cooking over medium-low heat, gently spooning the sauce over the eggs, until the eggs are piping hot. Sprinkle with the cilantro and serve immediately.

serves 2–4

Tamil Nadu

Molahuvarata Meen

pan-seared chile pepper fish

*The abundant fish found in the Bay of Bengal
is the primary food of the people of Tamil Nadu. The
most prized catch of all is pomfret, a flat, oval-shaped
fish about 12 inches (30 cm) long that is similar to
Dover sole. Tamilians call it vuvval and love its clean
structure and delicate flavor. Good substitutes are other
varieties of sole, flounder, or halibut. In this simple
everyday recipe, the fish is rubbed with spices, coated
with semolina, and shallow-fried. The crunch of the
spicy crust is a perfect contrast to the delicate, mild
interior. Serve the fish with a chutney and rice.*

4 skinless pomfret, sole, flounder, or halibut fillets,
about 1½ lb (750 g) total weight

1 tablespoon minced fresh hot green chiles such
as serrano

2 teaspoons minced garlic

15 fresh or 30 dried kari leaves, finely shredded
(page 248)

½–2 teaspoons cayenne pepper, to taste

1½ teaspoons paprika

3 tablespoons fresh lemon juice

½ teaspoon salt, or to taste

½ cup (3 oz/90 g) farina (fine-grind semolina)

¼ cup (2 fl oz/60 ml) vegetable oil

⚜ Lay the fish in a shallow dish. In a small bowl, combine the chiles, garlic, kari leaves, cayenne pepper to taste, paprika, lemon juice, and salt. Rub the spice mixture over the fish fillets and set aside to marinate for 30 minutes at room temperature.

⚜ Spread the semolina on a large plate.

⚜ Use 2 large nonstick frying pans, each big enough to hold 2 fillets without overcrowding. Add half the oil to each pan and warm over high heat. Meanwhile, dip the fish in the semolina, pressing down firmly so that the coating sticks. When the oil is very hot, add 2 fillets to each pan. Cook, shaking the pan so that the fish browns evenly, until the underside is brown, about 1 minute. Turn the fish with a spatula and continue cooking until lightly brown and crisp all over, about 1 minute longer. Transfer to a warmed platter and serve at once.

serves 4

Gujarat

Masaledar Paneer

braised cheese with herbs

A popular preparation of the Gujarati Jains, masaledar paneer *is very easy to make. The paneer cubes are simply tossed in spice-and-herb-infused oil, then served. Accompanied by plain or stuffed bread, this dish makes a lovely brunch or lunch. I also like to prepare it with Chinese firm tofu instead of* paneer, *although the flavor is completely different.*

2 tablespoons vegetable oil

½ teaspoon cumin seeds

½ teaspoon fennel seeds

½ teaspoon nigella seeds (page 250)

1 teaspoon peeled and grated fresh ginger

1 teaspoon minced garlic

1–2 fresh hot green chiles such as serrano, sliced

¼ cup (¾ oz/20 g) thinly sliced green (spring) onion, including tender green tops

2 cups (10 oz/315 g) fried paneer *cheese cubes (page 82)*

½ teaspoon salt, or to taste

½ cup (4 fl oz/125 ml) water

2 teaspoons lemon juice

❧ In a nonstick frying pan over medium–high heat, warm the oil. When hot, add the cumin, fennel, and nigella and cook, stirring, until the cumin turns a few shades darker, about 30 seconds. Add the ginger, garlic, chiles, and green onion and cook, stirring, until the spices are lightly fried, about 2 minutes.

❧ Add the *paneer,* salt, and water and cook, gently turning and tossing, until the water has evaporated and the spice flavors are absorbed into the cheese, about 6 minutes. Check and correct the seasonings. Serve sprinkled with the lemon juice.

serves 2–4

Delhi and Uttar Pradesh

Gosht

lamb curry with pumpkin

This is the quintessential dish of India, particularly in the north, where meat eating is more prevalent. Every family in northern India boasts a special way of cooking or seasoning gosht, *the secret of which is regarded as a prized possession and passed on from one generation to another with great traditional fanfare. But most Indians will agree that the people of Delhi, having inherited the Moghul legacy, have the most interesting interpretations of* gosht. *Among the Delhiites, any seasoned, spice-braised meat is called* gosht, *which literally means "meat" but usually refers to goat or sheep meat. Lamb makes a wonderful substitute.*

Gosht *can be prepared plain or include any number of ingredients. Vegetables such as potatoes, turnips, okra, or pumpkin; fruits such as plums, dried apricots, or raisins; or nuts such as cashews or walnuts are particularly popular. Like any braised dish,* gosht *tastes even better the next day.*

4 tablespoons (2 fl oz/60 ml) vegetable oil

1 lb (500 g) lean lamb shoulder meat, trimmed and cut into 1-inch (2.5-cm) cubes

1 cup (4 oz/125 g) chopped yellow onion

3 black or green cardamom pods

2 cassia leaves (page 244)

1 tablespoon peeled and grated fresh ginger

2 teaspoons minced garlic

2 tablespoons ground coriander

½ teaspoon ground turmeric

1 cup (6 oz/185 g) chopped tomato

1 tablespoon tomato paste

2 cups (16 fl oz/500 ml) chicken stock or water

1½ teaspoons salt, or to taste

1-lb (500-g) piece pumpkin or butternut squash, peeled, seeded, and cut into 1-inch (2.5-cm) pieces

1 tablespoon garam masala (page 249)

¼ cup (⅓ oz/10 g) chopped fresh cilantro (fresh coriander)

✤ In a large, heavy, flameproof baking dish over high heat, warm 2 tablespoons of the oil. When hot, add a few of the meat pieces and sear until they are lightly browned all over but not cooked through, about 3 minutes. Transfer to a bowl. Repeat with the remaining meat pieces.

✤ Add the remaining 2 tablespoons oil to the baking dish over medium-high heat. When hot, add the onion, cardamom, and cassia leaves and cook, stirring occasionally, until the onion is browned, about 8 minutes. Stir in the ginger, garlic, coriander, and turmeric.

✤ Return the browned meat to the baking dish along with the tomato, tomato paste, stock or water, and salt. Bring to a boil, then reduce the heat to low, cover, and cook until the meat is tender when pierced with a fork, about 2 hours. Alternatively, place the covered baking dish in an oven preheated to 350°F (180°C) for 2½ hours.

✤ About 20 minutes before the meat is done, stir in the pumpkin, re-cover, and continue cooking until the meat and pumpkin are tender and cooked through. Check and correct the seasoning. Transfer the curry to a warmed platter, taking care not to crush the pumpkin. Sprinkle with the garam masala and cilantro and serve.

serves 2–4

Tamil Nadu

Sambar

curried lentils with bell peppers

Many other vegetables can replace the bell peppers in this spicy southern Indian lentil stew. Particularly tasty are brussels sprouts, cauliflower, shallots, and radish.

1 cup (7 oz/220 g) pink or yellow lentils

3 cups (24 fl oz/750 ml) water

½ teaspoon ground turmeric

1 small yellow onion, cut into 1-inch (2.5-cm) pieces

2 green bell peppers (capsicums), cored and cut into 2-inch (5-cm) pieces

2 red bell peppers (capsicums), cored and cut into 2-inch (5-cm) pieces

24 fresh or 48 dried kari leaves (page 248)

2 teaspoons sambar powder (page 251) or curry powder (page 249)

1 tablespoon tomato paste

1½ teaspoons salt, or to taste

1 cup (8 fl oz/250 ml) tamarind water (page 251)

2 tablespoons light vegetable oil

1½ teaspoons brown mustard seeds

½ teaspoon powdered asafetida (see sidebar, page 144) or 1 teaspoon minced garlic

¼ cup (⅓ oz/10 g) chopped fresh cilantro (fresh coriander)

♨ Pick over the lentils, removing any stones or mis-shapen or discolored lentils. Rinse thoroughly and place in a deep pot. Add the water and turmeric and bring to a boil over high heat. Reduce the heat to medium and cook, uncovered, until the lentils are very soft, about 20 minutes. Add the onion, bell peppers, kari leaves, sambar or curry powder, tomato paste, and salt. Mix well, cover, and cook until the vegetables are soft, about 8 minutes. Add the tamarind water and cook for 2 minutes longer. Remove from the heat.

♨ In a small frying pan over medium-high heat, warm the oil. When hot, add the mustard seeds and cover the pan. When the seeds stop sputtering, after about 30 seconds, stir in the asafetida or garlic. Pour the entire contents of the pan over the lentils. Mix well. Sprinkle with the cilantro and serve at once.

serves 6

Karnataka

Tethi Kori

mangalore eggs with coconut

This spicy-hot Mangalorian egg dish will hit your palate like a bolt of lightning. Traditional accompaniments are rice, rice crepes, or bread.

8 eggs, preferably small, hard boiled and peeled

2 yellow onions

¼ cup (2 fl oz/60 ml) vegetable oil

2 teaspoons ground coriander

1 teaspoon ground cumin

¼ teaspoon ground fenugreek

pinch of ground cloves

½–1½ teaspoons cayenne pepper, to taste

¼ teaspoon ground black pepper

1 cup (8 fl oz/250 ml) coconut milk

1½ teaspoons salt, or to taste

1 cup (8 fl oz/250 ml) water

4 small potatoes, boiled and peeled, or 1 large potato, boiled, peeled, and cut into 4 pieces

2 tablespoons unsweetened grated coconut (optional)

♨ Place the eggs in a bowl with water to cover. Set aside until needed.

♨ Chop 1 onion very finely. Set aside. Slice the other onion thinly. In a wide, shallow frying pan over medium-high heat, warm the oil. When hot, add the sliced onion and cook, stirring frequently, until it turns caramel brown, about 9 minutes. Using tongs or a a slotted spoon, transfer to paper towels to drain. Set aside until needed.

♨ Add the chopped onion, coriander, cumin, fenu-greek, cloves, cayenne pepper, and black pepper to the remaining oil in the pan. Cook over medium-high heat, stirring, until the onion looks soft, about 4 minutes. Add the coconut milk, salt, and water and bring to a boil. Reduce the heat to low, cover, and simmer for 5 minutes to allow the flavors to blend.

♨ Drain the eggs. Add the eggs and potatoes to the sauce, cover, and cook for 5 minutes. Remove from the heat. Check and correct the seasonings. Fold the fried onion shreds very lightly into the eggs and sauce. Transfer to a shallow dish and serve sprinkled with grated coconut, if desired.

serves 4

Ganesha, the Elephant God

I remember, at the age of seven, sitting on a small mat in front of our family's *pujamandapam,* or ritual altar. The altar consisted of the *kuttivalaku,* the holy lamp; a framed photograph of my great-grandfather; and a statue of a pudgy figure with a human body and an elephant's head. This was Ganesha, my favorite Hindu god. He loved food and sweets (it is no surprise that Ganesha is the God of Food) and so did I. As you might expect, he was fat with a pot belly. I was, shall we say, rather round as well. In the Indian ethos, fatness is viewed as a good thing. It is a sign of prosperity and abundance, and often represents an appetite for good living and good cooking.

Statues of Ganesha are most common in home kitchens and by the cash register in restaurants, where they are thought to bring prosperity. Although today prosperity is associated with money, in ancient times it meant more cattle, more land, and therefore more food. Food and prosperity are inextricably linked in the Indian psyche, so Ganesha is worshipped as the provider of both. Good fortune is often attributed to Ganesha's grace, and people offer him food so that he will bless them and provide them with even more food.

On Ganesha Chaturthi, which falls during the month of Bhadon (corresponding to August or September in the Western calendar), Ganesha is celebrated with great festivities that include the consumption of *modakum,* considered to be one of his favorite sweets. *Modakum,* also known as *modak,* literally means "dumpling," and is similar to the Chinese dim sum. The wheat or rice flour dough is shaped into 2-inch (5-cm) rounds, stuffed with a sweet coconut mixture or with spicy beans, and then steamed.

Hindu children love the tale of Ganesha, whose father, Lord Shiva, one day mistook his son for an intruder and accidentally beheaded him. Ganesha's distraught mother, Parvati, demanded that he be restored, but even the gods could not find all the pieces. After searching the universe for the head of a newborn with the intelligence of a man, Lord Vishnu returned with that of an elephant, and thus Ganesha was reborn with a new identity.

Because of his association with prosperity, Ganesha is revered by the business community. Whenever the stockmarket drops, the statue of him is turned around in every brokerage house to symbolize his unhappiness at not having taken care of his subjects.

Kerala

Kalan

malabar pumpkin coconut stew

A traditional dish of the Namboodaris, Malabar Brahmins of Kerala, kalan is a delicately seasoned vegetable stew. Winter melon, plantains, potatoes, green mangoes, and pumpkin are popular vegetables in kalan, *although bell pepper, cauliflower, carrots, lima beans, endive, and artichoke hearts will also work quite well. It is the seasoning mixture, which includes chiles, turmeric, mustard seeds, fenugreek, and kari leaves, that transforms the simple yogurt-and-coconut sauce into a sublime dish. Kalan, like many Keralan vegetarian stews, has a soupy consistency that the Malabar people prefer. The following recipe has been modified for the Western palate to produce a thicker sauce with the same flavor and aroma.*

1-lb (500-g) piece pumpkin or 1 small butternut squash, about 1 lb (500 g)

1 zucchini (courgette)

1 cup (4 oz/125 g) firmly packed unsweetened flaked coconut, preferably fresh

4 fresh hot green chiles such as serrano, stemmed

1 teaspoon cumin seeds

1 teaspoon salt

½ cup (4 fl oz/125 ml) water, as needed, plus 1 cup (8 fl oz/250 ml)

1½ cups (12 oz/375 g) plain yogurt, whipped with a fork until smooth

½ teaspoon ground turmeric

½ teaspoon ground black pepper

3 tablespoons coconut oil or vegetable oil

1 teaspoon brown mustard seeds

1 dried red chile, broken in half, seeds discarded

¼ teaspoon fenugreek seeds

12 fresh or 24 dried kari leaves, finely shredded, plus fresh sprigs for garnish (optional; page 248)

☙ If using a piece of pumpkin, peel it, scrape out the seeds, and cut it into 1-inch (2.5-cm) pieces. If using a whole squash, first cut it in half. (Use a kitchen mallet to drive the knife through the tough skin.) Proceed as before. Halve the zucchini lengthwise, then cut it into 2-inch (5-cm) pieces.

☙ In a food processor or blender, combine the coconut, chiles, cumin, and salt and process until smooth. If necessary, gradually add a little water, but not more than ½ cup (4 fl oz/125 ml). Transfer to a small bowl and stir in the yogurt.

☙ In a saucepan over high heat, bring the 1 cup (8 fl oz/250 ml) water to a boil. Stir in the turmeric and pepper, then add the pumpkin and zucchini and mix to coat the vegetables with the turmeric water. Reduce the heat to low, cover, and simmer until the vegetables are soft, about 10 minutes. Add the coconut-yogurt mixture and mix carefully so as not to crush the vegetables. Check and correct the seasonings. Remove from the heat.

☙ In a small frying pan over high heat, warm the oil. When hot, add the mustard seeds and cover the pan. When the seeds stop sputtering, after about 30 seconds, uncover and add the chile pieces and fenugreek. Cook, stirring, until the fenugreek turns darker brown, about 15 seconds. Remove from the heat. Stir in the kari leaves and pour the entire contents of the pan over the pumpkin. Mix well, taking care not to crush the vegetables. If desired, serve garnished with kari sprigs.

serves 6

Uttaranchal

Paneer Cutless

cheese patties with cilantro

Patties of various kinds are known in India as cutless, *a mispronunciation of "cutlet" that originated among the English memsahibs' bearers, or servants, during the British Raj. Although the Raj is long gone, cutlets of all types live on in the menus of Indian armed services clubs and fancy restaurants. The paneer* cutlet *is one of them. It is essential to use the freshest of cheese for these* cutless *to taste delicious.*

1¼ cups (10 oz/315 g) chenna *cheese* or *crumbled* paneer *(page 82)*

2 baking potatoes, boiled, peeled, and mashed, to yield about 1½ cups (½ lb/250 g)

3 slices white bread, trimmed and finely crumbled

2 teaspoons fresh lemon juice

1 teaspoon cumin seeds, roasted (page 246)

1½ teaspoons salt, or to taste

3 tablespoons vegetable oil

¼ cup (¾ oz/20 g) minced green (spring) onion, including tender green tops

¼ cup (1⅓ oz/40 g) finely chopped roasted peanuts or cashew nuts

2–4 fresh hot green chiles such as serrano, seeded and thinly sliced

¼ cup (⅓ oz/10 g) finely chopped fresh cilantro (coriander)

Mint-Yogurt Salad (page 168) or Hot and Spicy Tomato Chutney (page 214) (optional)

❀ Using a food processor, blender, or sieve, cream the cheese and place it in a bowl. Add the potatoes, bread crumbs, lemon juice, cumin, salt, and 1 table-spoon of the oil. With your hands, knead the mixture until thoroughly blended. Add the green onion, peanuts or cashews, chiles, and cilantro and mix well. Divide the mixture into 8 equal portions. Form each portion into a 3-inch (7.5-cm) round patty.

❀ In a large frying pan, preferably nonstick, over medium-high heat, warm the remaining 2 table-spoons oil. When hot, add the patties in a single layer and cook until the underside has browned, about 5 minutes. With a spatula, turn the patties and brown the second side the same way. Transfer to a warmed platter and serve with the salad or chutney.

serves 4

Tamil Nadu

Kurma

madras-style meat with coconut

People from northern India always listen with certain misgivings when those from the south begin talking about korma, *the classic Moghul-style braised meat preparation of the north. First, there is the southern pronunciation,* kurma. *Then there is the addition of whole chiles and coconut—a distinctly southern way of flavoring. But long before the arrival of the Moghuls, South India had dishes similar to kormas. These recipes later underwent changes due to the influence of Moghul culture in the south during the seventeenth century.*

Kurma, a specialty of Tamil Nadu, is a rich and spicy preparation. Indian cooks usually make it with the fatty shoulder of the goat. Since this state is home to a large Christian population, beef, venison, and pork are not uncommon variations in this dish. The addition of fragrant spices such as aniseeds, clove, cinnamon, cardamom, and poppy seeds, coupled with prolonged slow cooking, produces an extremely tender and fragrant meat. You can make a vegetarian version of kurma *by replacing the meat with the same weight of potato, eggplant, cauliflower, okra, turnip, or brussels sprouts, in any combination. For best results, let the dish rest for a day in the refrigerator or at least thirty minutes at room temperature before reheating. Serve it with a rice dish or rice noodles.*

2 tablespoons poppy seeds

2 tablespoons coriander seeds

1 teaspoon aniseeds

¾ teaspoon ground turmeric

5 tablespoons (3 fl oz/80 ml) vegetable oil

2 lb (1 kg) lean lamb shoulder meat or beef, trimmed of fat and sinew and cut into 1-inch (2.5-cm) cubes

4 dried red chiles

1 cinnamon stick

3 green cardamom pods, lightly crushed

6 whole cloves

1 cup (4 oz/125 g) chopped yellow onion

1 teaspoon minced garlic

1 teaspoon peeled and minced fresh ginger

2 cups (16 fl oz/500 ml) coconut milk

1½ teaspoons salt, or to taste

❦ In a small, dry frying pan over medium–high heat, dry-roast the poppy seeds, coriander seeds, and aniseeds, shaking and tossing, until the spices are fragrant and turn a few shades darker, about 5 minutes. Transfer to a small bowl so that the spices are not cooked further by residual heat. Let cool, then transfer to a blender, mortar, grinding stone, or a coffee grinder reserved solely for spices and pound or process to a fine powder. Transfer to a small bowl and add the turmeric. Set aside.

❦ In a large, heavy nonstick frying pan over high heat, warm 2 tablespoons of the oil. When the oil is hot, add a few of the meat pieces and sear until they are lightly browned but not cooked through, about 2 minutes. With a slotted spoon, transfer to a bowl. Repeat in batches with the remaining meat pieces.

❦ To the same pan over medium–high heat, add the the remaining 3 tablespoons oil and the chiles, cinnamon, cardamom, and cloves. Cook until they are fragrant and look puffed, about 2 minutes. Add the onion and cook, stirring often, until it is light brown, about 7 minutes. Stir in the garlic, ginger, and reserved spice mixture. Mix well.

❦ Return the browned meat to the pan, add the coconut milk and salt, and bring to a boil over high heat. Reduce the heat to low, cover, and simmer until the meat is tender enough to be broken apart with a fork, about 1½ hours. Check and correct the seasonings, then serve.

serves 4

Uttar Pradesh

Rasedar

vegetables in
cumin-scented tomato gravy

Rasedar, *meaning "flavorfully sauced," well describes this combination of vegetables simmered in a delicately spiced gravy. The consistency can be varied according to the cook's preference. I usually prepare thicker dishes, as they are easier to scoop up with a piece of bread.*

2 tablespoons usli ghee *(page 247) or vegetable oil*

1 teaspoon cumin seeds

1 tablespoon peeled and finely chopped fresh ginger

1 tablespoon ground coriander

1½ teaspoons ground cumin

¾ teaspoon ground turmeric

½ teaspoon cayenne pepper

1 cup (5 oz/155 g) peeled, chopped boiling potatoes

2 tomatoes, puréed

2 cups (10 oz/315 g) chopped vegetables such as green beans, cauliflower, brussels sprouts, green peas, green bell pepper (capsicum), and kohlrabi, in any combination

2 cups (16 fl oz/500 ml) water or chicken stock

1½ teaspoons salt, or to taste

¼ cup (⅓ oz/10 g) chopped fresh cilantro (fresh coriander)

In a large frying pan over medium-high heat, warm the *usli ghee* or oil. Add the cumin seeds and cook, stirring, until they turn dark brown, about 15 seconds. Stir in the ginger, ground coriander, ground cumin, turmeric, and cayenne pepper. Cook, stirring, for 5 seconds, then add the potatoes, tomatoes, vegetables, water or stock, and salt.

Bring to a boil over high heat, reduce the heat to low, cover, and cook until the vegetables are very soft, about 15 minutes. With the back of a spoon, crush some of the vegetables, particularly the potatoes, to thicken the sauce. Check and correct the seasonings. Serve sprinkled with the cilantro.

serves 6

The Tandoor

Traditional Indian kitchens do not have conventional Western ovens. Yet Indians can still bake, broil, and roast their food. These basic cooking tasks are accomplished successfully in a tandoor, a clay-lined oven that is shaped like a barrel with a vent at the bottom. Several cultures, including the Syrian Bedouins and the Persians, devised a rudimentary tandoor, a shallow clay pit used primarily for baking breads.

The eastern Pashtun tribes of Pakistan refined the basic model to create the tandoor of today. In the oven's most common role, meat is marinated in a yogurt-spice mixture colored with an orange-red dye that identifies it as tandoor-cooked food, and then threaded onto skewers. The skewers are lowered into the searing heat of the oven where the meat grills, bakes, and smokes simultaneously, producing a unique flavor and remarkable tenderness.

Tandoori chicken and tandoori nan remain two of the most popular dishes served in Indian restaurants. But other foods, including fish and shellfish, vegetables, and cheese, take on the same earthy aroma and delicious flavor when cooked in this simple, yet ingenious, oven.

Delhi

Tandoori Murghi

tandoori chicken

This most popular of all Indian dishes takes its name from the tandoor, the clay oven in which it is baked. It can, however, be roasted very successfully using a conventional oven; the real secret of success is not so much a tandoor but the marinade and the way the chicken is prepared. Bone-in chicken is used because it retains moisture better than meat off the bone. Both whole and cut-up birds are acceptable, although larger pieces such as halves or quarters make for a more attractive presentation. The chicken pieces are skinned, pricked, and slashed before marinating to allow the marinade to penetrate the meat. I like to roast tandoori chicken in a 500°F (260°C) oven. The high heat gives a crusty exterior and seals in the succulent juices.

The creators of tandoori chicken, to ensure it was mistaken for no other, colored it bright red using edible dye. But the addition of color is entirely optional. To color chicken, add 1 teaspoon red food coloring and 2 teaspoons yellow to the marinade. Edible dyes are available in Indian grocery and speciality stores.

1 small chicken, about 3 lb (1.5 kg), cut into serving pieces, skinned, and trimmed of all visible fat

MARINADE

½ cup (4 oz / 125 g) plain yogurt

2 tablespoons fresh lemon juice or malt vinegar

1 tablespoon minced garlic

1 tablespoon peeled and grated or crushed fresh ginger

1 tablespoon ground cumin

1 teaspoon ground coriander

½ teaspoon cayenne pepper

¼ teaspoon ground cardamom

¼ teaspoon ground cloves

¼ teaspoon ground black pepper

2 teaspoons salt, or to taste

vegetable oil for brushing

fresh cilantro (fresh coriander) sprigs

slices of cucumber, red (Spanish) onion, tomato, and lemon

♚ Prick the flesh of the chicken all over with a fork, then, using a sharp knife, cut slashes in the flesh to allow the marinade to penetrate. Place the chicken in a large, shallow dish.

♚ To make the marinade, in a glass or ceramic bowl, combine the yogurt, lemon juice or vinegar, garlic, ginger, cumin, ground coriander, cayenne pepper, cardamom, cloves, black pepper, and salt. Stir until well mixed, then pour the mixture over the chicken and rub it into the flesh, turning the chicken several times. Cover and marinate in the refrigerator for 8 hours or overnight. (Do not marinate for longer than 2 days.) Remove the chicken from the refrigerator at least 30 minutes before cooking.

♚ The chicken may be grilled or roasted. If using a charcoal grill, prepare a fire for direct-heat cooking. Position the grill rack 5 inches (13 cm) from the fire. Allow the coals to burn until white ash covers them and the heat is moderate. Remove the chicken from the marinade, pressing lightly to extract excess marinade, and brush with oil. Place the chicken pieces on a well-oiled grill rack and grill, covered, with the vents open, turning 3–4 times, until the juices run clear when a piece is pierced near the bone with a knife, about 45 minutes.

♚ If roasting the chicken, preheat an oven to 450°F (230°C). Place the chicken on a rack in a roasting pan, brush with oil, and cook, turning once, until the juices run clear when a piece is pierced near the bone with a knife, 25–30 minutes.

♚ Serve with sprigs of cilantro and slices of cucumber, red onion, tomato, and lemon.

serves 4

The heated clay of the tandoor permeates the food with its special flavor and fragrance.

Karnataka

Usili

broccoli smothered in
spicy split pea nuggets

*A specialty of the city of Mysore, usili is yet another
imaginative way to serve legumes. The crumbly split
pea mixture laced with red chile and kari leaf adds
an interesting meatiness to this vegetable dish.
Any number of vegetables can be substituted for the
broccoli—particularly good choices are spinach, green
beans, cabbage, and bamboo shoots. This recipe comes
from my sister Chitra.*

1 cup (7 oz/220 g) yellow split peas (page 247)

*1 small bunch broccoli or 1 package (10 oz/
315 g) thawed frozen broccoli*

24 fresh or 48 dried kari leaves (page 248)

2 dried red chiles, broken into bits

1½ teaspoons salt

3 tablespoons vegetable oil

1 teaspoon brown mustard seeds

2 teaspoons white split gram beans (page 246)

½ teaspoon ground turmeric

*½ teaspoon powdered asafetida (see sidebar,
page 144) or 1 teaspoon minced garlic*

¼ cup (2 fl oz/60 ml) water

❧ Pick over the peas, removing any stones or mis-
shapen or discolored peas. Rinse thoroughly and
place in a deep pot. Add hot water to cover and let
soak for 1 hour.

❧ If using fresh broccoli, cut off the stem, peel it, and
cut it lengthwise into ½-inch (12-mm) slices.
Separate the broccoli head into florets and chop
them into 1-inch (2.5-cm) pieces. Rinse, drain, and
set aside until needed. If using frozen broccoli, allow
it to drain well. Set aside.

❧ Drain the peas. In a food processor or blender,
combine the drained peas, half of the kari leaves, 1 of
the chiles, and 1 teaspooon of the salt. Process until
coarsely ground. Stir in 1 tablespoon of the oil. Place
the split pea mixture in a steamer and steam for
15 minutes. Break up any lumps with a fork.

❧ In a nonstick frying pan over medium-high heat,
warm the remaining 2 tablespoons oil. When the oil
is hot, add the mustard seeds and the remaining chile
and cover the pan. When the seeds stop sputtering,
after about 30 seconds, uncover and add the white
split gram beans. Cook, stirring, until the beans are
lightly golden, about 15 seconds. Stir in the turmeric, asafetida or garlic, the remaining kari leaves, and
the remaining ½ teaspoon salt. Add the broccoli and
water, reduce the heat to low, cover, and cook until
the broccoli is soft, about 8 minutes. Fold in the pea
mixture, re-cover, and cook for 5 minutes longer.
Uncover and continue cooking, stirring to break up
the pea mixture, until lightly fried, about 5 minutes
longer. Remove from the heat. Check and correct
the seasonings. Allow to cool a little before serving.

serves 6

Versatile turmeric is used as
a spice, a dye, a paint pigment,
an antiseptic, a cosmetic.

Andhra Pradesh

Shikampuri Kabab

shikampur kabob with roasted chickpeas

On special occasions, these kabobs are stuffed with chopped, cooked egg whites, cilantro, and chiles. Try them rolled in Indian bread and accompanied with a salad and a chilled lassi.

1 lb (500 g) ground (minced) lamb or beef

1 small yellow onion, finely chopped

2 tablespoons roasted chickpeas (garbanzo beans), ground to a powder in a coffee grinder or blender

4 fresh hot green chiles such as serrano, thinly sliced

¼ cup (⅓ oz / 10 g) chopped fresh cilantro (fresh coriander)

2 tablespoons minced fresh mint

1 teaspoon garam masala (page 249)

1 teaspoon ground black pepper

1 teaspoon mango powder (page 248) or 2 teaspoons fresh lemon juice

1 tablespoon usli ghee (page 247) or unsalted butter, softened

1 egg

1½ teaspoons salt, or to taste

vegetable oil for frying

In a large bowl, combine the meat, onion, ground chickpeas, chiles, cilantro, mint, garam masala, pepper, mango powder or lemon juice, ghee or butter, egg, and salt. Knead with your hands until smooth. Divide the mixture into 12 portions. Roll each portion into a ball and press lightly to form a patty.

In a large nonstick frying pan, pour in oil to a depth of ¼ inch (6 mm) and heat to 375°F (190°C). When hot, add a few kabobs and cook, turning, until nicely browned and cooked through, about 6 minutes. Using tongs or a slotted spoon, transfer to paper towels to drain. Keep warm in a low oven, covered, while you cook the remaining kabobs the same way, adding more oil to the pan as necessary. Transfer to a warmed platter and serve at once.

serves 4

Maharashtra and Gujarat
Khatte Baigan

sindhi eggplant in sweet and sour tamarind sauce

A popular preparation in Bombay, khatte baigan is a classic dish of the Sindhis, an ethnic community that migrated to India from Sindh, in Pakistan, after partition in 1947. They arrived in Bombay, quickly established their new home, and adopted local ways, including integrating the local cooking style into their own Moghul-influenced cuisine.

The round variety of eggplant is more common in this dish, although the Japanese or Chinese long variety and small Italian eggplants also work very well. Select very fresh, firm eggplants that have a nice sheen. Stale eggplants, in addition to lacking flavor, tend to become mushy in braised dishes. Sindhi food is generally very hot, though pleasantly so because of the layering of sweet and sour flavors. If your palate agrees, use four very hot chiles, such as bird's eye, in this recipe.

6 tablespoons (3 fl oz/90 ml) vegetable oil

1 eggplant (aubergine), about 1½ lb (750 g), trimmed and cut into 2-inch (5-cm) pieces

1 teaspoon cumin seeds

½ teaspoon fennel seeds

¼ teaspoon fenugreek seeds

2 yellow onions, thinly sliced

2 baking potatoes, peeled and cut into 1-inch (2.5-cm) pieces

1 tablespoon ground coriander

1 teaspoon peeled and grated fresh ginger

1–4 fresh hot green chiles such as serrano, slit once down each side (see note)

2 tomatoes, finely chopped

salt to taste

20 fresh or 40 dried kari leaves (page 248)

2 cups (16 fl oz/500 ml) water

1 cup (8 fl oz/250 ml) tamarind water (page 251)

2 teaspoons jaggery (page 248) or brown sugar

½ cup (¾ oz/20 g) chopped fresh cilantro (fresh coriander)

※ In a large, wide pan over high heat, warm 2 tablespoons of the oil. When very hot, add half of the eggplant, placing it in a single layer. Let the eggplant fry, without stirring, for 1 minute, then turn and stir for 5 minutes to sear as many sides as possible. Transfer to a bowl. Add 2 more tablespoons oil to the pan. When hot again, add the remaining eggplant and sear it the same way. Transfer to the bowl holding the eggplant and set aside.

※ Add the remaining 2 tablespoons oil to the pan over high heat. When hot, add the cumin, fennel, and fenugreek and fry until they turn several shades darker, about 15 seconds. Add the onions, potatoes, ground coriander, ginger, and chiles. Reduce the heat to medium-high and cook, stirring often, until the vegetables are lightly browned, about 9 minutes.

※ Return the eggplant to the pan and add the tomatoes, salt, kari leaves, and water. Mix well and bring to a boil over high heat. Reduce the heat to low, cover, and simmer until the vegetables are tender, about 15 minutes. Stir in the tamarind water and jaggery or brown sugar and cook for 1 minute longer. Check and correct the seasonings.

※ Transfer to a warmed serving dish and serve garnished with the cilantro.

serves 6

Masalas are freshly ground every day using a different blend of spices for each dish.

Rajasthan

Bhindi Kadhi

marvari okra in yogurt sauce

*This hearty okra preparation is perfect served with
a rice dish or bread and green salad. For added flavor,
top with a tablespoon of usli ghee.*

1 cup (8 oz/250 g) plain yogurt

⅓ cup (1½ oz/45 g) chickpea (garbanzo bean)
flour

1 tablespoon ground coriander

½ teaspoon cayenne pepper

½ teaspoon ground turmeric

1½ teaspoons salt

1 cup (8 fl oz/250 ml) water

¼ cup (2 fl oz/60 ml) sesame oil or vegetable oil

1 teaspoon brown mustard seeds

1 teaspoon cumin seeds

1 teaspoon fennel seeds

1 yellow onion, finely chopped

1 lb (500 g) okra, stemmed

2 tomatoes, cut into 1-inch (2.5-cm) wedges

16 fresh or 32 dried kari leaves, finely shredded
(page 248)

❧ In a saucepan, combine the yogurt, chickpea
flour, coriander, cayenne pepper, turmeric, and salt.
Whisk until smooth. Stir in the water, place over
medium heat, and bring to a gentle boil. Reduce the
heat to very low and simmer, uncovered, until the
sauce is thickened, about 25 minutes. Keep the sauce
warm while you cook the okra.

❧ In a large frying pan over high heat, warm the oil.
When hot, add the mustard seeds and cover the pan.
When the seeds stop sputtering, after about 30 seconds, add the cumin, fennel, and onion. Reduce the
heat to low and cook, stirring, until the onion is
glazed and limp, about 3 minutes. Add the okra and
tomatoes and mix well. Cover and cook until the
okra is soft, about 20 minutes. Pour the entire contents of the pan over the yogurt mixture. Add the
kari leaves and mix well. Check and correct the seasonings, then serve at once.

serves 4

West Bengal

Machor Jhal

braised fish with
eggplant and potato

West Bengal is renowned for its many fish dishes. Machor jhal (machor means "made with fish" and jhal, "thin sauce") is an everyday classic which, to a Bengali, tastes best when made with the fish hilsa ilisha, known commonly as hilsa. This silvery green-and-purple fish grows to 15–20 inches (38–50 cm) long. Its flavor is wonderfully meaty but it has treacherous bones that make it extremely cumbersome to eat. Bengalis don't seem to mind the risk factor, since the reward is well worthwhile, but it makes the fish less popular with other Indians. Hilsa is available frozen in Indian grocery stores. Any oily fish, such as shad, carp, or mackerel, will make a fine substitute. Nonoily fish can be used, too. I like to prepare this dish with seabass, flounder, haddock, salmon, or cod for their light, superb texture and mellow flavor.

To add extra heat, Bengalis stir in sliced green chiles to the finished machor jhal. As I prefer a milder taste, I have eliminated that step, but you may add chiles to suit your taste. Although not traditional, I sprinkle a little chopped fresh cilantro on top before serving. Serve with plain boiled rice or coconut rice.

¾ *teaspoon ground turmeric*

1½ *teaspoons salt*

1½ *lb (750 g) fishsteaks such as* hilsa, sea bass, *flounder, or haddock*

4 *tablespoons (2 fl oz/60 ml) mustard oil or vegetable oil*

2 *dried red chiles*

2 *cassia leaves (page 244)*

2 *teaspoons* panch phoron *(page 249)*

1 *tablespoon prepared mustard*

1 *baking potato, cut into 8 pieces*

1 *small eggplant (aubergine), about ¾ lb (375 g), cut into 16 pieces*

3 *cups (24 fl oz/750 ml) water*

12 *large spinach leaves, fresh or thawed frozen*

¼ *cup (⅓ oz/10 g) fresh cilantro (fresh coriander) (optional)*

✿ In a small bowl, combine the turmeric and ½ teaspoon of the salt. Place the fish on a plate and rub each steak all over with the turmeric-salt mixture.

✿ In a large nonstick frying pan over high heat, warm 2 tablespoons of the oil. When the oil is very hot, add the fish and fry, turning once, until just lightly browned, about 1 minute total. Do not cook the fish all the way through. Transfer to a plate.

✿ Add the remaining 2 tablespoons oil to the pan. When very hot, add the dried chiles and fry, stirring, until they turn black, about 1 minute. Reduce the heat to medium-low, add the cassia leaves and *panch phoron*, and fry, stirring, until the spices turn several shades darker, about 20 seconds. Add the mustard, potato, eggplant, the remaining 1 teaspoon salt, and the water. Mix well, bring to a boil, then reduce the heat to low, cover, and cook until the vegetables are tender, about 20 minutes.

✿ Add the fish and the spinach leaves and carefully stir to submerge them in the sauce and vegetables. Cook briefly over medium heat until the fish is heated through, about 2 minutes. Check and correct the seasonings. Transfer to a warmed serving dish, sprinkle with the cilantro, if desired, and serve at once.

serves 4

Chiles

Today, India is the world's largest producer of hot chiles, which makes it difficult to believe that they were unknown on the subcontinent until the end of the fifteenth century, when the Portuguese came to colonize. It took until the late seventeenth century for chiles to be cultivated in the region. Nowadays, the addiction to their heat is so widespread that many Indians travel with a small bottle of the spice in case they're confronted with a "bland" meal.

Indians use chile in many forms: fresh green pods, dried red pods, red pepper flakes, and powder. Every level of heat, from that of sweet paprika to fiery bird's eye chiles, has its place in the kitchen.

Use fewer chiles than is stated in a recipe if a milder result is preferred. Chiles are appreciated for their flavor as well as their heat. For example, the taste of the milder árbol variety is often preferred over that of the very hot bird's eye chile.

Capsaicin, the chemical that gives chiles their characteristic heat, can cause painful burns, so pods should be handled very carefully. It is a good idea to wear kitchen gloves when you are chopping and seeding them.

Goa

Sorpotel

pork in hot and sour sauce

The Portuguese, who colonized and ruled Goa for 450 years, introduced the Goans to pork and the meat remains in high esteem. It features in chouriço, the garlicky sausage similar to the Spanish chorizo, and the world-famous vindaloo. But the dish most beloved of Goans is sorpotel, a stew of pork meat, lung, heart, and liver. The meat is seasoned and pickled with a special sweet-and-sour vinegar made of coconut palm sap and spices. This intensely flavored preparation tastes best when made with fatty, tender shoulder meat. If you enjoy very hot dishes, double the amount of cayenne pepper. Serve with coconut rice or bread.

1 pork liver (optional)

1 pork heart (optional)

1 pork lung (optional)

1½ lb (750 g) pork shoulder meat, cut into 1-inch (2.5-cm) cubes

2 cloves garlic, unpeeled, bruised

20 fresh or 40 dried kari leaves (page 248), or 2 cassia leaves (page 244)

3 cups (24 fl oz/750 ml) water

5 tablespoons (2½ oz/75 g) lard or usli ghee (page 247) or (2½ fl oz/75 ml) olive oil or vegetable oil

2 cups (10 oz/315 g) finely chopped yellow onion

1 tablespoon peeled and grated or crushed fresh ginger

2 teaspoons minced garlic

2 teaspoons cayenne pepper

1 teaspoon ground turmeric

½ teaspoon ground black pepper

½ teaspoon ground cumin

½ teaspoon ground cinnamon

½ teaspoon ground cloves

6 fresh hot green chiles such as serrano, seeded and sliced

¼ cup (2 fl oz/60 ml) coconut milk or red wine vinegar

¼ cup (2 fl oz/60 ml) tamarind water (page 251)

2 tablespoons jaggery (page 248) or maple syrup

1¼ teaspoons salt, or to taste

✿ If using the liver, heart, and lung, rinse them and pat dry on paper towels, then place in a deep pot. Add the pork shoulder meat, garlic, kari or cassia leaves, and water and bring to a boil over high heat. Reduce the heat to low and simmer gently, uncovered, occasionally skimming the froth off the top with a skimmer, until the meat is partially cooked, about 20 minutes. Using tongs or a slotted spoon, transfer the meat to a cutting board. Cut off and discard any membranes or sinews from the liver, heart, and lung, if used, then cut them into 1-inch (2.5-cm) pieces. Set aside with the shoulder meat.

✿ Strain the stock, return it to the pot, bring to a boil over high heat, and boil until reduced in volume to about 1 cup (8 fl oz/250 ml). Set aside.

✿ In a large, heavy frying pan over high heat, warm 2 tablespoons of the lard, *usli ghee*, or oil. When hot, add a few of the meat pieces and sear quickly until lightly browned, about 2 minutes. Using a slotted spoon, transfer the seared meat pieces to a bowl. Repeat in batches with the remaining meat pieces.

✿ Add the remaining lard, *usli ghee*, or oil and the onion, ginger, and garlic to the pan. Cook, stirring, until the onion is lightly browned, about 8 minutes.

Stir in the cayenne pepper, turmeric, black pepper, cumin, cinnamon, and cloves. Mix well. Return the cooked meat, with its juices, to the pan. Add the chiles, coconut milk or vinegar, tamarind water, jaggery or maple syrup, salt, and reserved pork stock. Bring to a boil over high heat, reduce the heat to medium-low, cover, and simmer until the meat absorbs much of the liquid and the sauce is thickened, about 30 minutes. Transfer to a warmed serving dish and serve at once.

serves 4–6

Portuguese colonists in Goa left a culinary legacy that includes pork, cashews, tomatoes, and the indispensable chile.

West Bengal
Jheenga Masala

shrimp in spiced cream sauce

Serve this flavorful dish from Calcutta with rice for a truly Indian-style meal. Or, for an elegant first course, plate the shrimp on a bed of salad greens.

¼ cup (2 fl oz / 60 ml) vegetable oil

½ cup (2½ oz / 75 g) finely chopped yellow onion

2 fresh hot green chiles such as serrano, thinly sliced

2 teaspoons paprika

1 teaspoon garam masala (page 249)

1 teaspoon minced garlic

¼ teaspoon ground turmeric

1 lb (500 g) medium-sized shrimp (prawns), peeled with the last shell segment and tail fin intact and deveined

½ cup (4 fl oz / 125 ml) light (single) cream

2 tablespoons minced fresh cilantro (fresh coriander)

coarse salt to taste

In a large frying pan over medium–high heat, warm the oil. When hot, add the onion and cook, stirring often, until it begins to brown, about 4 minutes. Stir in the chiles, paprika, garam masala, garlic, and turmeric.

✾ Add the shrimp and toss to coat with the spices. Cook, stirring, until the shrimp turn pink and begin to curl, 2–3 minutes. Stir in the cream, cilantro, and salt. Cook until the sauce is bubbling, about 1 minute more. Check and correct the seasonings. Transfer to a warmed platter and serve immediately.

serves 6

The fishing communities of India's southwest have many festivals and ceremonies dedicated to the sea.

Delhi

Murghi ka Chat

chicken chat

*Marinating diced, cooked tandoori chicken
in a tangy dressing of mango powder, roasted cumin,
and cayenne pepper creates this wonderfully smoky
and spicy chicken salad. The plump, moist chicken
pieces are layered with refreshing yogurt and ginger
before serving. I like to make the* chat *even more
complex by adding a sweet tamarind chutney, which
lifts the dish to new heights. In an emergency you can,
of course, use any ordinary roast chicken, but the salad
will not be as flavorful or appealing. You can make
a lovely meal of chicken* chat *by serving it in pita
pockets or rolled in chapatis.*

½ *recipe day-old Tandoori Chicken (page 96)
or Chicken Malai Kabob (page 113) or ¾ lb
(375 g) day-old grilled or roasted chicken
meat from your favorite recipe, cut into 1-inch
(2.5-cm) cubes*

*1 boiling potato, boiled, peeled, and diced
(¾-inch/2-cm dice)*

½ *cup (2 oz/60 g) diced red (Spanish) onion
(¾-inch/2-cm dice)*

*1 apple, preferably a crisp, tart variety such as
Granny Smith, or 1 Bartlett (Williams') pear,
peeled, cored, and sliced ¼ inch (6 mm) thick*

SOUR DRESSING
¼ *cup (2 fl oz/60 ml) water*

*2 teaspoons mango powder (page 248) or
2 teaspoons fresh lemon juice*

1 teaspoon dried mint leaves, crushed

½ *teaspoon cumin seeds, roasted and ground
(page 246)*

¼ *teaspoon ground black pepper*

¼ *teaspoon cayenne pepper*

¼ *teaspoon salt*

*8 large lettuce leaves, preferably oak leaf
or red leaf*

½ *cup (4 oz/125 g) plain yogurt*

1 teaspoon chopped fresh mint

¼ *cup (2 fl oz/60 ml) Tamarind Chutney
(optional; page 185)*

*1 tablespoon peeled and finely slivered fresh
ginger*

½ *cup (¾ oz/20 g) chopped fresh cilantro
(fresh coriander)*

☙ In a large bowl, combine the chicken, potato,
onion, and apple or pear.

☙ To make the sour dressing, in a measuring cup,
combine the water, mango powder or lemon juice,
dried mint, cumin, black pepper, cayenne pepper,
and salt. Pour over the chicken. Toss well, cover, and
set aside for 30 minutes at room temperature or up
to 2 hours in the refrigerator to let the flavors blend.

☙ When ready to serve, arrange the lettuce leaves on
a serving platter or individual plates. In a cup, combine the yogurt and mint. Pour the yogurt mixture
over the chicken, tossing carefully to coat the chick-
en and vegetables lightly with the sauce. Pile the
chicken mixture atop the lettuce.

☙ Distribute the tamarind chutney, if using, over the
salad. Sprinkle with the ginger slivers and cilantro,
then serve immediately.

serves 4

Tandoori Machi

tandoori grilled fish

Tandoori fish, a star item on the menus of Indian restaurants, is associated with light and healthy cooking. The delicate marinade, infused with ginger, garlic, and ajowan, adds wonderful flavor. I prefer to use sour cream instead of the more traditional yogurt because it lends a buttery flavor and an appealing sheen to the fish. Serve with a salad, rice dish, or bread.

2 salmon fillets, 12–14 oz (375–440 g) total weight

1 teaspoon fresh lemon juice

1 teaspoon minced garlic

1 teaspoon peeled and minced fresh ginger

½ teaspoon garam masala (page 249)

½ teaspoon ajowan seeds (page 244), bruised

¼ teaspoon cayenne pepper

½ teaspoon salt

1 tablespoon sour cream

1 tablespoon usli ghee (page 247) or olive oil

❀ Lay the fish in a shallow dish. In a cup, combine the lemon juice, garlic, ginger, garam masala, ajowan, cayenne pepper, and salt. Rub this mixture all over the fish. Coat the fillets with the sour cream, cover, and set aside to marinate for 30 minutes at room temperature or 3 hours in the refrigerator.

❀ The fish may be grilled or broiled. If using a charcoal grill, prepare a fire for direct-heat cooking. Position the grill rack 5 inches (13 cm) from the fire. Allow the coals to burn until white ash covers them and the heat is moderate. Liberally brush the fillets with the *usli ghee* or oil and place them on the grill rack. Grill, turning once and basting from time to time with more ghee or oil, until the fish is just cooked, about 6 minutes total.

❀ If using a broiler (griller), preheat it, positioning the broiler pan at least 5 inches (13 cm) from the heat. Brush the fillets with the *usli ghee* or oil and place them on the broiler pan in a single layer. Broil, turning once, until the fish is barely opaque, about 7 minutes total.

❀ Transfer to a warmed platter and serve at once.

serves 2

Maharashtra

Ekuri

spicy scrambled eggs

This is a specialty of the Bombay Parsis, followers of Zoroastrianism, who vary it infinitely, often adding slices of green mango or serving it with fried bananas.

2 tablespoons usli ghee *(page 247) or unsalted butter*

1 teaspoon cumin seeds

2 yellow onions, chopped

½ lb (250 g) okra or zucchini (courgettes), cut into slices ¼ inch (6 mm) thick

1 teaspoon finely chopped garlic

2 fresh hot green chiles such as serrano, thinly sliced

1 large tomato, finely chopped

1 teaspoon minced fresh mint, plus sprigs for garnish

2 tablespoons chopped fresh cilantro (fresh coriander), plus sprigs for garnish

¾ teaspoon salt, or to taste

6 eggs, lightly beaten

buttered toast or Paratha *(page 214)*

♔ In a large frying pan over medium heat, warm the *usli ghee* or butter. When hot, add the cumin, onions, and okra or zucchini and cook, stirring, until the vegetables are brown, about 8 minutes. Reduce the heat to low, cover, and cook until the vegetables are tender, about 10 minutes. Check them occasionally; if they look dry and begin to burn, add a little water.

♔ Uncover the pan, stir in the garlic and chiles, and cook for 1 minute. Add the tomato, mint, cilantro, and salt and stir to combine. Pour in the beaten eggs, distributing them evenly over the vegetables. Cook, mixing lightly to scramble the eggs, until the eggs are just set, about 2 minutes. Immediately remove the pan from the heat. Transfer the eggs to a warmed platter and garnish with the cilantro and mint sprigs. Serve immediately with toast or *Paratha*.

serves 4

Food and Religion

Of the innumerable religious Indian customs, none is more ancient than dietary taboos. For centuries, Hindus, Muslims, Jains, Sikhs, Christians, Parsis, and Jews have all managed to live within their respective religious dietary constraints while respecting the habits of others. The common denominator is that all Indians love to eat and prefer to do so in the traditional Indian style: sitting cross-legged on the floor, using the fingers to scoop food from a banana leaf or *thali*. Only the right hand is used to touch food; the left hand is considered unclean. Although this practice originated in ancient Hindu times, it is very much a part of contemporary Indian culture.

Food itself is governed by the dietary laws of each religious sect. Hindus, Jains, and Sikhs do not eat beef. Muslims and Jews omit pork from their diet. Indian Jews are strictly kosher; although rice can be eaten during Passover since wheat flour is uncommon in parts of India. Indian Muslims follow the rules of *halal* (religious slaughtering), but, out of respect for Hindus, many of them do not eat beef. Jains, on the other hand, are unwavering vegetarians governed by the principle of *ahimsa,* or nonviolence. Some ultraorthodox Jains go so far as to avoid roots and tubers, fruits, and vegetables in the rainy season, and to store their lentils in castor oil—all to avoid the possibility of causing harm to any insect.

Hindu Brahmins are strict vegetarians. Their dietary laws, written in the fourth century, are primarily a mixture of Jewish kosher and Chinese feng shui principles, along with Hindu Brahmin codes establishing health and hygiene concepts. In order to cook and consume healthful meals, everything from the location of the stove and the use of specific metal cooking pots to combinations of spices and ingredients and even the mood and demeanor of the cook are specified. An orthodox Hindu Brahmin's meal, called *kaccha khana* (*kaccha* means "raw" or "uncooked" and *khana* is "food") can be touched and consumed only by the immediate family. This antiquated practice is called *choot,* and it is rooted in the concept of cleanliness and avoidance of contaminants.

I think that one of the most inspiring food traditions is the weekly communal charitable feast of the Sikhs, known as *langar*. This free distribution of food to all castes and creeds promotes the idea of equality and brotherhood among all peoples.

Punjab

Saag Gosht

lamb with spinach

Saag gosht, a classic Moghul dish, can be made with lamb or beef. For variety, you can use a combination of greens such as spinach, mustard, kale, and purslane.

4 tablespoons (2 fl oz / 60 ml) vegetable oil

1½ lb (750 g) lamb shoulder or leg meat, trimmed of fat and sinew and cut into 1½-inch (4-cm) pieces

3 yellow onions, finely chopped

1 tablespoon peeled and grated fresh ginger

1 tablespoon minced garlic

3 tablespoons ground coriander

1 tablespoon paprika

½ teaspoon cayenne pepper

½ cup (4 oz / 125 g) plain yogurt, lightly beaten

2 tomatoes, finely chopped

1½ cups (12 fl oz / 375 ml) water

1½ teaspoons salt, or to taste

2 fresh hot green chiles such as serrano, minced

1 cup (7–8 oz / 220–250 g) packed chopped cooked spinach, coarsely puréed

2 teaspoons garam masala (page 249)

½ cup (¾ oz / 20 g) chopped fresh cilantro (fresh coriander)

☙ In a heavy nonstick pan over high heat, warm 2 tablespoons of the oil. When hot, add a few pieces of meat and sear, turning and tossing, until they are nicely browned all over, about 2 minutes. Transfer the seared meat pieces to a plate. Repeat in batches with the remaining meat pieces.

☙ Add the remaining 2 tablespoons oil and the onions to the pan and cook over medium-high heat, stirring often, until they turn caramel brown, about 15 minutes. Stir in the ginger, garlic, ground coriander, paprika, cayenne pepper, and yogurt. Cook, stirring occasionally, until the moisture evaporates and the yogurt begins to fry, about 3 minutes. Return the meat to the pan. Add the tomatoes, water, and salt and bring to a boil. Reduce the heat to low, cover, and simmer, stirring often, until the meat is cooked and very tender, about 1½ hours. Fold in the chiles, spinach, garam masala, and cilantro. Heat through briefly and serve at once.

serves 4

Punjab

Murgh Malai Kabab

chicken malai kabob

Punjabis love chicken preparations. These grilled kabobs may also successfully be roasted in the oven.

2 lb (1 kg) skinless, boneless chicken meat such as breast or thigh, cut into 1½-inch (4-cm) pieces

3 tablespoons fresh lemon juice

2 teaspoons salt

½ cup (4 oz / 125 g) plain yogurt

¼ cup (2 fl oz / 60 ml) sour cream

2 tablespoons minced fresh cilantro (fresh coriander)

1 tablespoon peeled and grated fresh ginger

2 teaspoons minced garlic

1 tablespoon garam masala (page 249) or cumin seeds, roasted and ground (page 246)

1 teaspoon cayenne pepper

½ teaspoon ajowan seeds (page 244) or 1 teaspoon minced fresh thyme

4 tablespoons (2 fl oz / 60 ml) vegetable oil

☙ Place the chicken pieces in a bowl and rub them with the lemon juice and 1 teaspoon of the salt. In a small bowl, combine the yogurt, sour cream, cilantro, ginger, garlic, garam masala or cumin, cayenne pepper, ajowan or thyme, and the remaining 1 teaspoon salt. Pour over the chicken and stir well to coat thoroughly. Carefully fold in 2 tablespoons of the oil. Cover and marinate for 1 hour at room temperature or overnight in the refrigerator.

☙ Preheat a broiler (griller) to maximum temperature and place the broiler pan 5 inches (13 cm) from the heat. Or, preheat an oven to 500°F (260°C).

☙ Thread 4 or 5 pieces of marinated chicken onto each of four 10-inch (25-cm) metal skewers, leaving about ¼ inch (6 mm) space between each piece. Brush with some of the remaining oil and broil or roast, turning and brushing occasionally with any remaining marinade, until the chicken is opaque throughout and firm to the touch, 7–9 minutes. Toward the end of the cooking time, and again just before serving, brush the kabobs with some of the remaining oil to give them extra gloss. Transfer to a warmed platter and serve immediately.

serves 4

Gujarat

Anda nu Popli

egg salad sandwich

During my school years in India, I sometimes stopped at my best friend's home after school for anda nu popli. Auntie Soharabji mixed hard-boiled eggs with cilantro sprouts, tiny chiles, and tomatoes until they looked like a fried chopped omelet. She served the sandwich open-faced, in the Indian style, on whole-wheat (wholemeal) bread tasting of honey and jaggery, which she bought from a nearby Indian Army canteen.

2 tablespoons usli ghee *(page 247) or unsalted butter*

1 yellow onion, finely chopped

1 teaspoon peeled and finely chopped fresh ginger

1 fresh hot green chile such as serrano, thinly sliced

¼ teaspoon cayenne pepper

⅛ teaspoon ground turmeric

8 eggs, hard boiled, peeled, and chopped into ½-inch (12-mm) pieces

¼ cup (1½ oz /45 g) finely diced tomato

¼ teaspoon salt, or to taste

¼ cup (⅓ oz /10 g) chopped fresh cilantro (fresh coriander)

6 slices bread, toasted

♨ In a nonstick frying pan over medium-high heat, warm the *usli ghee* or butter. When hot, add the onion and cook, stirring occasionally, until golden, about 5 minutes. Stir in the ginger, chile, cayenne, turmeric, and eggs. Mix well and cook, stirring gently, until the eggs are lightly fried, about 3 minutes.

♨ Fold in the tomato and turn off the heat. Add the salt and stir in the cilantro.

♨ To serve, pile the egg mixture onto the hot toast, dividing it evenly among the slices. If desired, cut each slice in half into rectangles.

serves 6

West Bengal

Baigan Bhaji

braised eggplant and potato
with spices

Bhaji *denotes a stir-fried or stewed vegetable with spices, and by far the most popular preparation is* baigan bhaji, *made with eggplant. I like the texture of large, round eggplants in this recipe, although all other varieties are acceptable. You can make this dish with other vegetables as well—squash, fragrant greens, okra, taro root, and plantains all work well. Bengalis simply adore potatoes, therefore no matter what* bhaji *the cook is making, a few potatoes will always be included.*

The classic recipe for baigan bhaji *calls for shallow-frying the eggplant slices. This is an essential step in Bengali cooking to add color and flavor to the vegetables. When fried on high heat and drained on paper towels, the vegetable slices are fairly oil-free, but if you prefer, they can be grilled or broiled, although there will be a difference in flavor. Bhaji is one of the typical dishes that are included in a Bengali-style* thali *meal. Serve with bread such as* poori, *a cool* raita, *and salad.*

vegetable oil for frying

2 eggplants (aubergines), about 2 lb (1 kg) total weight, quartered lengthwise and cut crosswise into slices ¼ inch (6 mm) thick

1 baking potato, peeled, halved, and cut into slices ¼ inch (6 mm) thick

½ cup (2½ oz/75 g) finely chopped yellow onion

1 tablespoon peeled and finely chopped fresh ginger

1 teaspoon finely chopped garlic

1 teaspoon cumin seeds

1 teaspoon fennel seeds

½ teaspoon ground turmeric

½ teaspoon cayenne pepper

2 tomatoes, finely chopped

2–4 fresh hot green chiles such as serrano, thinly sliced

1 cup (8 fl oz/250 ml) water, or as needed

1½ teaspoons salt, or to taste

½ teaspoon garam masala (page 249) or cumin seeds, roasted and ground (page 246)

¼ cup (⅓ oz/10 g) chopped fresh cilantro (fresh coriander)

☙ In a large frying pan, pour in oil to cover the bottom in a thin layer. Warm the oil over high heat. When hot, add a few of the eggplant and potato slices and fry until lightly browned, about 4 minutes. Use a slotted spoon to transfer the vegetable slices to several layers of paper towels to drain. Repeat in batches with the remaining slices, adding more oil as necessary. (This step is only to brown the vegetables lightly, not to cook them through; therefore, keep the heat high at all times.)

☙ There should be about 2 tablespoons oil in the pan; if not, add more as necessary. Reduce the heat to medium-high and warm the oil. When hot, add the onion, ginger, garlic, cumin, fennel, turmeric, and cayenne pepper. Cook, stirring often, until the onion is golden, about 6 minutes. Add the tomatoes and cook, stirring, until they begin to brown, about 5 minutes.

☙ Add the eggplant, potatoes, chiles, water, and salt and bring to a boil. Reduce the heat to low, cover, and cook until the vegetables are soft, about 8 minutes. Uncover, increase the heat to medium-high, and continue cooking, stirring, until the excess moisture evaporates and the sauce thickens to coat the vegetable pieces, about 3 minutes. Check and correct the seasonings. Sprinkle with garam masala or cumin and cilantro, mix gently, and serve.

serves 6

Haryana

Chana Masala

chickpeas in spicy sauce

For over half a century, the Kwality restaurant in the Connaught Place section of New Delhi has been serving chana masala that most Delhiites consider the best in the world. The secret is the local chickpeas, which are firmer and more intensely flavored than any others I have eaten. This recipe goes very well with fried bread such as poori or paratha. For a spicier version, fold in two to four minced fresh green chiles.

3 cups (21 oz/655 g) cooked chickpeas
(garbanzo beans), home-cooked or canned

¼ cup (2 fl oz/60 ml) vegetable oil

1 teaspoon cumin seeds

2 yellow onions, finely chopped

1 teaspoon peeled and grated fresh ginger

2 teaspoons ground coriander

½ teaspoon ground turmeric

½–1 teaspoon cayenne pepper

2 tomatoes, finely chopped

2 teaspoons tomato paste

1 teaspoon mango powder (page 248) or fresh lemon juice

½ cup (4 fl oz/125 ml) water

1 teaspoon garam masala (page 249)

¼ cup (⅓ oz/10 g) chopped fresh cilantro (fresh coriander)

☙ If you are using canned chickpeas, rinse them thoroughly in cold water and drain.

☙ In a large frying pan over medium–high heat, warm the oil. When hot, add the cumin and cook, stirring, until it turns darker, about 15 seconds. Add the onions and cook, stirring occasionally, until they turn light brown, about 10 minutes. Add the ginger, coriander, turmeric, cayenne pepper to taste, and the tomatoes and cook, stirring occasionally, until the tomatoes begin to brown, about 6 minutes.

☙ Add the chickpeas, tomato paste, mango powder or lemon juice, and water. Mix well and bring to a boil over high heat. Reduce the heat to low, cover, and simmer until the flavors are blended, about 5 minutes. Check and correct the seasonings. Transfer to a warmed serving dish, sprinkle with the garam masala and cilantro, and serve immediately.

serves 6

Chickpeas

Packed with rich flavor, protein, and nutrients, chickpeas, also known as garbanzo beans, serve as meat for Indian vegetarians. Afghan traders introduced the legumes to India, hence their name, *Kabuli chana,* from Kabul, the capital of Afghanistan, and *chana,* or peas. Each summer, northern Indians look forward to the arrival of green chickpea pods in the market. Later in the season, when the beans are mature, they are shelled and dried.

When I was living in New Delhi, I loved buying fresh chickpeas, which are crunchy like sugar snap peas. Vendors sold them in one-pound (500-g) bouquets accompanied with a secret dipping salt of what I believe was black salt and lemon crystals. The puffy, one-inch (2.5-cm) pods would pop when pressed, releasing the emerald green peas. Indian cooks like to stir-fry the fresh peas with spices or stuff them into breads.

Little known outside of India, except in Jerusalem, are *kala chana,* or black chickpeas. Small and spicy, they are a delicacy for the Punjabis, who braise them in tamarind sauce, and the southern Indians, who turn them into salads with coconut.

Kerala

Meen Pollichathu

malabar braised fish in sour gravy

Malabar's culture is a coastal one, so fish and seafood naturally play an important role in the region's cuisine. Throughout Kerala, karimeen, a carp-like fish, seer, a mackerel-like fish, and bahmeen, the Indian salmon, are served in various ways: lightly braised in sauce, steamed in banana leaves, batter-fried, or stir-fried. The spices most commonly used are mustard seeds, black pepper, turmeric, kari leaf, and hot chiles. There is also abundant use of coconut milk and fried onions.

A uniquely Keralan flavoring is kodampoli, a smoky-sour tasting fruit that is used in many fish preparations. In meen pollichathu, pieces of karimeen are braised in a spicy-sour kodampoli sauce. Carp or salmon are good substitutes, but I particularly like using gray sole. The mild flavor of the fish is a perfect counterpoint to the delicate coconut sauce.

1½ lb (750 g) skinless fish fillets such as gray or lemon sole, flounder, salmon, or haddock, cut into large serving portions

½ teaspoon ground turmeric

½ teaspoon cayenne pepper

½ teaspoon ground black pepper

½ teaspoon salt

4 tablespoons (2 fl oz/60 ml) vegetable oil

1 teaspoon brown mustard seeds

1 cup (3½ oz/105 g) thinly sliced yellow onion

1 teaspoon minced garlic

4 fresh hot green chiles such as serrano, seeded and slivered

18 fresh or 36 dried kari leaves or 8 kaffir lime leaves (page 248)

2 teaspoons ground coriander

1 kodampoli (see note) or unripe star fruit, sliced, or 1 teaspoon fresh lime juice

¾ cup (6 fl oz/180 ml) coconut milk

fresh kari sprigs (optional; page 248)

plain basmati rice (page 183) or Lemon Rice with Mustard Seeds (page 189)

☙ Place the fish on a plate. Combine the turmeric, cayenne pepper, black pepper, and salt. Rub each piece of fish thoroughly with the spices. Let the fish marinate for 10 minutes at room temperature.

☙ In a large frying pan over high heat, warm 2 tablespoons of the oil. When hot, add the fish and fry on one side until lightly browned, about 30 seconds. Using a spatula, turn and fry the other side for about 30 seconds. Do not fully cook the fish. Transfer to a plate and set aside.

☙ To the same pan over high heat, add the remaining 2 tablespoons oil and the mustard seeds and cover the pan. When the seeds stop sputtering, after about 30 seconds, uncover and add the onion, garlic, chiles, kari or kaffir lime leaves, and coriander. Reduce the heat to low and cook, stirring occasionally, until the onion is lightly colored, about 7 minutes.

☙ Return the fish to the pan. Add the *kodampoli*, star fruit, or lime juice and the coconut milk. Stir carefully to submerge the fish in the sauce. Cook briefly until the fish is just done, about 4 minutes. Check and correct the seasonings. Transfer to a warmed platter, garnish with the kari sprigs, if using, and serve immediately accompanied with rice.

serves 4

India's coastal regions, especially West Bengal, Goa, and Malabar, are noted for the sweet flavor of their seafood.

Karnataka
Muttakos Palusli

cabbage with indian cheese and kari leaf

This saladlike preparation is flavored in the southern style with dried chiles, asafetida, and white gram beans. Serve it with rice noodles or a pilaf.

1¼ cups (10 oz/315 g) chenna *cheese (page 82)*

4 tablespoons (2 fl oz/60 ml) usli ghee *(page 247) or vegetable oil*

1 teaspoon brown mustard seeds

2 dried red chiles, broken into bits and seeded

2 teaspoons white split gram beans (page 246)

½ teaspoon ground turmeric

½ teaspoon powdered asafetida (see sidebar, page 144) or 1 teaspoon minced garlic

1 small cabbage, 1–1½ lb (500–750 g), core and tough outer leaves discarded and chopped into ½-inch (12-mm) pieces

2–4 fresh hot green chiles such as serrano, thinly sliced

16 fresh or 32 dried kari leaves (page 248)

1½ teaspoons salt, or to taste

2–4 tablespoons water, if needed

juice of ½ small lime

❦ In a large nonstick frying pan over medium-high heat, combine the cheese and 2 tablespoons of the *usli ghee* or oil and cook, stirring, until lightly fried, about 5 minutes. The cheese will be crumbly and will pick up a few brown spots. Let the cheese stay lumpy. Transfer to a plate and set aside, uncovered, to allow it to dry out further.

❦ Wipe the pan clean, return it to high heat, and add the remaining 2 tablespoons oil. When hot, add the mustard seeds and cover the pan. When the seeds stop sputtering, after about 30 seconds, uncover and add the dried chiles and gram beans. Cook, stirring, until the beans turn light golden, about 20 seconds, then add the turmeric, asafetida or garlic, cabbage, and fresh chiles. Mix well and stir-fry until the cabbage wilts, about 5 minutes. Stir in the kari leaves and salt, reduce the heat to low, cover, and cook until the cabbage is soft, about 15 minutes. Uncover and check it from time to time; there will probably be enough moisture in the cabbage to let it steam itself, but if it looks dry, add 2–4 tablespoons water.

❦ Add the fried cheese and increase the heat to high. Mix, gently tossing and folding, until the cheese is evenly distributed and the excess moisture evaporates, about 5 minutes. Sprinkle with the lime juice, check and correct the seasonings, and serve.

serves 6

India, with its vast population of strict vegetarians, has produced the world's most diverse and imaginative vegetarian cuisine.

Karnataka

Denji Fry

spicy fish

This dish is a specialty of the Mangalorians who live along the Konkan coast. It is usually made with soft-shell crabs—those caught just after molting, when their new shells are still soft enough to be eaten. If they are out of season, fish fillets make a fine substitute.

1-inch (2.5-cm) piece tamarind

½ cup (4 fl oz / 125 ml) boiling water

¼ teaspoon salt

1 lb (500 g) skinless thin white fish fillets, such as sole or flounder, or 4 very fresh soft-shell crabs, about ¼ lb (125 g) each

⅓ cup (2 oz / 60 g) rice flour

2 teaspoons garam masala (page 249)

2 teaspoons cayenne pepper

½ teaspoon ground turmeric

3 tablespoons mustard oil or usli ghee (page 247)

☙ In a small bowl, soak the tamarind in the boiling water for 30 minutes. Squeeze and press to extract as much pulp as possible. Strain the liquid into a medium bowl. Discard the fibrous residue. Add the salt and mix. Add the fish fillets or crabs, gently mixing and turning to coat them with the tamarind water. Set aside to marinate for 30 minutes.

☙ When you are ready to cook the fish or crabs, combine the flour, garam masala, cayenne pepper, and turmeric on a plate. In a large frying pan over high heat, warm the oil or *usli ghee* until it begins to smoke. Remove from the heat and let the oil cool for about 30 seconds. Reheat it and, when it is hot, dip each fillet or crab in the seasoned flour to coat it completely. Add (shell side down, in the case of the crabs) to the oil. Cook, shaking the pan, until the underside is browned, about 3 minutes. Using tongs, turn and cook the second side to the same light brown crispness, about 3 minutes longer. Transfer to warmed serving plates and serve at once.

serves 2

Jammu and Kashmir

Dum Aloo

whole braised potatoes in moghul sauce

This dish is a specialty of the Kashmiri Brahmins. Don't be fooled by its deceptively plain appearance; both the sauce and the potatoes are quite delectable.

2 tablespoons mustard oil or olive oil

1 lb (500 g) very small Yukon gold or new potatoes, peeled and pricked all over with a fork

2 tablespoons usli ghee (page 247) or olive oil

3 black cardamom pods

3 whole cloves

1 tablespoon peeled and finely chopped fresh ginger

½ teaspoon black cumin seeds (page 246)

2 teaspoons ground coriander

1 teaspoon ground cardamom

1 teaspoon ground fennel

½ teaspoon ground cinnamon

½ teaspoon ground ginger

½ teaspoon cayenne pepper

1 tablespoon paprika

1½ teaspoons salt, or to taste

2 cups (16 fl oz/500 ml) water

½ teaspoon jaggery (page 248) (optional)

¼ cup (2 oz/60 g) plain yogurt, lightly beaten, or light (single) cream

¼ cup (⅓ oz/10 g) finely chopped fresh cilantro (fresh coriander)

In a heavy nonstick frying pan over medium-high heat, warm the oil. When hot, add the potatoes and cook, tossing and turning, until they are browned, about 7 minutes. Transfer to a bowl.

Add the *usli ghee* or oil to the pan along with the cardamom pods, cloves, fresh ginger, and cumin. Let the spices sizzle for 1 minute. Stir in the ground coriander, ground cardamom, fennel, cinnamon, ground ginger, cayenne pepper, paprika, salt, potatoes, and water. Mix well and bring to a boil. Reduce the heat to low, cover, and simmer until the potatoes are soft, about 20 minutes. Stir in the jaggery, if using, and the yogurt or cream. Transfer to a warmed platter, sprinkle with the cilantro, and serve at once.

serves 4

Delhi

Murgh Masala

chicken in tomato sauce

In this classic preparation, skinned chicken pieces are braised in a coriander-scented, garlicky tomato sauce. Indian cooks often add a few pieces of potato to soak up the luscious gravy. To give the sauce the desired reddish-brown color and proper depth of flavor, it is essential to cook the onions until they are caramelized.

¼ cup (2 fl oz/60 ml) vegetable oil

2 yellow onions, finely chopped

1 cinnamon stick

6 whole cloves

1-inch (2.5-cm) piece fresh ginger, peeled and finely chopped

4 cloves garlic, minced

1 tablespoon ground coriander

½–1 teaspoon cayenne pepper

½ teaspoon ground turmeric

1 small chicken, about 3 lb (1.5 kg), cut into serving pieces, skinned, and trimmed of all visible fat

4 tomatoes, 1–1¼ lb (500–625 g) total weight, puréed

1½ cups (12 fl oz/375 ml) water

2 teaspoons salt, or to taste

1 teaspoon garam masala (page 249)

¼ cup (⅓ oz/10 g) chopped fresh cilantro (fresh coriander)

In a large, heavy frying pan, preferably nonstick, over medium-low heat, warm the oil. When hot, add the onions, cinnamon, and cloves and cook, stirring occasionally, until the onion is caramel brown, about 8 minutes. Stir in the ginger, garlic, ground coriander, cayenne pepper to taste, and turmeric. Cook, stirring, until the spices turn several shades darker and are fragrant, about 5 minutes.

Add the chicken pieces and cook, turning and shaking, until the meat loses its pink color and is coated with the spices, about 5 minutes. Add the tomatoes, water, and salt. Mix well and bring to a boil over high heat. Reduce the heat to low, cover, and cook until very tender, about 45 minutes. Check and correct the seasonings. Sprinkle with the garam masala and cilantro and serve.

serves 6

Cashew Fruit Liquor

Mention Goa to an Indian and palm-fringed beaches, fiery vindaloos, haunting *mando* music, and sipping *fenni* come to mind. One seldom hears of *fenni* outside the state, however, because the Goans love the liquor so much that none is left for export.

There are two varieties of *fenni*: coconut and cashew. Centuries ago the Konkan people of Goa tapped and fermented coconut, turning it into mild-tasting coconut *fenni*. Cashew *fenni*, however, is relatively new. The Portuguese, who colonized Goa in 1510, introduced the cashew plant. Pear-shaped and juicy, the orange-yellow fruits were plucked when fully ripe and the nuts were separated. The fruit was processed in a manner similar to that for coconut *fenni*. Today, the strong and assertive cashew *fenni* (an acquired taste for some) is the favorite.

Purists prefer to sip *fenni* straight, like cognac, but the most popular way is to serve it with lime soda over ice. The cashew liquor is also the secret ingredient in many Goan marinades for seafood.

Goa

Richeiado

spice-rubbed grilled shrimp

Richeiado is a very popular and simple preparation that celebrates the succulent shrimp harvested along the shores of Goa. The shrimp are rubbed with the fiery-hot richeiado spice paste, then pan-grilled. The palm sugar in the spice rub not only tempers the heat in the shrimp but also adds distinctive flavor. These hot-and-spicy shrimp are wonderful eaten with tropical cocktails featuring Goa's fenni. You can also serve them accompanied with a salad and sweet dinner rolls such as pao.

1 lb (500 g) jumbo or large shrimp (prawns), peeled with the last shell segment and tail fin intact and deveined

SPICE PASTE
1 tablespoon minced garlic

1 tablespoon peeled and grated fresh ginger

2 teaspoons cayenne pepper

1 teaspoon ground black pepper

1 teaspoon ground cumin

½ teaspoon ground cinnamon

¼ teaspoon ground cloves

¼ teaspoon ground turmeric

2 tablespoons fenni (see sidebar, left) or gin

1 teaspoon palm sugar, jaggery (page 248), or dark brown sugar

2 tablespoons mustard oil or olive oil

1 tablespoon fresh lemon juice

green salad

dinner rolls

Place the shrimp in a shallow dish. To make the spice paste, combine the garlic, ginger, cayenne pepper, black pepper, cumin, cinnamon, cloves, turmeric, *fenni* or gin, and the palm sugar, jaggery, or dark brown sugar. Rub the paste evenly over the shrimp. Set aside for 30 minutes at room temperature.

In a large frying pan over high heat, warm the oil. When very hot, add the shrimp and cook, tossing, until they turn pink and curl, about 5 minutes. Sprinkle with the lemon juice. Serve immediately over a bed of green salad and accompanied with rolls.

serves 2

Gujarat

Pakode ki Bhaji

split pea fritters in spicy sauce

This dish was originally created to use up leftover split pea fritters, but the new invention was so tasty that Indian cooks began making the fritters just for this dish. Pakode ki bhaji really benefits from keeping. The fritters slowly soak up the sauce and turn even more flavorful, moist, and plump. To hasten the process, presoak the fritters in hot water for five minutes before adding them to the sauce. Serve with a rice dish, a stir-fried vegetable, and salad.

¼ cup (2 fl oz/60 ml) vegetable oil

2 yellow onions, sliced

1 teaspoon cumin seeds

1 tablespoon peeled and grated fresh ginger

1 tablespoon ground coriander

1 teaspoon minced garlic

½ teaspoon ground turmeric

2 tomatoes, finely chopped

3 cups (24 fl oz/750 ml) water

½ recipe Fragrant Split Pea Fritters with Cashew Nuts (page 65)

1 teaspoon garam masala (page 249)

2 tablespoon chopped fresh cilantro (fresh coriander)

❀ In a large frying pan over medium-high heat, warm the oil. When hot, add the onion and cumin and cook, stirring occasionally, until the onions are light brown, about 7 minutes. Add the ginger, ground coriander, garlic, and turmeric. Let the spices sizzle for a few seconds.

❀ Add the tomatoes and 2 cups (16 fl oz/500 ml) of the water and bring to a boil over high heat. Reduce the heat to low, cover, and cook until the sauce has the consistency of light (single) cream, about 10 minutes. Add the split pea fritters and the remaining 1 cup (8 fl oz/250 ml) water. Mix well, re-cover, and simmer for 10 minutes longer to blend the flavors. Sprinkle with garam masala and cilantro and serve at once.

serves 6

Madhya Pradesh

Gobhi Masala

fragrant cauliflower stew

*A favorite of Indian children, gobhi masala
is a delicately spiced cauliflower stew. Every region
in India has a special way to season this dish. In West
Bengal, for example, the local spice blend* panch
phoron *and red chile pods are added. In Rajasthan,
ajowan and mango powder are used. In Himachal
Pradesh, mustard and fennel are included. In this
recipe from Madhya Pradesh, the cauliflower is braised
in a lovely coconut sauce with caramelized onion,
tomatoes, and Moghul spices. The coconut milk adds
richness to the sauce, but chicken stock or water can
be substituted if you prefer.*

*Indian cauliflowers are generally small, about 1 pound
(500 g) in weight, and fragrant. For best results, use
the freshest available cauliflower. Indian cooks use the
entire cauliflower, florets, stems, leaves, and all. The
stems taste like kohlrabi and the leaves like cabbage.
I believe that using all parts of the vegetable adds
more depth to the sauce. Serve the stew with a rice
dish and a chutney.*

1 head cauliflower, about 2 lb (1 kg)

3 tablespoons usli ghee *(page 247) or vegetable
oil*

2 cassia leaves *(page 244)*

1 cinnamon stick

1 teaspoon cumin seeds

1 yellow onion, finely chopped

1 tablespoon peeled and grated fresh ginger

1 tablespoon ground coriander

1½ teaspoons salt

½–1 teaspoon cayenne pepper

2 tomatoes, finely chopped

1 cup (8 fl oz/250 ml) coconut milk or light
(single) cream

½ cup (4 fl oz/125 ml) water

1 tablespoon tomato paste

1 boiling potato, peeled and cut into 1-inch
(2.5-cm) pieces

1 teaspoon garam masala *(page 249)*

½ cup (¾ oz/20 g) chopped fresh cilantro
(fresh coriander)

⚜ Separate the cauliflower into florets and cut them
into 2-inch (5-cm) pieces. Peel the stem and cut
crosswise into slices ⅛ inch (3 mm) thick. Chop the
tender leaves into 2-inch (5-cm) pieces. Set aside
until needed.

⚜ In a large saucepan over medium heat, warm
the *usli ghee* or oil. When hot, add the cassia leaves,
cinnamon, and cumin and let the spices sizzle for
30 seconds. Add the onion and cook, stirring occasionally, until light brown, about 3 minutes. Stir in
the ginger, ground coriander, salt, cayenne pepper to
taste, tomatoes, ½ cup (4 fl oz/125 ml) of the coconut milk or cream, the water, and the tomato paste.

⚜ Add the cauliflower and potato, mix gently, and
bring to a boil over high heat. Reduce the heat to
low, cover, and cook until the vegetables are tender,
17–18 minutes. Uncover and add the remaining
½ cup (4 fl oz/125 ml) of the coconut milk or
cream, the garam masala, and half of the cilantro. Mix
well. Transfer to a warmed serving dish, sprinkle with
the remaining cilantro, and serve at once.

serves 6

Punjab

Makkhani Murgh

butter chicken

Punjabis are well known for their chicken preparations, and none is more famous than butter chicken. While Westerners in an Indian restaurant usually order tandoori chicken, Indians invariably ask for makkhani murgh. *Indians place a high value on the sauce in a dish, much more than on the main ingredient. The velvety sauce in butter chicken—consisting of tomatoes, cream, and spices—is held in particular esteem.*

6 tomatoes, 1½–1¾ lb (750–875 g) total weight, roughly chopped

1-inch (2.5-cm) piece fresh ginger, peeled and roughly chopped, plus 1 tablespoon, peeled and finely shredded

4 fresh hot green chiles such as serrano, stemmed

2 teaspoons ground coriander

salt and ground black pepper to taste

½ cup (¾ oz/20 g) chopped fresh cilantro (fresh coriander)

1 recipe day-old Tandoori Chicken (page 96) or Chicken Malai Kabob (page 113)

¼ cup (2 fl oz/60 ml) heavy (double) cream

¼ cup (2 oz/60 g) unsalted butter, softened

☙ Working in batches, in a blender or food processor, combine the tomatoes, chopped ginger, chiles, and ground coriander and process until smooth. Transfer the purée to a saucepan and bring to a boil over high heat. Reduce the heat to medium and cook, uncovered, until the sauce is reduced by half, about 10 minutes. Remove from the heat and strain through a fine-mesh sieve into a large frying pan.

☙ Add the shredded ginger, salt, pepper, half of the cilantro, and the chicken to the sauce. Cook over medium-low heat, stirring frequently to prevent sticking or burning, until the sauce comes to a boil. Reduce the heat to low, cover, and simmer until the chicken absorbs some of the sauce, about 5 minutes. Remove from the heat. In a small bowl, mix together the cream, butter, and the remaining cilantro. Pour over the chicken. Do not mix; the cream and butter should streak the tomato sauce. Transfer to a shallow serving dish and serve immediately.

serves 6

Tamarind

Indians are often surprised to discover that one of their beloved flavorings is not native to India. Introduced from Africa in prehistoric times, tamarind is valued for both its floral aroma and sweet-sour taste. Although popular throughout the country, the pulpy pods are primarily used in the southern kitchen, where they are indispensable in various preparations, including lentil stews (*sambar*), soups (*rasam*), and fish dishes. The flavoring is also valued for its cooling properties, and Indians typically sip iced tamarind tea or soda water to beat the summer heat.

Tamarind pods grow on large shade trees, *Tamarindus indica,* that dot the Indian countryside. While the pods are the most commonly used parts of the tree, Indians also employ the leaves and tender stems in cooking. The ripe pods are opened and seeded, and the pulp is pressed into blocks for sale. The soft, sticky brownish pulp is soaked in hot water and its juice extracted before use in cooking. Ready-made tamarind water and concentrated paste are also available in stores. In an emergency, processed or canned paste is an acceptable alternative.

Uttar Pradesh

Matar Paneer

peas and cheese in fragrant gravy

Matar paneer, like tandoori chicken and lamb with spinach, *is an Indian classic. The city of Varanasi is famous for its vegetarian cuisine, and this dish of braised cheese in a spicy tomato sauce is the jewel in its crown. You do not have to be a vegetarian to love it. Serve it with a rice dish, bread, or* pappadums.

2 teaspoons cumin seeds

3 tablespoons vegetable oil

2 yellow onions, finely chopped

2 tablespoons ground coriander

1 teaspoon ground turmeric

3 fresh hot green chiles such as serrano, minced

1 tablespoon peeled and grated fresh ginger

3 large tomatoes, puréed

1½ teaspoons salt or to taste

2 cups (16 fl oz/500 ml) water

2 cups (10 oz/315 g) fresh or thawed frozen green peas

2 cups (10 oz/315 g) fried paneer *cubes (page 82)*

1 teaspoon garam masala (page 249)

¼ cup (⅓ oz/10 g) chopped fresh cilantro (fresh coriander)

❦ In a wide, shallow frying pan over medium–high heat, warm the oil. When hot, add the cumin and cook, stirring, until it turns several shades darker, about 15 seconds. Add the onions and cook, stirring occasionally, until they turn caramel brown, about 8 minutes. Stir in the coriander, turmeric, chiles, and ginger and cook, stirring, until the ginger is lightly fried, about 2 minutes.

❦ Add the tomatoes and salt and cook until the tomatoes lose their raw aroma, about 5 minutes. Add the water and the fresh peas, if using. Bring the sauce to a boil, reduce the heat to low, cover, and simmer gently until the peas are cooked, about 5 minutes.

❦ Add the *paneer* and cook until it absorbs some of the moisture and puffs slightly, about 5 minutes. Add the garam masala, half of the chopped cilantro, and the thawed frozen peas, if using. Increase the heat to medium and cook until piping hot. Serve sprinkled with the remaining cilantro.

serves 6

Punjab

Murgh Hariali

chicken with green herbs

While Indian dishes are often garnished with chopped cilantro, this dish uses a Punjabi technique of adding the cilantro in two stages—first to the sauce as the chicken cooks, and later as a garnish. The two distinct flavors add a nice complexity. Dill, marjoram, parsley, and marigolds are all used in a similar fashion. Serve with a rice dish or fried bread, such as poori, *and a chutney.*

2 tablespoons vegetable oil

1 cinnamon stick

4 cardamom pods, preferably black

4 whole cloves

1 tablespoon peeled and grated fresh ginger

2 teaspoons minced garlic

1 yellow onion, sliced

4 fresh hot green chiles such as serrano, seeded and cut into long, wide slivers

1 chicken, about 3 lb (1.5 kg), cut into serving pieces, skinned, and trimmed of all visible fat

1 cup (8 fl oz/250 ml) coconut milk

1½ teaspoons salt, or to taste

1 cup (1½ oz/45 g) finely chopped fresh cilantro (fresh coriander)

1 cup (8 fl oz/250 ml) water

1 teaspoon ground black pepper

❦ In a large, shallow nonstick frying pan over medium–high heat, warm the oil. When hot, add the cinnamon, cardamom, cloves, ginger, and garlic. Cook, stirring, until the mixture is lightly fried, about 6 minutes.

❦ Add the onion, chiles, and chicken pieces. Mix well and cook, stirring, until the onion goes limp and the chicken loses its pink color, about 7 minutes. Add the coconut milk, salt, half of the cilantro, and the water. Mix well, increase the heat to high, and bring to a boil. Reduce the heat to low and cook, covered, until the chicken is tender, about 30 minutes. Remove from the heat and check and correct the seasonings. Sprinkle with the pepper and the remaining cilantro and serve immediately.

serves 6

SIDE DISHES

Salads, spiced dals, and other vegetable dishes showcase the rich diversity of farmland harvests.

Preceding pages: A girl harvests mustard seeds in Uttar Pradesh. Fields carpeted with these golden blooms are also a common sight in Madhya Pradesh, Punjab, Arunachal Pradesh, and Mizoram. **Above top:** Kanchenjunga, the world's third-highest mountain, seems to emit an eerie neon glow in the dawn light. **Above:** Garlic's most familiar role is in the kitchen, but strings of the bulbs are also hung in rural houses to ward off insects, snakes, and evil. **Right:** The New Gate in Jaipur, Rajasthan, is one of seven gateways into the city's eighteenth-century center.

TO MY MOTHER, the daughter of a landowner who produced export-quality tea and vegetables, an interest in the culinary world came naturally, and early on she recognized in me the same passion for food. As a child I saw garlic heads in place of minarets, *patisa* (flaky pastry) instead of the strata of slate, and *batasa* (cotton candy) in the clouds. Mother knew how to tease my senses with the perfume of freshly harvested *arhar dal* (yellow lentils from Uttar Pradesh), *nongu* (the ambrosial fruit of the palmyra, a native palm found in the lush Nilgiri Hills in the south), and frothy, warm milk, collected straight from the cow into my cupped hands. With her by my side, I knew I was always in for wonderful culinary adventures, so I followed her like a shadow.

When I was quite young, we took a trip to visit a family friend's vegetable farm on the outskirts of Kanpur, on the fertile floodplains of the Ganges in the northern state of Uttar Pradesh. Barely reaching my mother's waist, all I could see of the farm that day was a great expanse of emerald fields that stretched to the horizon. We strolled along the narrow pathways, Mother's silk sari ruffling in the summer

breeze. Every now and then she would look at me and, with eyes smiling with pleasure, point to tomatoes, eggplants (aubergines), okra, cauliflower, spinach, bottleneck squash, English peas, and green chiles. We picked young, tender chickpeas (garbanzo beans) to munch and dug up unripe peanuts that were as soft as peas. Although I had eaten singhara (Indian water chestnuts) before, this was the first time I'd seen them in their natural setting, growing like a weed in a pond next to some lotus. The farmer helped us gather a few, and I placed them in my pocket before deciding that they needed my immediate attention. I settled under a shady mango tree nearby. The leathery, moss-green skin came away easily, revealing the juicy, vanilla-scented, heart-shaped nut, which I quickly devoured.

Later that afternoon, we ate lunch in the farmer's mud-brick farmhouse, sampling the just-picked freshness of his produce, which had been transformed into many *bhaji* (stir-fried vegetable dishes), plus side dishes of braised and stewed vegetables and fragrant buttery dals. There were rich creamy *raitas,* or yogurt salads, too. The milk for the yogurt came from the farmer's water buffalo, which I had petted earlier. I had been careful to put my hand near her forehead, for unlike a horse or an elephant, water buffalo do not like to have their bodies touched. I learned this the hard way as a toddler. I had once stroked one of our buffalo near her hindquarters only to have her tail-whip me and send me flying.

When newcomers taste Indian yogurt for the first time, they are always struck by its

flavor and texture. Even people who take a tentative approach to yogurt become instant converts. Both cow's and buffalo's milk are commonly used, although the latter is becoming increasingly popular due to its richness. It produces a yogurt with a higher fat content— as much as 14 percent butterfat—which makes it thicker and creamier. Buffalo's milk is also high in lactic acid, the primary flavor component. Another factor that enhances flavor is the diet of the buffalo, which is supplemented by special greens such as fenugreek and, since the cattle are allowed to roam freely, wild grasses. Commercially available Western yogurt has little in common with the Indian product. Full-fat brands (3 to 4 percent) that have a pronounced tang are the best substitutes. If you are watching your calorie consumption,

Above top: Vendors sell vegetables from their boats, or *shikaras,* on Dal Lake in Kashmir's capital, Srinagar. **Above:** Here, many of the spices essential to Indian cooking are displayed in front of a shop in Old Delhi. Spices are valued not only for their flavor but also for their medicinal and digestive properties. Some, such as saffron and turmeric, have special places in religious worship as well. **Right:** A sari-clad villager in the central state of Madhya Pradesh smiles shyly for the camera.

low-fat or fat-free yogurt can be used, although there will be a compromise in flavor.

Yogurts made from the milk of sheep, goats, camels, or yaks are also popular in India, but only in the regions where they originate. Each type has a distinct flavor and aroma that most people outside the area do not like.

These regional preferences also apply to side dishes. Indian cooks will often prepare a main dish from another part of the country— a northern Indian may cook Goan *sorpotel* (hot and sour pork), or a southern Indian may make the Moghul classic *saag gosht* (lamb with spinach)—but when it comes to side dishes, they usually stay with the unique flavors of their region. Side dishes are the constants in a meal, linking Indians to their childhood heritage and ethnic and regional identity.

The amazing variety of these dishes is due to the use of seasonal vegetables and fruits and distinct regional combinations of flavors. A simple bowl of dal cooked with turmeric and salt will taste strikingly different when flavored with asafetida, cayenne, and green mango, as in *Banarasi dal;* with garlic, garam masala, and cumin, as in *Dilliwale dal;* or mustard seeds, jaggery, and dried red chiles, as in

Below: A woman harvests cardamom near Mercura, in the southern state of Karnataka. Many of the spices used in Indian cooking originated in the Mediterranean; only a handful, cardamom among them, are native to India.
Below bottom: On a terrace of the Rambagh Palace (once a residence of the Maharajah of Jaipur, now a luxury hotel), a cook bakes bread on a *chula,* a coal- or wood-burning mud stove. **Right:** On the summit of Shatrunjay Hill in Palitana, Gujarat, is an imposing complex of 863 Jain temples, some over one thousand years old. The Jains are a wealthy, ascetic, strictly vegetarian religious minority of about three million members, mostly in the trading communities of western India.

Gujarati dal. The same principles apply when preparing vegetables and *raitas,* too.

In general, the Indian kitchen enjoys an abundance of vegetables, legumes, and yogurt, which results in their being an integral part of every meal. Side dishes made from these ingredients are not regarded as inferior to main dishes, as they sometimes are in the West. Indian cooks know that some main dishes, especially those that are designed to impress with meat, poultry, and seafood, may not provide all the necessary nutrients, particularly protein. This is because such ingredients are expensive, so there is usually only enough for each person to have a small taste. Side dishes

are therefore crucial in making up any nutritional shortfalls. They are also valued for their interplay of tastes and textures, a factor that is important to the Indian enjoyment of food.

Knowing the importance of side dishes is one thing, but developing a taste for vegetables, legumes, and yogurt is a different matter entirely. Therefore, all Indian children are conditioned from a young age to do exactly that. An Indian infant's first solid food is lentils with rice. Soon after, a simple stir-fried vegetable is added, which then slowly evolves into a more complex and spicy version.

Indians have developed an especially ingenious way of incorporating yogurt, which

most consider an acquired taste, into their diet. Whatever their religion or level of education, all Indians are devout and superstitious. They believe that every important endeavor must be blessed by the gods to guarantee success, so Indian culture is full of good omen rituals that have been handed down through the ages. One such ritual is the consumption of a bowl of yogurt. Whether the occasion involves a child going abroad for studies, a business meeting with a tax collector, a son or daughter preparing for an arranged marriage meeting, or a tiny infant returning from a visit with grandparents, each event begins with a spoonful of yogurt.

Jammu and Kashmir

Baigan Dum

moghul pot-roasted eggplant

I first tasted this glorious dish in 1958 at the residence palace of the Maharaja of Jodhpur. It was part of a lavish Rajasthani buffet in honor of His Majesty the Maharaja's birthday. A striking dish, both in flavor and appeal, it is rather simply conceived and executed: Eggplant slices are first fried, then cooked dum-*style.*

Dum *is a classic Moghul technique of cooking food in sealed pots. In farm kitchens with wood-fired stoves, the pot, its lid tightly sealed with dough, is placed directly over hot ashes. After several hours the dish emerges with buttery soft pieces of vegetables that are imbued with heavenly scents. Often the dough seal cracks, allowing the smoke to penetrate the vegetables and adding yet another layer of flavor. Baigan dum, one of the most popular renditions of this technique, is prepared all over northern India, where the influence of Moghul cooking is dominant. For a complete meal, accompany the* baigan dum *with tandoori chicken and bread, or serve it on its own, with a rice dish.*

1 eggplant (aubergine), about 2 lb (1 kg)

1½ cups (12 oz/375 g) plain yogurt

1 tablespoon paprika

1½ teaspoons garam masala (page 249)

1 teaspoon salt, or to taste

½ teaspoon cayenne pepper

6 tablespoons (3 fl oz/90 ml) vegetable oil

1 teaspoon cumin seeds

1 tablespoon peeled and grated fresh ginger

2 teaspoons minced garlic

1 teaspoon ground turmeric

6 whole cloves

2 fresh hot green chiles such as serrano, sliced

2 tomatoes, cut into ½-inch (12-mm) wedges

½ cup (⅓ oz/10 g) chopped fresh cilantro (fresh coriander)

❦ Cut the eggplant lengthwise into quarters, then cut each quarter crosswise into slices ½ inch (12 mm) thick. In a small bowl, whisk together the yogurt, paprika, garam masala, salt, and cayenne pepper.

❦ In a large, shallow frying pan over high heat, warm 2 tablespoons of the oil. When hot, add a few eggplant slices. (Do not crowd the pan; they need ample room to fry properly.) Cook, stirring and turning, until they are fried and begin to soften, about 8 minutes. With a slotted spoon, transfer to paper towels to drain. Fry the remaining eggplant slices in the same way, adding more oil as necessary.

❦ Wipe the pan clean, return it to the stove over medium heat, and add 2 more tablespoons of oil. When hot, add the cumin seeds and fry, stirring, until they turn a little darker, about 30 seconds. Add the ginger, garlic, turmeric, cloves, and chiles. Mix well and let the spices fry for 30 seconds.

❦ Fold in the eggplant and the yogurt mixture and bring to a boil. Reduce the heat to medium-low and simmer, tightly covered, until the eggplant is cooked, about 12 minutes. Uncover and continue cooking until the excess moisture evaporates, about 15 minutes. During the last 5 minutes of cooking, add the tomatoes so that they soften but still hold their shape. Check and correct the seasonings. Fold half of the cilantro into the eggplant and sprinkle the remainder over the top of the dish just before serving.

serves 4

Traders and invaders, among them Moghuls, Arabs, Portuguese, and British, have all left their mark on Indian cooking.

Asafetida

To the six hundred million vegetarian Hindus and Jains in India, asafetida is a miracle spice. Before these religions adopted vegetarianism, their followers ate food, principally meat, that was seasoned lavishly with garlic and onion. New dietary laws came into force in the sixth century BC with the birth of a new religion, Jainism. It introduced the concept of *ahimsa* (*a* meaning "non" and *himsa*, "violence") and decreed that killing any living thing is an act of violence. The popularity of this concept led both Jains and Hindu Brahmins (the highest caste of Hindu) to adopt strictly vegetarian diets. The new dietary laws declared garlic and onion taboo, partly because they resembled a human head but mainly because they were associated with meat. Asafetida, with its garlic–onion flavor, was welcomed with open arms.

Asafetida is dried gum resin from the root of the ferula plant, a type of giant fennel grown mainly in Iran, Afghanistan, and Kashmir. It has a strong, fetid smell in its uncooked form. The presence of certain sulfur compounds gives the spice its odor, which is miraculously transformed during cooking into a sweet garlicky–onion aroma. Asafetida is available in both lump and powder form. There is little difference in quality, so it is more convenient to buy the spice already ground. Asafetida should be kept in an airtight jar to prevent the smell from lingering or permeating other foods.

Uttar Pradesh

Banarasi Dal

varanasi-style creamy red lentils with asafetida

Dal, the spice-laced legume purée, is the quintessential Indian food, though every region has its own special flavorings. In Uttar Pradesh, where I spent much of my childhood, green mangoes are added. In Varanasi (formerly known as Banaras) as in the rest of the region, mango trees color the landscape. Some of the crop is picked while the mangoes are immature, with their pits still soft enough to be cut through. These tiny, tart fruits are used as seasoning for dal, or dried for use when fresh mangoes are no longer in season.

Fresh green mangoes and dried green mango slices, called sabat amchoor, *are available in Indian grocery stores. An equal quantity of tart apples, star fruit, or 2 teaspoons of mango powder make fine substitutes.*

1½ cups (10½ oz/330 g) pink or red lentils

½ teaspoon ground turmeric

1 small unripe mango, peeled, pitted, and sliced (about ⅓ cup/3 oz/90 g; optional)

4 cups (32 fl oz/1 l) water

1½ teaspoons salt, or to taste

3 tablespoons usli ghee (page 247) or vegetable oil

1 teaspoon cumin seeds

½ teaspoon cayenne pepper

½ teaspoon powdered asafetida (see sidebar, left) or 1 teaspoon minced garlic

¼ cup (⅓ oz/10 g) finely chopped fresh cilantro (fresh coriander)

❦ Pick over the lentils, discarding any stones or misshapen or discolored lentils. Rinse and place in a deep pot. Add the turmeric, mango, if using, and water. Bring to a boil over high heat, then reduce the heat to low. Simmer gently, uncovered, stirring occasionally, until the lentils are tender, about 25 minutes. Remove from the heat and add the salt.

❦ In a small frying pan over medium-high heat, warm the ghee or oil. When hot, add the cumin and sauté until it turns very dark, about 30 seconds. Add the cayenne pepper, asafetida, and cilantro. Pour the entire contents of the pan over the lentils and mix well. Check and correct the seasonings. To serve, ladle into small bowls such as *katori*.

serves 4

Rajasthan

Bhindi ke Lachche

crisp shoestring okra

When I first tasted this dish of shimmering, crisp-fried okra shreds with the spicy aroma of chat masala *and* asafetida, *I was enraptured. It was at the Indian restaurant Chor Bizarre, in London's prestigious Ritz Carlton Hotel, that I found the best rendition of this preparation. The spaghetti-thin shreds of okra were crunchy, spicy, and very addictive. The dish is surprisingly easy to make once you have a batch of garden-fresh, tender okra. The trick to keeping okra from becoming slimy is to salt it after cooking.*

2 lb (1 kg) young, tender okra

2 teaspoons mango powder (page 248) or lemon juice

1 teaspoon garam masala (page 249)

¼ teaspoon powdered asafetida (see sidebar, page 144) or 1 teaspoon minced garlic

½ cup (2½ oz/75 g) chickpea (garbanzo bean) flour

1½ teaspoons salt, or to taste

2 teaspoons chat masala *(page 244) or 1 teaspoon ground black pepper*

vegetable oil for deep-frying

♛ Stem the okra and slice each pod lengthwise into quarters. Place the pieces in a large bowl.

♛ In a small dish, mix together the mango powder, garam masala, and the asafetida or garlic. Sprinkle over the okra, then toss and rub to coat the okra thoroughly with the spice mixture. Transfer to a large baking sheet and spread the okra in a single layer. Sprinkle the okra with the chickpea flour, preferably using a fine-mesh sifter or a sieve. Toss and roll the pieces to coat all of them with a light, even layer of the flour.

♛ In a mortar, blender, or coffee grinder reserved solely for spices, combine the salt and *chat masala* or black pepper and pound or process until finely powdered. Set aside until needed.

♛ In a large pan, pour in vegetable oil to a depth of 1 inch (2.5 cm) and warm over medium-high heat to 375°F (190°C) on a deep-frying thermometer. When the oil is ready, add some of the okra and fry, stirring and turning with tongs, until cooked and browned, about 5 minutes. Using the tongs or a slotted spoon, transfer to paper towels to drain, then immediately sprinkle the okra with the spiced salt. Keep warm in a low oven while you fry the remaining okra in the same way. Transfer to a warmed serving dish and serve immediately.

serves 4

In some regions, a stone mortar and pestle are a traditional part of a bride's dowry.

Tamil Nadu

Pattani Varutadu

green peas and carrots with spices

This simple yet tasty dish traditionally uses Indian sweet peas (similar to sugar snap peas) and Indian red carrots. Roasted rice grains add a lovely smokiness.

2 tablespoons vegetable oil

½ teaspoon brown mustard seeds

1 teaspoon white rice

½ teaspoon ground turmeric

1 teaspoon curry powder (page 249)

12 fresh or 24 dried kari leaves (page 248)

1 cup (5 oz / 155 g) chopped carrot

1 cup (5 oz / 155 g) fresh or thawed frozen green peas

½ teaspoon salt, or to taste

½ cup (4 fl oz / 125 ml) water

2 tablespoons finely chopped fresh cilantro (fresh coriander) (optional)

In a large frying pan over medium heat, warm the oil. When hot, add the mustard seeds and cover the pan. When the seeds stop sputtering, after about 30 seconds, uncover and add the rice. Cook until the rice turns light brown, then add the turmeric, curry powder, kari leaves, carrots, and peas. Mix well and stir-fry until the vegetables are well coated with spices, about 4 minutes.

Stir in the salt and water and cover the pan. Lower the heat and cook until the vegetables are soft, about 8 minutes. Uncover and continue cooking until the excess moisture evaporates and the rice is cooked, about 2 minutes. Check and correct the seasonings. Serve sprinkled with the cilantro, if desired.

serves 4

Lentil Wafers

Pappadums, papad, and *aplaam* are some of the names for these crisp, dinner-plate-sized wafers. Indian meals traditionally include them to add texture and flavor to the dishes. They also make a fine addition to tiffin, afternoon tea, or cocktails. Anytime of the day, whenever hunger pangs suddenly strike, I reach for *pappadums* for a satisfying nibble.

Although referred to as lentil wafers, *pappadums* are actually made from beans, specifically mung beans *(moong dal)* and black gram beans *(urad dal)*. They can also be made with rice, potato, or tapioca, but these forms are not as common or as popular. Some are mild and fragrant, seasoned with cumin, garlic, or cilantro, while others are hot and spicy, spiked with black pepper, green chiles, or cayenne pepper.

Traditionally, *pappadum* making has been the responsibility of the senior ladies of the household. When I was a child, I would watch and help my grandmother, mother, and great-aunt painstakingly hand-roll, one by one, hundreds of thin circles of *pappadums*. They were laid out to dry atop clean, colorful saris under the hot Indian summer sun. Before the ants and birds could begin feasting on our precious wafers, my grandmother quickly gathered them into neat stacks and placed them in tall brass containers that were put away in our cool, dark storeroom beside the pickles, chutneys, and preserved vegetables. I have fond memories of munching wafers as after-school snacks, drizzled with warm *usli ghee*.

Things have changed in the last half century. *Pappadum* making is no longer a family activity but is handed over to cottage industries in villages of rural India. The dried *pappadums* sold in markets come wrapped in packs of ten; stored in an airtight container, they will keep for a year. Before serving, they are cooked by briefly roasting them over a live flame, deep-frying in oil, or baking in the oven.

Delhi

Dilliwale Dal

delhi-style lentils

Side-dish dals are generally very soupy and best served in small bowls and eaten with a spoon. For extra flavor, top with a little usli ghee *just before serving.*

1½ cups (10½ oz/330 g) pink, red, or yellow lentils

½ teaspoon ground turmeric

4 cups (32 fl oz/1 l) water

1½ teaspoons salt, or to taste

1 tomato, finely chopped

3 tablespoons vegetable oil

1 teaspoon cumin seeds

1 yellow onion, finely chopped

4 cloves garlic, thinly sliced

½ teaspoon cayenne pepper

1 teaspoon garam masala (page 249)

¼ cup (⅓ oz/10 g) finely chopped fresh cilantro (fresh coriander)

♨ Pick over the lentils, discarding any stones or misshapen or discolored lentils. Rinse and place in a deep pot. Add the turmeric and water and bring to a boil over high heat. Reduce the heat to low and gently simmer the lentils until they are tender, about 25 minutes for pink or red lentils and 40 minutes for yellow. Add the salt and tomato and cook until the tomato is soft, about 5 minutes. Reduce the heat to very low to keep the lentils warm while you make the spice-infused flavoring.

♨ In a small frying pan over medium-high heat, warm the oil. When hot, add the cumin and sauté until it turns very dark, about 30 seconds. Add the onion and garlic and cook, stirring, until they are light golden, about 6 minutes. Stir in the cayenne pepper and garam masala and pour the entire contents of the pan over the lentils. Add the cilantro and mix well. Check and correct the seasonings and serve ladled into small bowls such as *katori*.

serves 4

Tamil Nadu

Takkalipayam Pachadi

tomato and yogurt salad

Pachadi *is the southern Indian version of the northern Indian yogurt salad* raita. *This recipe from Tamil Nadu is made with ripe tomatoes, yogurt, and oil infused with mustard seeds. A cool and refreshing side dish, it can also be transformed into a complete meal when served with stuffed bread, a pilaf, or a grain dish.*

1½ cups (12 oz/375 g) plain yogurt

½ teaspoon salt, or to taste

¾ lb (12 oz/375 g) cherry tomatoes, halved

1 tablespoon vegetable oil

½ teaspoon brown mustard seeds

¼ teaspoon powdered asafetida (see sidebar, page 144) or ½ teaspoon minced garlic

1 fresh hot green chile such as serrano, thinly sliced

8 fresh or 16 dried kari leaves (page 248)

※ In a bowl, combine the yogurt and salt and whisk until smooth. Add the tomatoes, mixing carefully so as not to crush them.

※ In a small frying pan over medium-high heat, warm the oil. When hot, add the mustard seeds and cover the pan. When the seeds stop sputtering, after about 30 seconds, uncover and add the asafetida or garlic, chile, and kari leaves. Let the spices sizzle for 10 seconds, then pour the entire contents of the pan over the yogurt. Mix well and serve, or cover and refrigerate for up to 3 days.

makes 3 cups (24 fl oz/750 ml); serves 4

Tamil Nadu

Keerai Masial

tanjore wilted spinach

A classic Tamil way of cooking greens, masial *is best
made with very fresh greens. I still remember my
elder sister asking one of our kitchen helpers to pick
a bunch of spinach from her vegetable garden, just
moments before she started the actual cooking. The
greens are wilted in oil scented with smoked chiles and
mustard seeds. The pure, clean flavor is phenomenal.*
Keerai masial *goes well with dishes such as Spice-
Rubbed Grilled Shrimp, Whole Braised Potatoes
in Moghul Sauce, Butter Chicken, and Mangalore
Eggs with Coconut.*

2 lb (1 kg) spinach

1 tablespoon Indian sesame oil or vegetable oil

1 dried red chile

1 teaspoon brown mustard seeds

*3 cloves garlic, thinly sliced, or ½ teaspoon
powdered asafetida (see sidebar, page 144)*

½ teaspoon salt, or to taste

❀ Remove any very tough stems from the spinach,
but otherwise leave the stems intact. Rinse the
spinach thoroughly and drain. Set aside.

❀ In a large *karhai* or frying pan over high heat,
warm the oil. When very hot, add the chile and fry,
stirring, until it turns very dark brown, about
1 minute. Add the mustard seeds and cover the pan.
When they stop sputtering, after about 30 seconds,
uncover and add the garlic or asafetida. Cook, stirring, until the garlic turns golden, about 1 minute, or
until the asafetida releases an onionlike aroma.

❀ Add the spinach, a handful of leaves at a time, and
mix with a folding motion. As soon as the spinach
leaves wilt, add more. When all of the spinach leaves
have been added, mix thoroughly and add the salt.
Cook, stirring, until all of the excess moisture evaporates, about 5 minutes. Serve hot, at room temperature, or cold.

serves 4

Gujarati Dal

ahmedabad lentils with jaggery

Dals from Gujarat contain jaggery, the Indian natural cane sugar, which tastes like maple syrup. I like my dals thick and full-bodied, but if you prefer a soupy consistency, add a cup of water to the finished dal.

1½ cups (10½ oz / 330 g) yellow lentils

1 teaspoon ground coriander

1 teaspoon ground cumin

½ teaspoon ground turmeric

2 fresh hot green chiles such as serrano, minced

5 cups (40 fl oz / 1.25 l) water

1½ teaspoons jaggery (page 248) or brown sugar

1 teaspoon salt, or to taste

2 tablespoons peanut oil

1 teaspoon brown mustard seeds

1 dried red chile

½ teaspoon powdered asafetida (see sidebar, page 144) or 1 teaspoon minced garlic

¼ cup (⅓ oz / 10 g) finely chopped fresh cilantro (fresh coriander)

❧ Pick over the lentils, discarding any stones or misshapen or discolored lentils. Rinse and place in a deep pot. Add the ground coriander, cumin, turmeric, fresh chiles, and water. Bring to a boil over high heat, then reduce the heat to medium and cook at a low boil, uncovered, until the lentils are very soft, about 50 minutes. Check and stir often to ensure that they are not burning.

❧ When the lentils are soft, beat them with a wooden spoon to make a smooth purée. The consistency should be thin; if necessary, add more water. Add the sugar and salt and mix until the sugar dissolves. Reduce the heat to very low to keep the lentils warm while you make the spice-infused flavoring.

❧ In a small frying pan over medium-high heat, warm the oil. When hot, add the mustard seeds and cover the pan. When the sputtering stops, after about 30 seconds, uncover and add the dried chile. Continue frying until the chile turns almost black, about 30 seconds longer. Add the asafetida and immediately pour the entire contents of the pan over the lentils. Mix, ladle into small bowls such as *katori*, and serve garnished with the cilantro.

serves 6

Indian Cattle

No animal has so revered a place in Indian culture as the cow. Eight hundred million Indians lead an agrarian life in which cattle are vital as beasts of burden, for their labor in the fields, and for their milk and the products that it yields. This usefulness has led to their being revered as animals whose every gift is a life source.

For the Hindus and Sikhs, the eating of beef is prohibited because the cow is a sacred animal in Indian mythology. For Indians of all religions, cattle are treated like family members. Their status is as high as that of a son. They are brought inside the house in bad weather, but are otherwise allowed to roam freely. Most choose to stay near their home, but those that wander off will be fed by strangers, as it is considered a privilege to provide for them.

Cow dung is another essential resource. *Goitha,* a form of natural cooking fuel, is made from sundried disks of shredded hay mixed with dung. For the millions of Indians who live in treeless deserts and other barren areas, this is the only form of fuel.

Cow dung also has a religious significance. All Hindu Brahmin religious ceremonies must use *goitha* when starting a *havan* (holy fire). It also has a function in many festivals. For example, during *Pongal,* the rice harvest festival, statuettes of Lord Ganesha, the god of food, are fashioned from cow dung.

Aloo Gobhi

cauliflower and potatoes with spices

In this Punjabi recipe, cauliflower and potatoes are cooked in oil laced with cumin and turmeric until smoky and golden yellow. Aloo gobhi is traditionally a mild dish, and a favorite of Indian children. It is one of the first dishes offered to an Indian child to acclimatize his or her palate to spices and ready it for the much spicier food that will follow later in life. The addition of bread, a rice pilaf, and a sweet, fruity chutney makes aloo gobhi *into a complete meal.*

1 head cauliflower, 1½–2 lb (750 g–1 kg)

2 tablespoons vegetable oil

1 teaspoon cumin seeds

3 boiling potatoes, peeled and cut into 1-inch (2.5-cm) pieces

2–4 tablespoons peeled and finely shredded fresh ginger

2 teaspoons minced garlic

¾ teaspoon ground turmeric

½ teaspoon cayenne pepper

1½ teaspoons salt, or to taste

¾ cup (6 fl oz / 180 ml) water

¼ cup (⅓ oz / 10 g) finely chopped fresh cilantro (fresh coriander)

½ teaspoon garam masala (page 249) or cumin seeds, roasted and ground (page 246)

❧ Separate the cauliflower florets and cut them into 1½-inch (4-cm) pieces. Peel the stem and cut crosswise into slices ⅛ inch (3 mm) thick. Chop the leaves, if any, and add to the cauliflower.

❧ In a large saucepan over medium-high heat, warm the oil. When hot, add the cumin and fry until it turns several shades darker, about 30 seconds. Add the potatoes and stir-fry until they are lightly crisped, about 5 minutes. Add the ginger, garlic, turmeric, and cayenne pepper and mix well.

❧ Add the cauliflower, salt, and water and mix well. Reduce the heat to low, cover, and cook until the cauliflower is very soft, about 7 minutes. Uncover the pan, increase the heat to medium–high, and cook until the excess moisture evaporates, about 5 minutes. Check and correct the seasonings. Sprinkle with cilantro and *garam masala* or cumin and serve.

serves 6

Delhi

Gharki Dal

everyday favorite lentils

*A very tasty and satisfying dal, gharki dal is
a family favorite. It has two ingredients of which I am
particularly fond—garlic and cilantro. For variation,
substitute yellow mung beans for the red lentils.
I like to spoon this dal over plain basmati rice and
accompany it with a vegetable.*

1 cup (7 oz/220 g) red lentils

1 tablespoon peeled and grated fresh ginger

1 teaspoon ground turmeric

4 cups (32 fl oz/1 l) water

1½ teaspoons salt, or to taste

1 tablespoon mustard oil or vegetable oil

½ teaspoon panch phoron *(page 249)*

1 dried red chile

4 large cloves garlic, thinly sliced

¼ cup (⅓ oz/10 g) chopped fresh cilantro
(fresh coriander)

❦ Pick over the lentils, discarding any stones or mis-
shapen or discolored lentils. Rinse and place in a
deep pot. Add the ginger, turmeric, and water and
bring to a boil over high heat. Reduce the heat to
medium and boil gently, uncovered, until the lentils
are very soft, about 25 minutes. Check and stir often
to ensure that they are not burning. Stir in the salt
and reduce the heat to very low to keep the lentils
warm while you make the spice-infused flavoring.

❦ In a small frying pan over high heat, warm the oil
until it begins to smoke, then immediately remove
the pan from the heat. When the smoking stops, after
about 30 seconds, reduce the heat to medium, return
the pan to the stove, and add the *panch phoron* and
dried chile. When the spices turn several shades darker, after about 1 minute, add the garlic and cook until
it turns light brown, about 1 minute. Remove from
the heat and pour the entire contents of the pan over
the lentils. Add the cilantro, mix thoroughly, and
serve ladled into small bowls such as *katori*.

serves 4

Andhra Pradesh

Narial Raita

coconut and smoked chile yogurt salad

To grate fresh coconut, crack open a coconut and pry away the meat. Peel off the brown skin and grate the meat on a box grater or in a food processor.

1 cup (8 oz/250 g) plain yogurt

1 cup (5 oz/155 g) packed grated fresh coconut

1 tablespoon peeled and finely diced fresh ginger

1–2 fresh hot green chiles such as serrano, minced

¼ cup (⅓ oz/10 g) finely chopped fresh cilantro (fresh coriander)

½ teaspoon salt, or to taste

⅓ cup (2 oz/60 g) chopped roasted cashew nuts

1 tablespoon vegetable oil

½ teaspoon brown mustard seeds

1 teaspoon white split gram beans (page 246)

1 dried red chile

In a small bowl, combine the yogurt, coconut, ginger, fresh chiles, cilantro, and salt and whisk until smoothly blended. Add the cashew nuts and mix.

In a small frying pan over medium-high heat, warm the oil. When hot, add the mustard seeds and cover the pan. When the seeds stop sputtering, about 30 seconds, uncover and add the white gram beans and dried chile. Cook, stirring, until the beans turn light golden, about 30 seconds, then immediately pour the entire contents of the pan over the yogurt mixture. Mix well and serve, or cover and refrigerate for up to 1 week.

makes 2 cups (16 fl oz/500 ml); serves 4

Gujarat

Sak

cauliflower with spices

The city of Surat, on the coast of Gujarat, is home to Hindu Vaishnavites, who are known for their vegetarian cooking. It is also famous for its vegetable gardens, which supply the entire region. Vaishnavas generally do not use garlic because of its association with meat, but this is changing due to recent medical reports on garlic being good for the heart. This utterly delicious recipe comes from my Surati friend Vinod Patel, and, much to my delight, includes garlic.

1 cauliflower, 1½–2 lb (750 g–1 kg)

2 tablespoons vegetable oil

1 teaspoon brown mustard seeds

1 tablespoon peeled and grated fresh ginger

2 teaspoons minced garlic

2 teaspoons ground coriander

½ teaspoon cayenne pepper

¼ teaspoon ground turmeric

¾ cup (4½ oz/140 g) fresh or canned chopped tomatoes

2 teaspoons tomato paste

1¼ teaspoons salt, or to taste

¾ cup (6 fl oz/180 ml) water

¼ cup (⅓ oz/10 g) chopped fresh cilantro (fresh coriander)

☙ Trim the cauliflower and separate it into small florets. Peel the stem and cut it crosswise into slices ⅛ inch (3 mm) thick.

☙ In a large sauté pan, warm the oil over high heat. When very hot, add the mustard seeds and cover the pan. When the seeds stop sputtering, after about 30 seconds, uncover and add the ginger, garlic, ground coriander, cayenne pepper, and turmeric. Reduce the heat to low and cook, stirring, for 10 seconds. Stir in the tomatoes, tomato paste, salt, and water.

☙ Add the cauliflower pieces and stir thoroughly to coat them with the tomato-spice mixture. Increase the heat to medium-high, cover, and cook until the cauliflower is tender, about 20 minutes. Uncover and continue cooking until the excess moisture evaporates and the cauliflower is coated with a thick gravy, about 5 minutes longer. Fold in half of the fresh cilantro and serve garnished with the remainder.

serves 4

Tamil Nadu

Muttakos Kari

tossed cabbage with mustard and coconut

You can make an equally delicious kari, or stir-fry, using kohlrabi or brussels sprouts. Both are favorite vegetables of the people of Tamil Nadu.

2 tablespoons usli ghee (page 247) or vegetable oil

1 teaspoon brown mustard seeds

1 cup (5 oz/155 g) finely chopped shallots

20 fresh or 40 dried kari leaves (page 248) or 4 cassia leaves (page 244)

½ teaspoon ground turmeric

2 fresh hot green chiles such as serrano, seeded and slivered

1 small cabbage, 1–1½ lb (500–750 g), cored and cut into ½-inch (12-mm) pieces

1¼ teaspoons salt, or to taste

½ cup (4 fl oz/125 ml) water

¼ cup (1 oz/30 g) unsweetened coconut flakes

2 tablespoons chopped fresh cilantro (fresh coriander)

☙ In a large sauté pan over medium-high heat, warm the usli ghee or oil. When hot, add the mustard seeds and cover the pan. When the seeds stop sputtering, after about 30 seconds, uncover and add the shallots, kari or cassia leaves, turmeric, and chiles. Cook, stirring occasionally, until the shallots are lightly fried, about 5 minutes.

☙ Add the cabbage and salt and sauté, turning and tossing, until the cabbage wilts, about 5 minutes. Stir in the water and cover the pan. Reduce the heat to low and cook until the cabbage is very soft, about 10 minutes. Uncover, lightly mix in the coconut and cilantro, and serve.

serves 6

The coconut palm is known as the tree of wealth, as every part can be turned to profit.

Maharashtra

Tori Moong

mung beans and squash with mustard seeds

Tori, a type of ridged squash, is a popular vegetable in the southern and southwestern regions. This dal is just as good made with other varieties of squash.

1 cup (7 oz/220 g) yellow mung beans

¼ teaspoon ground turmeric

4 cups (32 fl oz/1 l) water

2 cups (10 oz/315 g) diced squash, such as peeled silk squash, peeled and seeded butternut squash, or unpeeled snake squash or zucchini (courgette) (½-inch/12-mm dice)

2 tablespoons peeled and finely chopped fresh ginger

2 fresh hot green chiles such as serrano, minced

1 tablespoon fresh lemon juice

1 teaspoon salt, or to taste

2 tablespoons peanut oil

1 teaspoon cumin seeds

1 teaspoon coarsely ground black pepper

½ teaspoon powdered asafetida (see sidebar, page 144) or 1 teaspoon minced garlic

¼ cup (⅓ oz/10 g) finely chopped fresh cilantro (fresh coriander)

❦ Pick over the beans, discarding any stones or mis-shapen or discolored beans. Rinse and place in a deep pot. Add the turmeric and water and bring to a boil over high heat. Reduce the heat to medium and boil gently, uncovered, until the beans are half done, about 10 minutes. Add the squash, ginger, chiles, lemon juice, and salt. Cover and cook, stirring often, until the beans and squash are soft, about 10 minutes longer, or 20 minutes for butternut squash. Check and correct the seasonings. Keep warm over very low heat while you make the spice-infused flavoring.

❦ In a small frying pan over medium-high heat, warm the oil. When hot, add the cumin and fry until it turns several shades darker, about 30 seconds. Add the pepper and asafetida or garlic and immediately pour the entire contents of the pan over the beans. Mix well. Serve garnished with the cilantro.

serves 6

An Indian Kitchen

The family kitchen of my childhood was a big, airy room with a movable wood-fired stove, in front of which the cook squatted on the floor. In one corner of the room, next to the water faucet, sat two huge grinding stones. Known as *ami* or *sil-batta* and *kallural,* these stones were used for making *masalas,* chutneys, and batters of puréed beans. Pots and pans made of clay, brass, zinc, and silver sat on a concrete shelf. Another shelf, right above it, held brass vessels containing spices and seasonings for use in everyday cooking. Staples such as flour, rice, and sugar were kept in an adjacent storeroom, away from the kitchen's heat and light.

For me, and for most children, the indelible sights, sounds, smells, and activities of the childhood kitchen contributed to an image of family that has lingered throughout life. The fragrance of tamarind, turmeric, cilantro, and kari, of steaming lentils and smoky breads will be with me forever. I remember sitting on mats, near the stove, barefoot (the Hindu kitchen forbids entering with shoes because of the fear of pollution) and with my *thali* (rimmed dinner plate) and several *katori* (tiny bowls) placed in front of me. Our family cook would first fill the *katori* with a variety of curries—some with sauce, others stir-fried. While I waited, she made breads, wonderful whole-wheat *phulka*s, and roasted them one by one on the embers of the fire. I watched the breads heat and puff into delightful balloons and then I devoured them with those delicious curries of cauliflower, green beans, and potatoes.

Although the curries tested a child's tolerance for heat, I seldom reached for water because it was always warm, even at the height of summer. That was my father's rule. He believed that cold water contributed to a sore throat and other coldlike ailments. I, too, am a strong proponent of drinking warm water with meals. I understand the Ayurvedic reasoning behind my father's rule. Warm water enters the blood stream more quickly and therefore helps with digestion—a simple concept that makes sense.

For an Indian, it is the kitchen that is at the center of the family and binds the roots and traditions of survival. Kitchen memories, whether sweet or sad, become the bedrock of one's collective cultural heritage.

Karnataka

Kela Raita

banana and green chile raita

Bananas, one of the oldest fruits on Earth, have been in India since the beginning of Hindu civilization. They are an object of great reverence, and as such are eaten on all auspicious occasions. Special banquets and religious feasts generally include a banana raita. This recipe of the Mangalorians is sometimes made with the extremely sweet and fragrant finger bananas. Some red-colored varieties look particularly attractive in the ivory-white yogurt. Finger or red bananas may be found at specialty produce grocers.

1½ cups (12 oz/375 g) plain yogurt

2 teaspoons sugar

½ teaspoon cumin seeds, roasted and ground (page 246)

¼ teaspoon salt, or to taste

3 fresh hot green chiles such as serrano, thinly sliced

¼ cup (1 oz/30 g) finely chopped walnuts

3 ripe bananas, peeled and cut into 1-inch (2.5-cm) cubes

☙ In a bowl, combine the yogurt, sugar, cumin, salt, and chiles and whisk until smoothly blended. Add the walnuts and bananas and mix well. Serve at once, or refrigerate for up to 6 hours (if left any longer, the bananas will begin to discolor).

makes 3 cups (24 fl oz/750 ml); serves 4

Prayers and offerings are made in the hope of a good monsoon and bountiful harvest.

Maharashtra

Alu-Sem nu Saag

beans and potato with kokum

This is a typical vegetable stir-fry of Maharashtra. It is a fragrant and mild dish of potatoes, green beans, spices, and kokum, a sour fruit used as seasoning. Maharashtrian cooks, famous for the use of kokum, add it whole or torn into large pieces to lend color and texture to the dish. Although safe to eat, kokum is seldom eaten raw because its leathery texture is hard to chew. Cooking renders kokum soft and enables its distinct flavor to leach into the sauce. To vary the texture of this dish, the kokum may be sliced into very fine slivers rather than added in large pieces. Kokum is available in Indian grocery stores.

1 lb (500 g) boiling potatoes, boiled, peeled, and cut into 1-inch (2.5-cm) pieces

1 teaspoon ground cumin

1 teaspoon ground coriander

½ teaspoon cayenne pepper

¼ teaspoon ground turmeric

1 teaspoon salt, or to taste

2 tablespoons peanut oil

1 teaspoon brown mustard seeds

½ lb (250 g) green beans, trimmed and cut into ½-inch (12-mm) pieces

3 pieces kokum (page 248), each cut in half, or 1½ teaspoons lemon juice

1 teaspoon jaggery (page 248) or brown sugar

3 cups (24 fl oz/750 ml) water

☙ Place the potatoes in a bowl and sprinkle with the cumin, coriander, cayenne pepper, turmeric, and salt. Mix well and set aside.

☙ In a nonstick frying pan over medium-high heat, warm the oil. When hot, add the mustard seeds and cover the pan. When the sputtering stops, after about 30 seconds, add the potatoes and cook, turning and tossing, until evenly coated with the oil and lightly browned. Add the beans, *kokum* or lemon juice, sugar, and water and bring to a boil over high heat. Reduce the heat to low, cover, and simmer until the beans are cooked, about 10 minutes. Check and correct the seasonings, then serve.

serves 6

Gujarat

Aam Raita

mango yogurt salad

This simple raita *is ravishing when you choose the correct mango. It is essential that the mango be fiberless. The Haden variety, known in America as Mexican mangoes, is similar to the Indian Langra or Alphonso varieties. They are generally fiberless, with smooth and creamy flesh.*

Select a fully ripe mango, as only then will it impart the sweet perfume we so dearly associate with this fruit. Firmness, too, is important, because very soft flesh often falls apart and makes the raita *murky. Canned mangoes in syrup are too soft and sweet to work well in this recipe. To intensify the mango flavor in the* raita, *add a spoonful of peach liquor or, if you want to avoid alcohol, peach nectar.*

1½ cups (12 fl oz/375 ml) plain yogurt

1 teaspoon fresh lemon juice

1 teaspoon cumin seeds, roasted (page 246)

½ teaspoon coarse salt

¼ teaspoon cayenne pepper

¼ teaspoon ground black pepper

1 teaspoon minced fresh mint or kari leaves (page 248)

2 medium or 1 large ripe mango, peeled, pitted, and cut into ½-inch/12-mm dice, to make about 1½ cups (12 oz/375 g)

In a bowl, combine the yogurt, lemon juice, cumin, salt, cayenne pepper, black pepper, and mint or kari and whisk until smoothly blended. Fold in the mango, cover, and refrigerate until ready to serve. It will keep for up to 2 days in the refrigerator.

makes about 3 cups (24 fl oz/375 g); serves 4

West Bengal

Alurbhaja

potatoes with panch phoron

These potatoes are delicious hot, at room temperature, or straight from the refrigerator. They are great in pita pockets with sliced tomatoes and lettuce, and perfect to take along on a picnic because the Bengali spice blend panch phoron *helps keep the potatoes from spoiling.*

2 tablespoons mustard oil or vegetable oil

2 dried red chiles

1 teaspoon panch phoron *(page 249)*

2 yellow onions, finely chopped

1–2 fresh hot green chiles such as serrano, thinly sliced

½ teaspoon ground turmeric

1½ lb (750 g) boiling potatoes, boiled, peeled, and cut into 1-inch (2.5-cm) cubes

1½ teaspoons salt, or to taste

2 tablespoons chopped fresh cilantro (fresh coriander)

In a large nonstick frying pan over medium heat, warm the oil. When hot, add the dried chiles and fry, stirring, until they are very dark, almost black, about 1 minute. Add the *panch phoron* and let the spices sizzle until they turn several shades darker, about 30 seconds. Add the onions, fresh chiles, and turmeric and cook, stirring, until the onions are lightly fried and golden, about 5 minutes.

Add the potatoes and salt, mix well, and cook until the potatoes are heated through. Check and correct the seasonings and fold in the cilantro. Serve hot, at room temperature, or cold.

serves 6

Punjab

Dahi Bhalla

lentil dumplings and yogurt salad

Dahi bhalla (called dahi bara or dahi vada in other regions) is a classic Indian vegetarian preparation. In this composed raita, fried puffs made with puréed whole gram beans are combined with spiced yogurt and fresh herbs. Typically Dahi bhalla is not an everyday dish, as one needs to have the readymade bean puffs on hand. It is also costly. Raisins and yogurt are expensive items in India and are used with discretion. As a rule, wedding feasts, buffets, and traditional vegetarian meals all feature dahi bhalla.

Fried Bean Puffs with Ginger and Raisins (page 58)

3 cups (24 oz/750 g) plain yogurt

1½ teaspoons sugar

1 teaspoon cumin seeds, roasted and lightly crushed (page 246)

½ teaspoon salt

½ teaspoon black pepper

½ teaspoon ground black salt (see sidebar, right) or chat masala (page 244) (optional)

2 teaspoons peeled and shredded fresh ginger

1 teaspoon sliced fresh hot green chiles such as serrano

½ teaspoon cayenne pepper or paprika

2 tablespoons chopped fresh cilantro (fresh coriander)

✼ Place the bean puffs in a large bowl, add hot water to cover, and let soak for 30 minutes. Drain them, then gently squeeze out the excess water.

✼ In another large bowl, combine the yogurt, sugar, half of the cumin, the salt, black pepper, and black salt or chat masala, if using, and whisk until thoroughly blended. Add the bean puffs, cover, and set aside for 1 hour at room temperature so that the bean puffs absorb some of the yogurt.

✼ To serve, arrange the bean puffs in a shallow dish. Pour any remaining yogurt over them. Sprinkle with the remaining cumin, the ginger, chiles, cayenne pepper or paprika, and cilantro. Serve immediately or refrigerate, covered, for up to 3 days.

serves 8–12

Black Salt

My first taste of kala namak (literally, "black salt") came as a young child. Just outside the schoolyard vendors sold treats. My favorite was churan, a sweet, hot, fudgelike concoction made of minced dates, golden raisins (sultanas), spices, and black salt. I could never get enough of it. As an adult I discovered the properties of black salt as a flavor enhancer and appetite stimulant.

Black salt is not a true sodium salt at all but a sulfur compound or deposit. This is the reason black salt has the taste and smell of boiled eggs with onions. The salt is mined from underground deposits in central India, Pakistan, and Afghanistan. It is brownish black in its natural form, hence its name. When ground, however—the form in which the salt is commonly sold—the crystals become a light pink.

Black salt is usually sprinkled over appetizers, snacks, and starters. The spice blend chat masala, used in various appetizer salads called chat, traditionally contains black salt.

Bihar and Madhya Pradesh

Podine ka Raita

mint-yogurt salad

This is a rustic, farmhouse recipe from Patna, given to me by my friend Arun Sinha, whose family have been landowners in Bihar for generations. There is nothing technically complicated about the recipe, but it requires the best ingredients. The yogurt must be fresh, with a pronounced lactic aroma, and the mint should smell distinctly minty when chopped. Indian cooks use intensely aromatic spearmint sprigs.

1½ cups (12 oz/375 g) plain yogurt

2 teaspoons finely chopped fresh mint

1 teaspoon minced garlic

¼ teaspoon salt, or to taste

¼ teaspoon ground white pepper

¼ cup (1 oz/30 g) dried cranberries or raisins

In a medium bowl, combine the yogurt, mint, garlic, salt, and pepper and whisk until smooth, then stir in the cranberries or raisins. Refrigerate, covered, for 30 minutes before serving so the fruit can soften and the flavors blend. It will keep, covered, for up to 3 days in the refrigerator.

makes about 2 cups (16 fl oz/500 ml); serves 4

No Indian celebration, ritual, or pageant begins without first paying homage to food.

West Bengal

Bhaja Monger Dal

roasted mung bean purée

Roasting the beans before cooking a dal is a classic technique of West Bengal's cuisine. The beans lose some of their starchiness and taste spicier. Some cooks dry-roast the beans, which lends a totally different aroma, but I like to roast them in a skillet with a little oil. This method is easier, faster, and browns the beans evenly. For variation, red lentils can replace the mung beans. This soupy dal is best served with dishes such as Shrimp in Spiced Cream Sauce, Braised Eggplant and Potatoes with Spices, Mint-Yogurt Salad, Radish Pickle, Plain Basmati Rice, and Balloon Bread.

1¼ cups (10 oz/315 g) yellow mung beans

4 tablespoons (2 fl oz/60 ml) usli ghee (page 247) or vegetable oil

4 cups (32 fl oz/1 l) water

1 teaspoon ground turmeric

3 dried red chiles

2 cassia leaves (page 244)

1 cinnamon stick, broken into a few pieces

1½ teaspoons cumin seeds

½ cup (4 fl oz/125 ml) coconut milk

1½ teaspoons salt, or to taste

1 teaspoon sugar

Pick over the beans, discarding any stones or mis-shapen or discolored beans. Rinse, drain, and pat dry on paper towels. In a deep pot over medium-high heat, warm 2 tablespoons of the *usli ghee* or oil. When hot, add the mung beans and cook, stirring, until they are light brown, about 8 minutes. Add the water and turmeric and bring to a boil over high heat. Reduce the heat to low and simmer gently, uncovered, until the beans are very soft, about 30 minutes. Crush some of the beans to give the dal a slightly creamy consistency.

In a small frying pan over medium-high heat, warm the remaining *usli ghee* or oil. Add the dried chiles, cassia leaves, cinnamon, and cumin. Fry, stirring, until the seeds turn several shades darker and are fragrant, about 1 minute. Immediately pour the entire contents of the pan over the beans. Add the coconut milk, salt, and sugar and mix well. Serve immediately.

serves 4

Karnataka

Okra Thel Pyau

mangalore braised okra with coconut

Here is a simple, unique way to cook okra. While other regional Indian cuisines stir-fry and glaze vegetables with spices, the Christian Mangalorians of Karnataka steam-cook them. Isobel Nazareth of Mangalore gave me this recipe in which tender, whole okra is steamed with onion, garlic, chiles, and kokum, *a souring agent. It is served garnished with coconut.*

1¼ lb (625 g) young, tender okra, stemmed

1 large yellow onion, halved and sliced

3 cloves garlic, thickly sliced

6 fresh hot green chiles such as serrano, stemmed and slit lengthwise

2 pieces kokum *(page 248) or 1 teaspoon lemon juice*

1¼ *teaspoons salt, or to taste*

1 cup (8 fl oz/250 ml) water

⅔ *cup (2½ oz/75 g) unsweetened grated coconut*

☙ In a saucepan, combine the okra, onion, garlic, chiles, *kokum* or lemon juice, salt, and water and bring to a boil over high heat. Reduce the heat to medium, cover partially, and cook until the okra is very tender but not mushy, about 15 minutes. If there is excess moisture in the okra, uncover the pan completely during the last few minutes of cooking to allow it to evaporate.

☙ Remove from the heat and fold in half of the coconut. Sprinkle the remaining coconut over the top of the dish just before serving.

serves 4

Serpent Worship

There are few sights more exotic and intriguing to the Western eye than the Indian snake charmer. Snakes have long been both feared and worshipped in India. Their importance to the culture is celebrated in various rituals that are linked to both milk and grain and thus, in Indian thinking, to life itself. Cobras live in rice fields and protect the grain by eating the rodents that might otherwise destroy the crop. In return for this service they are never harmed; indeed, they are often offered milk and milk products such as *usli ghee* and sweets.

Cobra worship is a pagan ritual that was fairly common among ancient Indian pastoral peoples. They particularly dreaded king cobras, which inhabited farm fields. As is often the case in many cultures, this fear of a mortal enemy gave rise to its deification. When the Aryans arrived in 2500 BC and gave root to Hindu culture in India, *Nagpooja*—the worship of cobras and other snakes—became part of the religious pantheon. Serpent worship is still practiced today, particularly on Nag Panchami, the fifth day of the month of Sravana (corresponding to July and August on the Western calendar). Hindu women pray to the snake god Naga to protect their *suhag*, or married state, by giving long life to their husbands. (In Hindu mythology, Naga is immortal, because it is rejuvenated with the sloughing off of its skin.)

The Naga ceremony is, in fact, an indirect ceremony of milk, the food which is offered to the serpents. The milk used for the ceremony is only cow's milk, never buffalo's. The cow, unlike the buffalo, is a sacred animal, so only its milk is considered fit to be offered to the cobra, which is also sacred. The milk is ceremonially prepared:

First, the kitchen is freshly whitewashed, then decorated with designs made out of rice flour colored with turmeric. The women participating in the ceremony fast beforehand, ritually bathe, then dress in purified saris. Afterward, no one may touch them until their fast is broken and the ceremony over; they must remain "pure" throughout the ceremony.

Once the kitchen and the participants are readied, the milk is boiled for the cobras. Various sweets are also prepared: *jalebi* (syrup-soaked pastries), *laddoo* (sweet balls), and *barfi* (milk fudge), all of which contain milk. The milk and sweets are offered to the cobras, who eat their fill then leave. There is a superstition that if the milk is not prepared correctly and offered to the cobras with due ceremony, the next day fifty or sixty vengeful snakes will return and wreak havoc.

Any food that is left is considered blessed and the women consume it to break their fast. Afterward there is a celebration and feasting. Ceremonies such as this, and similar ones in the innumerable temples and shrines in India that are devoted to cobras and other snakes, result from the Indian desire to maintain a balance between man and nature. Indians believe that if they respect and do not harm the cobras, the snakes will do the same for them.

ACCOMPANIMENTS

Tangy relishes and rice
or freshly made bread are
essential to every table.

Preceding pages: Well protected against the Kashmir cold, a young woman sells bread in the capital, Srinagar.
Above top: A vendor sifts grain in Jodhur's grain market.
Above: Turmeric gives an earthy taste and bright color to many curries, pickles, and *masalas*. It has a tenacious pigment that stains the clothes and hands of those who process it and that also makes a good dye. Right top: Keralan schoolgirls seek shelter from the monsoonal rain.
Right bottom: A stone bridge spans the Betwa River at Orchha, Madhya Pradesh.

I AM VERY FOND of the traditional Indian style of dining, in which one sits on the floor with a banana leaf as a plate. No one made this custom come alive more expressively and sensuously than my cousin Kunja when I visited her in Trichinapoly, which is situated amid the palm forests and rice fields of Tamil Nadu, in the south. First, a neatly trimmed two-foot (60-cm) piece of banana leaf was placed on the mud-plastered floor. Then Kunja spooned out a little tasting portion of pudding—a *prasadam,* or offering blessed by the gods—to begin the feast. The accompaniments followed. Kunja placed three types of pickle on my banana leaf: one made of tart green mangoes the size of bing cherries; one made of small Indian limes, similar to key limes; and one made with vegetables. All were laced with spices such as fenugreek, mustard, turmeric, the special crimson chiles of southern India, and *gingeli yennai* (virgin sesame oil). Next, she spooned out several sweet-spicy chutneys. Some were dry powders made with roasted lentils, while others were chunky, fruity, and spiced. One consisted of fresh green herbs, and she also included my favorite, made with fresh coconut from her backyard.

On a large *thali,* or individual platter, Kunja laid out fragile *varuval* (chips and wafers) and *pappadums,* which southerners consider a bread. Then grain dishes such as *tenga sevai* (rice noodles with coconut) preceded the final, most important accompaniment, the rice. Kunja brought the *vengalapanai* (rice pot) and, using the traditional rice spoon, served up a steaming mound of southern rice. Westerners are always surprised to learn that basmati rice is eaten mainly in the north, and that the rice served in the south is quite different, being more like Thai jasmine rice. Southern Indians are great rice eaters. They adore its texture, flavor, and visual appeal, and therefore exercise little restraint when serving it.

Even before a single main dish had been brought from the kitchen, my banana leaf looked full and aesthetically complete. With the sun's rays penetrating the cracks in the roof panels and falling on my food, the beautiful arrangement seemed like a painting in motion. What a feast for the senses, I thought,

and a wonderful prelude to the many other culinary pleasures to come.

As this complex but by no means unusual meal illustrates, Indians like many flavor and texture contrasts on their palate: hot against cool, fiery against sweet, soft against crunchy, and mellow against assertive. To achieve this, meals usually include a few chutneys and pickles. All such condiments combine fruit, vegetables, nuts, or herbs and are flavored with a multitude of spices and seasonings to stimulate the taste buds.

Chutneys can be an uncooked blend of ingredients such as puréed herbs, spices, and coconut or tamarind. They can also be fully cooked like a fruit preserve, or partially cooked and seasoned with spiced oil. In India, all cooked chutneys are made when fruits and vegetables are plentiful, so that great quantities can be prepared economically. Large amounts of salt and sugar are added to prevent spoilage and increase shelf life. (These can be reduced to moderate amounts with no loss of flavor, as long as the chutneys are kept refrigerated.) The texture of a chutney depends upon its use: A mint chutney to accompany a fritter is

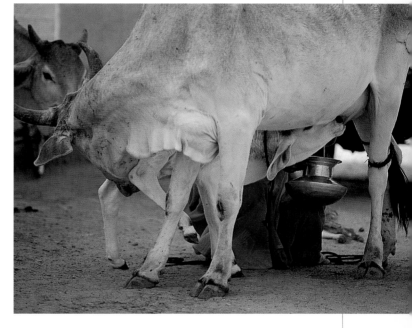

Left: Festive garlands are offered for sale in Haridwar, in Uttar Pradesh. **Above top:** Workers sift flour in the bakery of Amritsar's Golden Temple. The bakery serves the *langar,* or communal dining room, in which volunteers feed up to thirty-five thousand people a day. All colors, castes, and creeds are welcome; all sit on the floor and eat communally, in contrast to the tenets of Hinduism, which prohibit people of different castes from eating together. **Above:** A calf and its owner share the milk from a compliant cow. Although many Indians do not eat beef, people of all religions enjoy dairy foods.

Above top: The Samode Palace near Jaipur, once the residence of Rajasthani nobles, is now a luxury hotel. Its magnificent Durbar Hall is hand-painted in exquisite detail. **Above:** Piles of spices (from left: green cardamom pods, dried mace, pepper, and cassia) are set out at a stall in Old Delhi. **Right:** A roadside tandoori chef bakes roti, a type of flat bread. The tandoor, a clay-lined oven, is not a feature of most Indian homes, because it is expensive to build and run. It is more common in the north of the country. In the south, its use is limited to the more exclusive restaurants.

fairly thin and used as a dip, while a chunky hot-and-spicy tomato chutney can almost pass for a side dish.

Pickles range from mildly spicy to very hot, although there are a few sweet ones, too. Chunks of vegetables or fruits, nuts, or berries are marinated in a briny solution laced with fragrant spices. The marination can last for up to six months, and each Indian family has its own secret recipe.

Grains play an even more critical role in the Indian diet. Rice and bread are considered more than mere accompaniments. They are essential underpinnings, the foils upon which vibrant, spicy foods can come alive. Breadmaking dates back to the Indus Valley civilization, when breads baked from millet were a dietary staple. Today in India, greetings are often followed by the phrase *"Roti khai-lo?"* which means "Have you eaten bread?" Similar associations exist for rice, an equally old and important grain. Any dish, whether it be a rich butter chicken or a simple *sambar* (curried lentils), is not considered a complete meal until rice or bread accompanies it. The inclusion of these two staples is not just desirable, but necessary to mellow and round off flavors and provide nutritional balance.

During an Indian meal, it is the breads that typically steal the show. Their appeal is due to their attractive appearance, delicious flavor, and the ease with which they can be prepared at home. Most are unleavened flat breads made with whole-wheat (wholemeal) flour. Regional variations are made using other flours, such as those milled from corn, millet, barley, chickpeas (garbanzo beans), rice, and chestnuts. They are generally baked in wood-fired stoves called *chulha* that imbue them with an irresistible, faintly smoky flavor.

Although plain roti or chapatis and flaky, layered *parathas* (whole-wheat/wholemeal flat breads) are the daily fare in my home, my son's eyes light up when I serve balloon bread, *poori,* or puffy yogurt bread, *bhatoora.* A universal favorite is the leavened bread nan, which is baked in a large, clay-lined oven called a tandoor. All these breads are perfect with any Moghul or northern Indian dishes, particularly tandoori chicken and kabobs.

Of all the many varieties of rice cultivated in India, the best known is the beautifully flavorful and fragrant basmati, which is grown along the foothills of the Himalayas. This is the favorite accompaniment to the Moghul cuisine of northern India, but there are other, equally delicious varieties grown in different regions, each one of which pairs wonderfully with that region's classic dishes. Kerala's red rice, Kashmir's black rice, and the pearl rice of Madras are just three examples. Kashmiri red rice is another. It is relatively unknown outside the Jammu and Kashmir region, because it is grown exclusively for local consumption. Round, fat, and delicately perfumed, it is ideal with Kashmiri foods such as *haak* (flat-leaf kale) or seared river trout. The rice is packed into fresh bamboo pipes then steamed, which infuses the grain with a deep floral aroma. Rice prepared in this way is both a staple and a local specialty in the mountainous northeastern states of Arunachal Pradesh, Nagaland,

Above: Outside the Chotiwala restaurant in Rishikesh, Uttar Pradesh, a man is employed to sit as an unusual living advertisement. **Right:** An open-air stall displays chunks of jaggery, dehydrated sugarcane juice. It is as important as sugar in Indian cookery, adding a distinctive flavor as well as sweetness. **Far right top:** A man leads a cow to drink in a Karnatakan village. Ancient Indian artworks depicting similar long-horned, hump-backed cattle have been found, showing that such cattle have been domesticated since at least the times of the Indus Valley civilization, over four thousand years ago. **Far right bottom:** The village of Khajuraho, in Madhya Pradesh, is famous for its vast temple complex dating from the eleventh and twelfth centuries. Here, sandstone bas-reliefs from the Lakshmana Temple depict divinities and mythical figures.

Manipur, Mizoram, Tripura, Assam, and Meghalaya. The people along the southern coastal regions of Andhra Pradesh, Tamil Nadu, Karnataka, Goa, and Kerala also steam rice, as well as boiling, baking, and frying it.

Plain cooked rice, without salt or fat, is generally eaten on a regular basis. For important occasions, rice is prepared using saffron, mint, coconut, tamarind, or lemon. It is cooked with innumerable other seasonings and ingredients as well, such as garlic, cumin, ginger, onions, vegetables, fruits, and nuts. These more elaborate recipes, called *pulao, bhat, tehri,* or *biriyani,* are excellent served alone or with a *raita.* Rice and other grains are also turned into breakfast cereal, flakes, puffs, noodles, pasta, powder, and flour and served as puddings, fluffy pilafs, crepes, pancakes, and dumplings. With such an array of culinary possibilities, the accompaniments in an Indian meal ensure that the palate is never bored, but rather, piqued and ultimately satisfied.

Gujarat

Gajjar Achar

carrot pickle

During summer, Indian cooks spend much of their time outdoors, feverishly pickling vegetables. The sun's fierce heat helps kill bacteria, thus prolonging the shelf-life of the produce. Indian pickles are highly seasoned and assertive, so serve them in moderate portions.

¼ cup (2 fl oz/60 ml) vegetable oil

2 tablespoons yellow mustard seeds, crushed

2 large cloves garlic, thickly sliced

1 teaspoon ground turmeric

1 lb (500 g) carrots, peeled and cut into matchsticks

8 fresh hot green chiles such as serrano, halved lengthwise

1 tablespoon jaggery (page 248) or brown sugar

1 tablespoon salt

3 tablespoons fresh lemon juice

❧ In a small pan over medium heat, warm the oil. When hot, add the mustard seeds, garlic, and turmeric. Let the spices sizzle and fry until the garlic is translucent but not brown, about 1 minute. Add the carrots, chiles, sugar, salt, and lemon juice. Mix well to coat the vegetables with the spiced oil. Cook, stirring, until the ingredients are heated through, about 2 minutes.

❧ Remove from the heat, transfer to a bowl, and let cool completely before serving. The pickle will keep, covered, in the refrigerator for up to 2 weeks.

makes about 2 cups (1 lb/500 g

Uttaranchal

Sada Chawal

plain basmati rice

Many varieties of rice are used in India—long-, medium-, and short-grained, colored, glutinous, and scented. But to make a great bowl of scented, long-grain rice in which each grain is separate, you must use basmati. For best results, rinse the rice of clinging starch and soak it before cooking. The quantities in this recipe can be successfully doubled or tripled.

1 cup (7 oz/220 g) basmati rice
2 cups (16 fl oz/500 ml) water

☼ Rinse the rice thoroughly in cold water. In a small saucepan, combine the rice and water and let soak for 30 minutes.

☼ Place the saucepan over medium-high heat and bring the water and rice to a boil, stirring occasionally to ensure that the rice is not settling to the bottom of the pan. Reduce the heat to medium and boil gently, without stirring, until most of the water evaporates and the surface of the rice is covered with steaming holes, about 6 minutes.

☼ Cover the pan tightly and reduce the heat to the lowest point. (If the pan lid does not fit tightly, place a sheet of aluminum foil over the pan before putting on the lid.) Cook for 5 minutes longer, then remove from the heat and let the rice rest, covered, for 5 minutes. Serve immediately, or use in making flavored rice dishes.

makes 2½ cups (12½ oz/390 g); serves 2–4

Rice, the staple food of two-thirds of the population, has been cultivated in India for over six thousand years.

Basmati Rice

In India, rice is more than a grain. It is *annabrahma*, the god of life. Consuming it creates a cosmic connection with divinity, hence all Hindu Brahmin religious celebrations include rice. It is the first food of an Indian baby and the last to honor the dead.

The tradition of tossing rice at newlyweds originated in India, but a wedding is the only time that an Indian willingly tosses away the kernels. I remember once throwing out a rack of lamb because it was past its best, but when it came to disposing of a few spoonfuls of rice, my heart missed a beat. This reverence for the grain has resulted in the creation of many elaborate rice dishes that are showcased during regional festivals and feasts.

Countless varieties of rice are used in India, but none is more venerated than basmati. Grown along the Himalayan foothills, basmati, the queen of rice (*bas* means "fragrance" and *mati* means "leader" or "queen") has long, slender grains and a delicate almond-butter aroma that make it the ideal choice for pilafs and *biriyani*s. The flavor is so compelling that I like it cooked absolutely plain, without any salt or fat.

Tamil Nadu

Opma

semolina pilaf

Opma, a classic cereal dish from Salem, in south India, resembles couscous. It is a delicate, very fragrant preparation, flavored in the southern style with popped mustard seeds, white gram beans, and kari leaf. Although referred to as a pilaf, opma won't fluff as rice pilaf will, especially when hot. Its texture is traditionally soft. For this reason, allow opma to rest and cool for a few minutes before serving it.

3 tablespoons Indian sesame oil or vegetable oil

1 teaspoon brown mustard seeds

2 teaspoons white split gram beans (page 246)

1 yellow onion, chopped

2 fresh hot green chiles such as serrano, thinly sliced

1 cup (6 oz/185 g) fine-grind semolina (farina)

1¾ cups (14 fl oz/440 ml) hot water

16 fresh or 32 dried kari leaves (page 248)

1 teaspoon salt, or to taste

½ cup (2½ oz/75 g) cooked fresh or thawed frozen green peas (optional)

¼ cup (1 oz/30 g) grated coconut or (1⅓ oz/40 g) finely chopped roasted cashew nuts

In a large, shallow pan over medium–high heat, warm the oil. When hot, add the mustard seeds and cover the pan. When the seeds stop sputtering, after about 30 seconds, uncover and add the white split gram beans. Cook until the beans are lightly golden, about 15 seconds, then add the onion and chiles. Cook, stirring, until the onion is limp and translucent, about 3 minutes.

Add the semolina and mix well to coat it evenly with the spiced oil. Add the water, kari leaves, salt, and the green peas, if using. Mix well and bring to a boil. Still over medium–high heat, cook, stirring, until the semolina thickens to a puddinglike consistency, about 2 minutes. Reduce the heat to low, cover, and steam the semolina until the grains are fully cooked and expanded, about 8 minutes.

Uncover and let rest for 5 minutes, then stir with a fork to fluff the pilaf. Stir in the coconut or cashew nuts and serve at once.

serves 4

Gujarat

Imli Chatni

tamarind chutney

Unless you are a farmer with access to fresh pods, you will most likely see tamarind in a processed form. It is available as compressed tamarind pulp, tamarind juice, or tamarind paste. Any form is acceptable, as long as it is free of additives and salt. Because tamarind is an organic product, its sourness will vary from one batch to the next. Always taste the tamarind to assess its acidity before using: It should be about as sour as sour prunes or plums. If it is any more sour, use less tamarind to the same amount of water.

1½ cups (12 fl oz/375 ml) tamarind water (page 251)

8 pitted dates

1 teaspoon cumin seeds, roasted and ground (page 246)

1 teaspoon cayenne pepper

1 teaspoon salt

In a food processor or blender, combine the tamarind water, dates, cumin, cayenne pepper, and salt and process until liquefied and smooth. Serve at once, or cover and refrigerate for up to 1 week.

makes about 2 cups (1 lb/500 g)

The sour tang of tamarind asserts itself in many dishes of India's south.

Delhi

Bhatoora

puffy yogurt bread

Bhatoora is a Punjabi classic, but the place best known for serving it is the Kwality restaurant in the Connaught Place section of New Delhi. This spongy, deep-fried bread is made with yogurt and leavened dough. In the hot Indian climate, the dough naturally leavens and lightens when left at room temperature. Elsewhere, it needs a little assistance, so this recipe includes self-rising flour. Recently, many Indian cooks have started adding spices to bhatoora to enhance its flavor and visual appeal. I particularly like whole nigella seeds, fennel seeds, and ajowan. Bhatooras generally puff unevenly, with small bubbles. Serve this bread with any sauce-based dish to mop up the juices.

1 cup (5 oz / 155 g) chapati flour or all-purpose (plain) flour, plus extra for dusting

1 cup (5 oz / 155 g) self-rising flour

1 teaspoon nigella seeds (page 250)

½ teaspoon fennel seeds

pinch of ajowan seeds (page 244)

⅓ cup (3 fl oz / 80 ml) plain yogurt

⅔ cup (5 fl oz / 160 ml) water

vegetable oil for deep-frying

To make the dough by hand, in a bowl, combine the chapati flour, self-rising flour, nigella, fennel, and ajowan. In a cup, mix the yogurt and water and add to the flour. Mix until the dough forms a mass, then turn out onto a lightly floured surface and knead for 2 minutes. Cover and let rest for 15 minutes.

Alternatively, to make the dough in a food processor, combine the chapati flour, self-rising flour, nigella, fennel, and ajowan in a food processor and process until the flours are blended. In a cup, mix the yogurt and water and, with the machine running, add the mixture through the feed tube until a ball of dough forms on the blade. Using a pulse action, process the dough for 30 seconds longer. Turn out onto a lightly floured work surface and knead for 2 minutes. Cover and let rest for 15 minutes.

Divide the dough into 16 equal pieces. Using your hands, roll each piece into a ball and dust generously with flour. Using a rolling pin, roll out each ball into a 5-inch (13-cm) circle. As the circles are formed, keep them covered with a damp cloth until you are ready to cook them.

In a *karhai,* deep-fryer, or large, deep saucepan, pour in oil to a depth of 3 inches (7.5 cm) and heat to 375°F (190°C) on a deep-frying thermometer. When the oil is ready, gently slip 1 bread into the oil. Fry the bread, turning once, until cooked and lightly browned, about 40 seconds total. Using tongs or a slotted spoon, transfer to paper towels to drain. The bread will be light and spongy. If serving hot, keep warm in a low oven while you fry the remaining breads the same way. Serve hot, warm, or at room temperature.

makes 16

Tamil Nadu

Phalsa Chatni

hot-and-sour cranberry chutney

Phalsa, a sour-tasting wild berry, is not available outside India. However, Tamilians in the United States have developed a particular fondness for cranberries, which are similar, and have started using them in South Indian-style chutneys.

¾ lb (375 g) cranberries, halved

2 fresh hot green chiles such as serrano, thinly sliced

¼ cup (2 oz / 60 g) sugar

2 teaspoons salt

1 tablespoon vegetable oil

1 teaspoon brown mustard seeds

20 fresh or 40 dried kari leaves (page 248) or 2 cassia leaves (page 244)

In a bowl, combine the cranberries, chiles, sugar, and salt and toss well.

In a small pan over high heat, warm the oil. When hot, add the mustard seeds and cover the pan. When the seeds stop sputtering, after about 30 seconds, remove from the heat. Uncover, add the kari or cassia leaves, and cover the pan again. Let the leaves sizzle for 15 seconds. Pour the contents of the pan over the cranberries. Mix thoroughly and set aside. Let the chutney stand for 30 minutes before serving, to allow the flavors to develop. It may also be refrigerated, covered, for up to 3 weeks.

makes about 2 cups (16 oz / 500 g)

The Rice Harvest Festival

Pongal, the rice harvest festival, is one of the oldest Indian celebrations, predating the arrival of the Aryans in 2500 BC. A strictly southern Indian holiday (*pongal* is a Tamil word meaning "overflowing" or "upsurge"), the festival, also known as *Sankranti*, is observed in Tamil Nadu, Karnataka, and Andhra Pradesh. Full of ancient pagan rituals, *Pongal* is celebrated in January, marking the end of the dreary winter monsoons and heralding spring, with its plentiful sun and the rice harvest season.

Pongal festivities span three days, beginning with *Bhogi Pongal*, a celebration of the family home. Houses are cleaned and painted and homage is paid to Indra (god of the seasons) for blessing the earth and for *annabrahma*, the life source rice (*anna* means "grain" and *Brahma* means the supreme creator of the universe).

Day two is the heart of the *Pongal* celebration, when Surya Pongal (god of the sun) is worshipped. House entrances are decorated with *kolam*, the beautiful ritual designs made from rice powder and paste. Newly harvested rice is cooked with milk and jaggery (maple-flavored sugar) in pots decorated with turmeric plants and paste. People go from house to house ask-ing *"Pongaladu?,"* which means "Has the rice boiled?" The answer is always yes. Singing and rejoicing are followed by feasts of rice dishes, including sweet *Pongal* rice, tamarind rice, lemon rice, lentil rice, and coconut rice.

The third day, my favorite, is called *Mattu Pongal* (*mattu* means "cow" or "cattle"). This day is set aside for worshipping cattle. Aside from being useful, these revered animals are associated with Lord Shiva. Nandi, the holy bull, grandson of the ocean, is Lord Shiva's companion. On this day the cattle are bathed with sandalwood-scented water and festooned with bells and garlands of flowers. The same newly harvested rice offered to the deity is also offered to the cattle, accompanied with many other rice dishes.

During the holiday, villages are a cheerful, colorful sight. Brilliant yellow and orange pumpkin blossoms are used to decorate the statues of Lord Ganesha, the god of food, wisdom, and prosperity. My family has its own temple in which communal feasts are held that are open to anyone who wishes to take part in the celebrations—rich, poor, family members, or the passing traveler.

Karnataka

Nimboo Bhat

lemon rice with mustard seeds

This sixteen-hundred-year-old recipe for refreshing lemon rice can be made with any ordinary cooked rice, although the grains will not be as pretty as basmati.

Plain Basmati Rice (page 183)

2 tablespoons Indian sesame oil or vegetable oil

½ teaspoon brown mustard seeds

½ cup (2½ oz/75 g) raw peanuts, skinned

2 teaspoons white split gram beans (page 246)

1 tablespoon peeled and minced fresh ginger

1 teaspoon sugar (optional)

½ teaspoon powdered asafetida (see sidebar, page 144) or 1 teaspoon minced garlic

½ teaspoon ground turmeric

½ teaspoon cayenne pepper

16 fresh or 32 dried kari leaves (page 248)

2 fresh hot green chiles, thinly sliced

1 teaspoon salt, or to taste

5 tablespoons (2½ fl oz/75 ml) fresh lemon juice

¼ cup (2 fl oz/60 ml) water, if needed

✹ If the rice is freshly made, spread it on a large plate and let cool completely.

✹ In a large frying pan over medium-high heat, warm the oil. When hot, add the mustard seeds and cover the pan. When the seeds stop sputtering, after about 30 seconds, uncover, add the peanuts, and stir-fry until they turn light brown, about 2 minutes. Reduce the heat to medium and add the white split gram beans. Cook, stirring, until the gram beans turn golden, about 1 minute. Stir in the ginger, sugar (if using), asafetida or garlic, turmeric, cayenne pepper, kari leaves, chiles, salt, rice, and lemon juice. If the rice looks dry, add up to ¼ cup (2 fl oz/60 ml) water. Mix well and cook, stirring, until the seasonings are evenly distributed and the flavors have blended, about 5 minutes.

✹ Check and correct the seasonings. Serve hot, at room temperature, or cold.

serves 2–4

Poori

balloon bread

Poori, *the most popular Indian bread, originates from the bread-loving northern region of Haryana. It goes well with dishes that have rich, creamy sauces.*

1½ cups (7½ oz/235 g) whole-wheat (whole-meal) flour, preferably chapati flour (page 244)

½ cup (4 fl oz/125 ml) warm water, or more as needed

1 tablespoon vegetable oil, plus extra for brushing and deep-frying

½ teaspoon salt, or to taste

all-purpose (plain) flour for dusting

❧ Place the flour in a large, shallow bowl. Combine the water, 1 tablespoon oil, and salt in a measuring cup and pour over the flour. Using your hand, mix the ingredients so that they adhere together into a mass. A dough ball should form; if not, add a few tablespoons more water. Gather the dough together, turn out onto a floured work surface, and knead until smooth, about 5 minutes, dusting with all-purpose flour if it sticks. Brush the dough with oil, cover with plastic wrap or a clean, damp cloth, and set aside to rest at room temperature for 15 minutes.

❧ In a *karhai,* deep-fryer, or large, deep pan, pour in oil to a depth of 3 inches (7.5 cm) and heat to 385°F (195°C) on a deep-frying thermometer. Meanwhile, divide the dough into 2 equal portions. On a floured surface, using your hands, roll each portion into a rope 8 inches (20 cm) long. Cut each rope into 8 equal pieces and roll each piece into a smooth ball. Working with 1 ball at a time and using a rolling pin, roll out each ball into a 5-inch (13-cm) circle, dusting often with flour to prevent sticking. Repeat with the remaining balls.

❧ When the oil is ready, gently slip 1 bread into the hot oil. Press the top lightly with a flat slotted spoon; this will enable the bread to puff up. When the bread is puffed and the underside cooked, about 30 seconds, turn it with tongs and cook the second side for 30 seconds, using another spoon to gently baste the bread with the oil. Using tongs, transfer the bread to paper towels to drain briefly. Keep the cooked breads warm in a low oven while you fry the remaining breads the same way. Serve immediately.

makes 16

Delhi

Pulao

spiced basmati pilaf

Pulao, or pilaf, is a classic Moghul dish originating in the royal kitchens of Delhi. It is prepared by cooking rice in a broth scented with Moghul spices such as clove, cardamom, cinnamon, and cassia leaf. Basmati rice is essential in this dish. No substitute is adequate.

1 cup (7 oz/220 g) basmati rice

2 cups (16 fl oz/500 ml) water

1 tablespoon usli ghee *(page 247)* or vegetable oil

4 whole cloves

2 black or green cardamom pods

1 cassia leaf

1 cinnamon stick

1 teaspoon coarse salt

☼ Rinse the rice thoroughly, place in a bowl, and add the water. Let soak for at least 30 minutes, but no more than 2 hours.

☼ In a saucepan over medium heat, warm the *usli ghee* or oil. When hot, add the cloves, cardamom, cassia leaf, and cinnamon and fry until the spices are fragrant, about 3 minutes. Add the rice, its soaking water, and the salt and bring to a boil. Still over medium heat, boil gently, without stirring, until most of the water evaporates and the surface of the rice is covered with steaming holes, about 6 minutes.

☼ Reduce the heat to the lowest point, cover the pan tightly, and cook for 10 minutes longer. (If the pan lid does not fit tightly, place a sheet of aluminum foil over the pan before putting on the lid.) Remove from the heat and let the rice rest, covered, for 5 minutes before serving.

serves 2–4

Jammu and Kashmir

Sev Chatni

plum and apple chutney

Kashmir is famous for the many fruits grown in its valley. Best known are apples, which are consumed in many forms. Sev chatni combines apples, plums, and spices into a spicy, compote-like chutney. It is great served with grilled meats, in traditional thali meals, slathered on bread, or even spooned over vanilla ice cream. Also delicious is a spoonful on wheat crackers, topped with a slice of sharp cheddar.

1½ teaspoons cumin seeds

1½ teaspoon fennel seeds

1 teaspoon cardamom seeds

1 teaspoon black peppercorns

1 teaspoon ground ginger

1 teaspoon dry mustard

¼ cup (2 fl oz/60 ml) white vinegar

1½ cups (12 oz/375 g) sugar

1 lb (500 g) plums, peeled, pitted, and sliced, about 2 cups

2 tart apples, such as Granny Smith, peeled, cored, and sliced (about 2 cups), tossed in 1 tablespoon fresh lemon juice

¾ cup (3 oz/90g) chopped walnuts

¾ cup (4½ oz/140 g) raisins

☼ In a dry frying pan over high heat, toast the cumin, fennel, cardamom, and peppercorns until they are fragrant and change color, about 4 minutes. Transfer to a bowl, let cool, then coarsely crush using a mortar and pestle, kitchen mallet, or rolling pin. Add the ginger and mustard and set aside.

☼ In a nonaluminum pan, combine the vinegar and sugar and cook over medium heat, stirring, until the sugar melts. Bring to a boil, reduce the heat to low, and simmer, uncovered, until the syrup is thick and sticks to the back of a metal spoon, about 20 minutes. Stir in the spices.

☼ Add the plums and apples and continue cooking, uncovered, until the fruits are soft, about 15 minutes. Remove from the heat and fold in the walnuts and raisins. Let cool completely, then cover and refrigerate. For the best flavor, allow the chutney to rest for 1 day before serving. It can be refrigerated, covered, for up to 3 weeks.

makes about 4 cups (2 lb/1 kg)

Karnataka

Rava Dosa

semolina crepes with bell peppers

In southern India, where rice is the staple, cooks have developed ingenious ways to make bread with rice flour. One example is this ancient crepe recipe.

⅔ cup (4 oz/125 g) fine-grind semolina (farina)

⅓ cup (2 oz/60 g) rice flour

¼ cup (1½ oz/45 g) all-purpose (plain) flour

2 cups (16 fl oz/500 ml) water

1 tablespoon vegetable oil, plus extra for frying

1 red bell pepper (capsicum), seeded and finely diced

1 green bell pepper (capsicum), seeded and finely diced

4 shallots, chopped (about ½ cup/2½ oz/75 g)

3–4 fresh hot green chiles such as serrano, thinly sliced

1 tablespoon chopped fresh cilantro (fresh coriander)

1 teaspoon cumin seeds, crushed

½–1 teaspoon red pepper flakes

1½ teaspoons salt, or to taste

☙ In a bowl, combine the semolina, rice flour, all-purpose flour, and water. Whisk until well blended and smooth. Cover and set side for 1 hour to allow the semolina to thicken.

☙ In a nonstick frying pan over medium-high heat, warm the 1 tablespoon oil. When hot, add the red and green bell peppers, shallots, chiles, cilantro, cumin seeds, and red pepper flakes. Fry, stirring frequently, until the vegetables are partially cooked, about 5 minutes. Pour the contents of the pan over the semolina. Add the salt and mix well.

☙ Wipe the pan clean and heat it over medium-high heat until very hot. Brush the surface of the pan with a little oil. Pour about ⅓ cup (3 fl oz/80 ml) of batter into the pan. Quickly tilt the pan to coat it evenly with the batter. Cook until the underside of the crepe is browned, about 2 minutes, adding a little more oil to ensure that it browns nicely. Flip the crepe and cook the second side until lightly browned, 30–45 seconds longer. Keep warm in a low oven while you cook the remaining crepes in the same way.

makes 8; serves 4

The Spice Box

Long ago, when a girl in an Indian village got married, a *masaladani*, or "spice box," was included in her dowry. This covered container with several small compartments could be a simple vessel carved out of wood or an elaborate affair of molded gold studded with precious jewels. It contained spices that the bride was to take to her new family and new home.

Even though spice boxes are no longer a standard dowry item (handheld beaters and mini processors have replaced them), their use in an Indian kitchen remains as traditional as ever. The spice box enables one to keep as many as seven spices essential to Indian recipes close to the cooking area. A diligent search might turn up a brass or copper box, but stainless steel or wood are the more commonly used materials. I prefer spice boxes with an inner lid. These provide added cover, helping to keep the spices fragrant for a longer period.

Gujarat

Chapati

pan-fried whole-wheat bread

In most homes in northern India, breads are baked at least twice a day, but commercial baking is also done on a regular basis. Chapatis, commonly known as roti, are baked by rotiwalas, who belong to a special sub-caste. The men are the bakers, while the responsibility for mixing and kneading the dough and cooking the stuffing often falls to female members of the family. The rotiwalas often work for small eateries called dhabas, where chapatis accompany all dishes. I still remember one morning on a narrow street of Chor Bazaar, in Siliguri, as some friends and I watched the rotiwala bake thin, delicate chapatis with lightning speed.

1½ cups (7½ oz/235 g) chapati flour or whole-wheat (wholemeal) flour, plus extra for dusting

½ teaspoon salt

¼ cup (2 fl oz/60 ml) usli ghee (page 247) or unsalted butter, at room temperature

1 tablespoon milk

½ cup (4 fl oz/125 ml) water, or as needed

☙ Place the flour and salt in a large bowl. In a cup, combine 1 tablespoon of the *usli ghee* or butter with the milk. Add it to the flour and rub the liquid into the flour using your hands. Add the ½ cup (4 fl oz/ 125 ml) water and mix, gathering and pressing, until the flour adheres together. If the dough looks very dry, add 1–2 tablespoons more water. Be careful not to add too much, however, or the dough will become too soft and sticky to roll.

☙ Transfer the dough to a lightly floured work surface and knead for 3 minutes. Cover the dough with plastic wrap or a damp cloth and let it rest at room temperature for 15 minutes. Divide the dough into 12 equal portions. On a floured surface, using your hands, roll each portion into a neat ball. Using a rolling pin, roll out each ball into a 6-inch (15-cm) circle, dusting often with flour.

☙ Heat a dry Indian *tava* griddle or frying pan over high heat until very hot, then reduce the heat to medium-high and place 1 bread on the hot griddle or pan. Cook until brown spots appear on the underside, about 30 seconds. Using tongs, turn the bread over and cook until the second side is spotted with brown, about 30 seconds longer. Using a clean kitchen towel, press and pat one corner of the surface of the bread. This is to make the trapped steam

separate the bread into layers and make it puff. (It is not essential that the breads puff, although it enhances their appearance.) Transfer the cooked bread to a work surface, brush lightly with some of the remaining *usli ghee,* and place in a covered container lined with a clean cloth napkin or paper towels (this absorbs any condensation that would make the bottom breads soft). Repeat with the remaining breads. Serve at room temperature.

makes 12

Punjab

Nimboo ka Achar

delhi sweet-and-sour lemon pickle

This mildly sweet lemon pickle is more like a stewed chutney. Punjabis enjoy their pickles and chutneys best with bread, particularly paratha, to mop up the juices. For best results, use the juiciest lemons you can find.

6 lemons, halved

½ cup (4 oz/125 g) sugar

1 teaspoon cardamom seeds, preferably from black cardamom

1 teaspoon black peppercorns

4 whole cloves

2 tablespoons salt

☙ Squeeze the lemons and pour the juice into an enamel or other nonaluminum pan. Reserve the skins. Add the sugar, cardamom, black pepper, and cloves to the pan. Mix well, cover, and set aside.

☙ Using a spoon or knife, scrape out and discard the inner fibrous membrane of the lemon skins, leaving the white pith intact. Cut the skins into ¼-inch (6-mm) wide strips. Add the skins to the pan.

☙ Place the pan over medium-low heat and cook the lemon mixture, stirring constantly, until the sugar dissolves and the mixture comes to a boil. Boil until the skin is partially cooked, about 2 minutes. Remove from the heat and, when completely cool, transfer to a covered dish and refrigerate. The pickle needs at least 1 day, preferably 3 days, of ripening before it can be served. It will keep, refrigerated, for up to 3 months.

makes about 2 cups (14 oz/440 g)

Tamil Nadu

Tenga Sevai

madras stir-fried rice noodles with coconut

Southern Indians in rice-growing areas have a century-old tradition of serving rice noodles, in every conceivable form, as a staple. This popular recipe works well with all southern dishes.

½ packet (8 oz/250 g) Thai or Chinese thin rice noodles

2 tablespoons finely diced carrots

2 tablespoons light vegetable oil

2–4 dried red chiles

1 teaspoon brown mustard seeds

1 tablespoon white split gram beans (page 246)

18 fresh or 36 dried kari leaves (page 248)

1 teaspoon salt, or to taste

¼ cup (2 fl oz/60 ml) coconut milk

½ cup (2 oz/60 g) packed unsweetened grated coconut

❦ In a bowl, soak the noodles in a large quantity of hot water until softened, about 5 minutes. Drain and refresh under cold water.

❦ Blanch the carrots: Bring a pan of water to a boil. Have ready a bowl of cold water and ice cubes. Add the diced carrots to the boiling water and cook for 1 minute. Remove with a slotted spoon and immediately plunge the carrots into the ice water to stop the cooking. Drain and set aside.

❦ In a large nonstick frying pan over medium heat, warm the oil. When very hot, add the dried chiles and fry, tossing and turning, until almost black, about 1 minute. Add the mustard seeds and cover the pan. When the seeds stop sputtering, after about 30 seconds, uncover and add the white split gram beans and kari leaves. When the beans turn golden, about 15 seconds, add the noodles, salt, and coconut milk. Stir-fry until the noodles are coated with spices and the coconut milk is absorbed, about 6 minutes. Fold in the carrots and coconut. Check and correct the seasonings, then serve.

serves 4

Maharashtra

Tori Chatni

silk squash chutney

This is a typical preparation of the Bene Israel Jewish community. Silk squash, or tori, looks like long, ridged zucchini. It has a cucumber-like flavor and spongy interior, and is available from Indian grocers. Zucchini may be substituted. For Passover, replace the bread with ⅓ cup (2 oz/60 g) matzo meal.

1 tablespoon vegetable oil

1 yellow onion, chopped

1–2 fresh hot green chiles such as serrano, seeded and sliced

2 large silk squash or zucchini (courgettes)

1 slice white bread, trimmed and torn into pieces (about ⅓ cup/1 oz/30 g), or 1 tablespoon chopped blanched almonds

¼ cup (1½ oz/45 g) packed fresh cilantro (fresh coriander)

1 tablespoon fresh lemon juice

¼ teaspoon cumin seeds, roasted and ground (page 246)

¼ teaspoon ground black pepper

½ teaspoon salt

☙ If using silk squash, cut off the ridges, peel it, and cut it into ½-inch (12-mm) dice. If using zucchini, cut it into ½-inch (12-mm) dice without peeling it.

☙ In a large frying pan over medium heat, warm the oil. When hot, add the onion and chiles and cook, stirring constantly, until soft and glazed, about 4 minutes. Make sure they do not brown. Add the squash, stir-fry for 2 minutes, and cover the pan. Reduce the heat to low and cook until the squash is soft, about 5 minutes. Uncover, stir in the bread or almonds, and remove from the heat.

☙ In a food processor or blender, process the cilantro until finely chopped. Transfer to a bowl and fold in the cilantro, lemon juice, cumin, pepper, and salt. (The texture should be similar to that of a chunky salsa.) Serve immediately, or cover and refrigerate for up to 4 days.

makes about 2 cups (1 lb/500 g); serves 8

Andhra Pradesh

Kesar Bhat

saffron basmati pilaf

Kesar bhat *is the Hindu version of* zarda, *the classic saffron pilaf prepared by the Muslim Shia community in India and Pakistan. While* zarda *contains sugar and tastes more like a dessert,* kesar bhat *is sugarless. Cooked pilaf-style, in the Moghul tradition, it contains onions and the highly aromatic spices cardamom, cinnamon, clove, and saffron. This dish is popular in regions where there is a sizable Muslim community. It often goes by other names, such as* kesar chawal, kesar pulao, *and* zaffran pulao. *Serve* kesar bhat *with Moghul dishes and grilled meats.*

1 cup (7 oz/220 g) basmati rice

2 cups (16 fl oz/500 ml) water

½ teaspoon saffron threads, lightly crushed

2 tablespoons usli ghee (page 247) or vegetable oil

2 tablespoons minced yellow onion

3 green cardamom pods

3 whole cloves

1 cinnamon stick

⅓ cup (2 oz/60 g) raisins

¾ teaspoon salt

❦ Rinse the rice thoroughly in cold water. In a small bowl, combine the rice, water, and saffron and let soak for 30 minutes.

❦ In a saucepan over high heat, warm the *usli ghee.* When hot, add the onion, cardamom, cloves, and cinnamon and cook, stirring, until the onion is limp, about 2 minutes.

❦ Add the rice, its soaking water, the raisins, and salt and bring to a boil. Reduce the heat to medium and boil gently, without stirring, until most of the water is evaporated and the surface of the rice is covered with steaming holes, about 6 minutes. Cover tightly, reduce the heat to the lowest point, and cook the rice for 5 minutes longer.

❦ Remove the rice from the heat and let rest, covered, for 5 minutes. Serve immediately.

serves 2–4

Saffron

Surprising as it seems, it is harder to grow cilantro (fresh coriander) in your backyard than to cultivate the flower that yields saffron. But turning the stigmas of the *Crocus sativus* into the world's most expensive spice is a tedious process. Roughly six hundred stigmas from 150 crocuses are needed to produce just one gram of the deep orange spice. Spain and Kashmir, its main producers, think the effort worthwhile because of the high prices that saffron fetches. The spice is an essential ingredient in Spanish paellas and Indian *biriyanis.*

Saffron has been used in India since antiquity. It reached its zenith during the Moghul period in the seventeenth century, when it scented lavish basmati and pheasant casseroles, roast venison, and flaky shortbread.

Available in both thread and powder form, saffron comes in small packages of one to two grams. It is preferable to buy threads, since the powder is often adulterated with cheaper spices that imitate the color of the spice but lack its unique aroma and flavor. Stored in a sealed container in a cool, dry place, it will keep indefinitely.

Kerala

Narial Chatni

coconut chutney

Unless you can obtain coconuts with really fresh, fragrant, and sweet-tasting flesh, I suggest using a packaged variety; those containing the superb Hawaiian coconut meat are best. This classic Keralan recipe is lovely served with fish and rice dishes.

1 cup (8 oz/250 g) packed unsweetened shredded coconut

2 fresh hot green chiles such as seerrano, stemmed

½-inch (12-mm) piece fresh ginger, peeled

2 teaspoons fresh lemon juice

½ cup (4 fl oz/125 ml) water

½ teaspoon salt

2 tablespoons roasted split peas (optional; page 247)

1 tablespoon sesame oil or vegetable oil

1 teaspoon brown mustard seeds

❦ In a food processor or blender, combine the coconut, chiles, ginger, lemon juice, water, and salt and process until smooth. If you are using the roasted split peas, process them in a mortar or coffee grinder until finely powdered. Add to the coconut mixture and mix well. Transfer to a bowl.

❦ In a small frying pan over high heat, warm the oil. When hot, add the mustard seeds and cover the pan. When the seeds stop sputtering, after about 30 seconds, pour the entire contents of the pan over the coconut. Mix well. Serve immediately, or cover and refrigerate for up to 5 days.

makes about 1½ cups (12 oz/375 g)

Tamil Nadu and Andhra Pradesh
Manga Orha

tanjore mango pickle

This is a popular southern Indian pickle of tender, young green mangoes. It is sometimes referred to as a relish or salad because the mangoes are not cooked; the pickle is created by tossing them in spices and spiced oil. Although it is not traditional, I like to use medium-ripe mangoes to give a sensational hot, sour, and sweet play on the palate. The recipe also works well with pineapple, peaches, and nectarines.

1 large or 2 medium unripe or medium-ripe tart mangoes

1 tablespoon cayenne pepper

1½ teaspoons salt

¾ teaspoon ground turmeric

12 fresh or 24 dried kari leaves (page 248)

1 tablespoon sesame oil or vegetable oil

½ teaspoon powdered asafetida (see sidebar, page 144) or 1 teaspoon minced garlic

☙ Peel the mango(es) and remove the flesh in large pieces from around the pit(s). Discard the pit(s). Cut the flesh into ½–inch (12-mm) pieces. Transfer the pieces to a bowl, add the cayenne pepper, salt, turmeric, and kari leaves, and toss well to mix.

☙ In a small frying pan over medium-high heat, warm the oil. When hot, add the asafetida or garlic and let sizzle until lightly fried, about 15 seconds. Pour the entire contents of the pan over the mango mixture. Mix well and serve at room temperature or refrigerate for up to 5 days.

makes about 1½ cups (8 oz / 250 g)

Gujarat and Maharashtra

Khichra

whole mung bean and basmati pilaf

Driving through Gujarat, particularly the northern part, one is struck by the number of farms that dot the landscape. A variety of legumes and grains is grown in this area. Mung beans are greatly cherished and used in myriad ways: steamed, fried, boiled, sprouted, ground into flour, in fermented batters, and as a spice and snack. In this classic preparation, whole mung beans are cooked with rice in a spiced broth. Khichra, a Gujarati version of the pilaf, is one of the standard dishes of a classic Gujarati thali meal. It contains a nominal amount of mung beans, just enough to add a meaty flavor to the rice. Serve it with sauce-based dishes to soak up the sauce.

¼ cup (2 oz/60 g) whole green mung beans (page 247)

1 cup (7 oz/220 g) basmati rice

2 tablespoons usli ghee (page 247) or vegetable oil

¼ cup (1½ oz/45 g) minced yellow onion

3 green cardamom pods

2 cassia leaves (page 244)

2½ cups (20 fl oz/625 ml) water, plus extra as needed

1½ teaspoons salt, or to taste

❦ Pick over the beans, removing any stones or mis-shapen or discolored beans. Rinse the rice and beans and place them in a bowl with water to cover them by 1 inch (2.5 cm). Let soak for 30 minutes. Drain, discarding the soaking water, and set aside.

❦ In a saucepan over high heat, warm the *usli ghee* or oil. When hot, add the onion, cardamom, and cassia leaves and cook, stirring, until the onions are limp, about 2 minutes. Add the rice-bean mixture and sauté until the grains are well coated with the oil, about 1 minute.

❦ Add the water and salt and bring to a boil. Reduce the heat to low, cover, and cook until the rice and beans are very soft, about 17 minutes. Check the grains during cooking; if the evaporation is too quick, add 2–4 tablespoons more water. Serve the pilaf immediately.

serves 4

Meghalaya and Tripura

Aam Chatni

mango chutney

Mangoes are relatively new to the West, but have been highly esteemed in India for more than five thousand years. This chutney uses medium-ripe mangoes that have a sweetish-sour taste. Unlike unripe green mangoes, which stay firm when cooked, these turn soft and creamy—exactly the texture desired.

1 tablespoon vegetable oil

1 teaspoon cumin seeds

2-inch (5-cm) piece fresh ginger, peeled and cut into thin shreds

2 medium or 1 large medium-ripe mango, peeled, pitted, and cut into ½-inch (12-mm) pieces

2 fresh hot green chiles such as serrano, thinly sliced

2 tablespoons fresh lemon juice

⅓ cup (3 oz/90 g) sugar

¼ teaspoon salt

❦ In a small pan over medium-high heat, warm the oil. When hot, add the cumin and fry, stirring, until lightly colored, about 30 seconds. Add the ginger and stir for 30 seconds. Add the mango, chiles, lemon juice, sugar, and salt. Mix well and reduce the heat to low. Cook, stirring occasionally, until the mango is translucent, about 15 minutes. Serve hot, at room temperature, or chilled. The chutney can be refrigerated, covered, for up to 5 days.

makes about 2 cups (1 lb/500 g)

The blend and balance of flavor and texture are of paramount importance.

Madhya Pradesh

Chilla

millet and chickpea pancakes with fenugreek

Millet, believed to be India's oldest grain, is mentioned in the Hindu sacred text Rig-Veda. Madhya Pradesh is the millet-producing region, where the grain is put to good use in recipes such as these wheat-free pancakes.

½ cup (2½ oz/75 g) millet flour

½ cup (2½ oz/75 g) chickpea (garbanzo bean) flour

1 teaspoon minced garlic

¾ teaspoon cumin seeds, crushed

2 fresh hot green chiles, seeded and thinly sliced

¼ cup (⅓ oz/10 g) chopped fresh fenugreek or fresh cilantro (fresh coriander)

1 teaspoon salt, or to taste

2 tablespoons vegetable oil, plus extra for frying

½–¾ cup (4–6 fl oz/125–180 ml) water

✤ In a bowl, combine the millet flour, chickpea flour, garlic, cumin, chiles, fenugreek or cilantro leaves, salt, the 2 tablespoons oil, and the water. To make thick pancakes, add ½ cup (4 fl oz/125 ml) water; for thinner pancakes, use ¾ cup (6 fl oz/ 180 ml) water. Whisk until thoroughly blended.

✤ Heat a nonstick frying pan over medium-high heat until very hot. Brush the surface with a little oil. Pour about ¼ cup (2 fl oz/60 ml) of batter into the pan. Quickly tilt the pan to coat it evenly with the batter. Cook until the underside of the pancake is browned, about 2 minutes, adding a little oil around the pancake during cooking to ensure that it browns nicely. Flip the pancake and cook on the second side until browned, 30–45 seconds longer. Transfer to a plate and keep warm in a low oven while you cook the remaining pancakes the same way.

makes 8; serves 4

After-Dinner Digestives

One of India's oldest traditions is the chewing of *pan,* the astringent leaf of the *Piper betle* plant, as an after-dinner digestive. Both the holy Hindu Veda and Buddhist Jataka texts refer to offerings of *pan* to the gods. In contemporary India, no social, religious, or official function is considered complete or auspicious without its inclusion.

The word *pan* comes from the Sanskrit *parna,* meaning "leaf." Also known as betel leaf, *pan* is usually chewed slathered with *chuna,* "slaked lime," and *supari,* "areca nut" (*Areca catechu*). This composed betel quid is called *pan-supari* or simply *pan.* To counter its astringent taste, *pan* is embellished with various sweet and aromatic spices and conserves, such as fennel seeds, cardamom seeds, candied rose buds, *kewra,* scented anise, and coconut shreds.

Even on informal, more intimate occasions, *pan* plays a significant and symbolic role. For instance, when my mother once gave me a gift of a gold chain and bracelet, she placed them over betel leaves and alongside areca nuts, turmeric root, and vermilion.

Hindu Brahmins of South India offer honored guests the ceremonial *pan* as a gesture of respect, similar to the Chinese custom of offer-ing visitors special teas. The Moghuls took such a liking to the *pan*-chewing tradition that Akbar the Great commissioned the best craftsmen to design beautiful jeweled containers to hold *pan* for use in the royal courts. Today, such boxes, called *pandan,* are an integral part of the Indian cultural heritage.

Pan is highly regarded for its medicinal properties, and for its ability to freshen the breath. Most Indians do not think about the medical benefits of chewing *pan,* but rather the enjoyable experience that it delivers. To an Indian gourmet, a meal isn't quite complete until one has chewed a *pan* or two, especially in the company of friends. Every city and village in India has its *panwala* (shops specializing in *pan*). No matter what cuisine has been consumed—be it Indian, Chinese, or even French—Indians look forward to ending the meal at a *panwala.*

To Westerners, chewing *pan* may not seem a pleasant or healthful habit. It is true that chewing several *pans* over a period of many hours can stain the mouth red, but few people feel the need to chew for a long time. Should they do so, however, the redness is only temporary and neither the color nor the ingredients that comprise the *pan* are injurious to one's health.

Delhi

Podina Nan

tandoori mint bread

I always wondered why, the moment I landed in Delhi and breathed its air, I would feel a sense of nostalgia at my homecoming. I later realized the emotion was triggered by the scent of smoke and roasting breads emanating from the city's thousands of tandoors. This recipe attempts to replicate the smoky air of the tandoor in a conventional oven.

½ cup (2½ oz/75 g) finely diced yellow onion

2 tablespoons finely chopped fresh mint

1 teaspoon dried mint, crushed

½ cup (4 oz/125 g) unsalted butter, melted

1 cup (8 oz/250 g) plain yogurt

½ cup (12 fl oz/375 ml) boiling water

1 tablespoon sugar

2 teaspoons active dry yeast

1½ teaspoons salt

1 egg

3 cups (15 oz/470 g) all-purpose (plain) flour, plus up to 1¼ cups extra for dusting

vegetable oil as needed

2 teaspoons chat masala *(page 244) or mango powder (page 248) mixed with 1 tablespoon vegetable oil (optional)*

❀ In a small frying pan over medium heat, combine the onion, fresh mint, dried mint, and 2 tablespoons of the butter and cook, stirring, until the onion is soft but not brown, about 4 minutes. Remove from the heat and let cool completely.

❀ In a large bowl, whisk together the yogurt and water. Add the sugar, yeast, salt, remaining butter, and egg. Mix thoroughly. Add the 3 cups (15 oz/370 g) flour and the cooked onion and mix with your hands just until the dough adheres into a mass; it will be extremely wet and sticky. Wipe your hands clean and oil them generously. Knead the dough in the bowl until smooth and satiny, about 10 minutes, oiling your fingers and adding extra flour as necessary. Cover the bowl and let the dough rest in a warm place until doubled in volume, about 4 hours.

❀ If you have a baking stone, place it in the oven. Preheat the oven to 500°F (260°C) or to the maximum heat. Punch down the dough, knead for 1 minute, and divide it into 16 equal portions. With

a rolling pin, quickly roll out each ball into a 5-inch (12.5-cm) round. With your fingers, stretch each round into a 5–7 inch (13–18 cm) oval. Arrange a few of the breads in a single layer on ungreased baking sheets or directly on the baking stone and bake until they are slightly puffed and brown, 4–5 minutes. Repeat with the remaining breads.

❀ Preheat a broiler (griller) to the maximum heat. Transfer a few of the baked breads to the broiler pan and broil for 15–20 seconds to brown the tops. Brush the tops lightly with the *chat masala* oil, if desired. Repeat with the remaining breads.

makes 16

Arunachal Pradesh and Orissa

Mooli Achar

radish pickle

Achar *means "pickle." Indians love pickled vegetables as much as fresh. Mild daikon radishes are best in this recipe, though common red radishes are acceptable.*

1 daikon, peeled and thinly sliced (about 2 cups/ 8 oz/250 g)

1 teaspoon cayenne pepper

¼ teaspoon ground turmeric

1 teaspoon salt

3 tablespoons mustard oil or vegetable oil

1½ teaspoons panch phoron *(page 249) or ½ teaspoon each cumin seeds, fennel seeds, and nigella seeds (page 250)*

❀ In a bowl, combine the radish, cayenne pepper, turmeric, and salt and toss until well mixed.

❀ In a small pan over high heat, warm the oil until it begins to smoke. Immediately remove the pan from the heat and let the oil rest for 30 seconds. Reduce the heat to medium, return the pan to the stove, and add the *panch phoron*. Stir-fry until the spices turn several shades darker, about 20 seconds. Add the radish and stir well to coat it with the spiced oil.

❀ Cook, stirring constantly, until heated through, about 3 minutes. Transfer to a bowl and, when completely cool, serve or refrigerate for up to 5 days.

makes about 1½ cups (8 oz/250 g)

Madhya Pradesh

Gobhi Pulao

cauliflower pilaf

Madhya Pradesh ("central province") is the largest state in India. Until Independence in 1947, this region consisted of several separate royal kingdoms, resulting in a rich cultural heritage and an understated yet eloquent royal Hindu cuisine. Sharing borders with seven states, each with its own distinctly different cuisine, has added a depth and richness to the food of Madhya Pradesh. The coconut in this pilaf adds just that element of fusion and mystique. I like to cook the pilaf in oil, but a purist will insist upon usli ghee.

3 yellow onions

1 small cauliflower, about 1½ pounds (750 g)

1½ cups (10½ oz/330 g) basmati rice

2 cups (16 fl oz/500 ml) water

5 tablespoons (2½ fl oz/75 ml) vegetable oil or (2½ oz/75 g) usli ghee (page 247)

2 teaspoons peeled and grated fresh ginger

1 teaspoon minced garlic

6 whole cloves

½ teaspoon cayenne pepper

¼ teaspoon ground turmeric

1 cup (5 oz/155 g) cooked fresh or thawed frozen green peas

1 cup (8 fl oz/250 ml) coconut milk

2 teaspoons salt, or to taste

1 teaspoon fresh lemon juice

꙳ Thinly slice 2 of the onions and set aside. Finely chop the third onion and set aside separately. Separate the cauliflower into florets and cut them into 1½-inch (4-cm) pieces. Peel the stem and cut crosswise into thin slices. Rinse the rice thoroughly, place in a bowl, and add the 2 cups (16 fl oz/500 ml) water. Set aside until needed.

꙳ In a large pan over high heat, warm 3 tablespoons of the oil or *usli ghee*. When hot, add the sliced onions. Reduce the heat to medium-high and fry, stirring often, until the onions are caramel brown, about 12 minutes. Using a slotted spoon or tongs, transfer to paper towels to drain. Add the cauliflower to the pan and stir-fry, turning and tossing, until slightly streaked with brown and lightly fried, about 8 minutes. Transfer to a plate and set aside.

꙳ Wipe the pan clean, add the remaining 2 tablespoons oil or *usli ghee*, and place over medium-high heat. Add the chopped onions and cook, stirring, until limp and light golden, about 5 minutes. Stir in the ginger, garlic, cloves, cayenne, and turmeric. Add the cauliflower, rice and its soaking water, green peas, coconut milk, salt, and lemon juice. Bring to a boil over high heat, then reduce the heat to low, cover, and cook until all the liquid is absorbed and the cauliflower and rice are tender, about 18 minutes.

꙳ Remove the pan from the heat and let the rice rest, covered, for 5 minutes before serving. Transfer the pilaf to a platter, sprinkle the fried onion shreds on top, and serve.

serves 6

Punjab

Podina Chatni

mint chutney

Mint and cilantro give this chutney its emerald green color. Serve it with kabobs, samosas, fritters, or breads.

2 yellow onions, finely chopped

4 fresh hot green chiles such as serrano, stemmed

2 teaspoons ground pomegranate seeds (page 250) or lemon juice

1¼ teaspoons salt

1 small unripe mango, peeled, pitted, and chopped (about ½ cup/4 oz/125 g), or 1 tart apple, peeled, cored, chopped, and mixed with 1 tablespoon fresh lemon juice

1 cup (2 oz/60 g) firmly packed fresh mint leaves

½ cup (1½ oz/45 g) firmly packed fresh cilantro (fresh coriander) leaves

1–2 tablespoons water, if needed

꙳ In a food processor or blender, combine the onions, chiles, pomegranate seeds, and salt. Process until the ingredients are finely minced. Add the mango or apple, a few pieces at a time, and continue processing until puréed. Add the mint and cilantro, a little at a time, and process until a smooth paste forms. If the machine labors, add the water. Serve at once, or cover and refrigerate for up to 5 days.

makes about 2 cups (16 oz/500 g)

Maharashtra

Aval

rice flake pilaf with shallots

Aval, available at Indian grocery stores, consists of fermented, cooked rice pressed flat into flakes. Fermentation lends it a distinct aroma, similar to that of rice wine, which is highly regarded by Indian cooks. Everything from fried snacks, fluffy pilafs, scrumptious puddings, and luscious sweets is made using aval. Since aval is fragile, it should be soaked briefly and handled gingerly so that it won't crumble. This classic recipe of the Poone Maharashtrians is flavored with asafetida, kokum, coconut, and kari leaves. It is a delicately spiced dish that can be served on its own or with a vegetable, a chutney, and a raita.

2 cups (6 oz/185 g) rice flakes (see note)

¼ cup (2 fl oz/60 ml) usli ghee (page 247)

1½ teaspoons cumin seeds

1 cup (4 oz/125 g) chopped shallots

½ cup (2½ oz/75 g) chopped roasted cashew nuts

½ teaspoon powdered asafetida (see sidebar, page 144) or 1 teaspoon minced garlic

¼ teaspoon ground turmeric

16 fresh or 32 dried kari leaves (page 248)

4 pieces kokum (page 248), thinly sliced, or 1 tablespoon fresh lemon juice

½ teaspoon salt, or to taste

½ cup (2 oz/60 g) unsweetened grated coconut

✤ Place the rice flakes in a bowl, add water to cover, and soak for 20 seconds. Drain and set aside.

✤ In a large nonstick pan over medium–high heat, warm the *usli ghee*. When very hot, add the cumin seeds and cook, stirring, until they turn several shades darker, about 30 seconds. Add the shallots, cashew nuts, asafetida, turmeric, and kari leaves. Stir-fry until the shallots are soft and lightly fried, about 5 minutes.

✤ Add the soaked rice flakes, *kokum* or lemon juice, and salt. Mix well and cook, stirring, until the flakes look dried and fried, about 10 minutes. Check and correct the seasonings. Fold in the coconut and serve at once.

serves 4

The Spice Grinder

I like to think of the *sil-batta,* or "grinding stone," as an old-fashioned food processor. It can be used for grinding, mincing, and pulverizing everything from grains and legumes to vegetables, herbs, and spices. Traditionalists maintain that Indian food tastes better when *masalas* (spice blends) are ground on *sil-batta,* but nowadays convenience rules. Blenders and food processors are the *sil-batta* of contemporary times.

This is not to say that the grinding stone is becoming extinct, however. Its other, far more important role in Indian Hindu society is firmly entrenched. In the holy Vedic scriptures, the *sil-batta* is equated with the mountains of central Asia, the place from where the Vedic Indians (the Hindus' ancestors) came. No Hindu Brahmin ritual—birth, marriage, or death—can be performed without the presence of a *sil-batta,* since it symbolizes the connection to the Vedic homeland.

Made of granite, a *sil-batta* consists of two parts: a heavy, flat rectangle about fifteen inches by ten inches (38 cm by 25 cm) that sits on the ground, and a rolling-pin-like cylinder about ten inches (25 cm) long. The latter is moved back and forth with both hands across the top of the lower slab to get the job done.

Punjab

Paratha

flaky layered bread

Paratha, *meaning "turned" or "folded," describes how this common North Indian flatbread is made. A piece of dough is rolled into a circle, brushed with* usli ghee, *folded, and then rolled out again. The layers separate during cooking, lending a delicious flakiness.*

Indian cooks prefer to use atta, *or chapati flour, in* parathas *because it gives a better flavor and texture. Ajowan seeds are not essential, but they add an interesting flavor. For variation, substitute nigella seeds. Or, like my friend Micki Trager, a devoted Indian cook, use both, plus some cumin seeds.*

2 cups (10 oz/310 g) chapati flour (page 244) or whole-wheat (wholemeal) flour, preferably atta, *plus extra for dusting*

¾ teaspoon salt

½ teaspoon ajowan seeds (page 244)

⅔ cup (5 fl oz/160 ml) water, or as needed

½ cup (4 oz/125 g) usli ghee (page 247), melted, or (4 fl oz/125 ml) vegetable oil

♨ In a large, shallow bowl, stir together the flour, salt, and ajowan. In a measuring cup, mix the water with 1 tablespoon of the *usli ghee* or oil and pour over the flour. Mix, adding a little more water only if necessary, until the flour adheres together into a mass and can be kneaded. Gather the dough together, turn out onto a floured work surface, and knead until smooth, about 5 minutes, dusting with flour as necessary to prevent sticking. Cover with plastic wrap or a clean, damp cloth and set aside to rest for 15 minutes at room temperature.

♨ Divide the dough into 8 equal portions. Using your hands, roll each into a ball. With a rolling pin, roll each ball into a circle 6 inches (15 cm) in diameter, dusting often with flour. Brush the top of the dough circle lightly with *usli ghee* or oil and fold it in half. Brush the top of the semicircle with *usli ghee* or oil and fold again to form a triangle. Dust with flour and roll into a 7-inch (18-cm) long triangle. Roll the remaining bread in the same way, keeping it covered with a damp kitchen towel until ready to cook.

♨ Heat a dry Indian *tava* griddle or frying pan over high heat until hot. Add a bread triangle and reduce the heat to medium-high. Cook until the underside of the bread is spotted, about 2 minutes. Turn and cook the other side in the same way. Brush the side

that was cooked first with *usli ghee* or oil, then flip and brush the second side with *usli ghee* or oil, and flip again. Cook until the bread is nicely fried and brown on both sides, about 1 minute. Remove from the heat and set aside. If serving the breads hot, keep them warm in a low oven while you cook the remaining dough. Serve hot or at room temperature.

makes 8

Tamil Nadu

Takkalipayam Chatni

hot and spicy tomato chutney

My grandmother used to make this chutney from an original Tamil Nadu recipe. She did not add garlic, though; that is my mother's touch. Serve with paratha *or* poori, salad, *and a* lassi.

¼ cup (2 fl oz/60 ml) vegetable oil

1 teaspoon cumin seeds

¼ teaspoon powdered asafetida (see sidebar, page 144) or 1 teaspoon minced garlic

1 teaspoon curry powder (page 249)

8 fresh hot green chiles, slivered

1-inch (2.5-cm) piece fresh ginger, peeled and slivered

1½ lb (750 g) tomatoes, cored and cut into ½-inch (12-mm) thick wedges

½ teaspoon salt, plus extra to taste

1 tablespoon fresh lemon juice

♨ In a frying pan over high heat, warm the oil. When hot, add the cumin and fry, stirring, until it turns several shades darker, about 30 seconds. Add the asafetida, curry powder, chiles, and ginger and stir-fry for 2 minutes. Add the tomatoes and ½ teaspoon salt and mix well, then let the tomatoes cook, undisturbed, for 2 minutes. Carefully stir and turn the tomatoes and continue cooking until they are soft but still hold their shape, about 10 minutes. Sprinkle with the lemon juice and add more salt to taste. Serve hot, at room temperature, or cold. The chutney can be refrigerated, covered, for up to 5 days.

makes about 1½ cups (12 oz/375 g)

SWEETS, DESSERTS, AND BEVERAGES

Cardamom, saffron, and rose water flavor sweet treats and fragrant teas.

IT WAS TO BE A ROUTINE FLIGHT from Varanasi to Delhi on Indian Airlines. The group of travelers I had brought to India had just completed a visit that included exploring the old part of the holy city of Varanasi on the banks of the Ganges, where wonderful sweets are made using centuries-old recipes. *Lal peda,* "red fudge," is the jewel of Varanasi. To make it, pure cow's milk is cooked over very low embers for a day or longer until it colors and develops *khoya,* a caramelized milk flavor, then jaggery and spices are added. Rust-colored and shaped into two-inch (5-cm) patties, *lal peda* is indescribably delicious and synonymous with Varanasi.

The plane door was shut and locked as we settled in for our journey. Suddenly, the crew announced a short delay in takeoff. As we waited and chatted, whiling away the time, a flight attendant approached me. She held a beautiful gold-colored box decorated with

Preceding pages: In a shop window, a stack of the chickpea (garbanzo bean) sweets known as *Mysore pak* makes a striking display. **Above top:** A street stall equipped with a sugarcane pulper provides fresh sugarcane juice to passersby. **Above:** India boasts a wide range of rich, sticky sweetmeats, such as these *gulab jamuns,* dumplings soaked in a rose-water-scented sugar syrup. **Right:** Most of the houses in small villages do not have running water. These Rajasthani women carry brass pots, *ghara,* that they will fill at the communal well and then take back to their kitchens.

a picture of Shiva, the patron god of Varanasi. Handing it to me, she smiled knowingly and said, "You were leaving without this, ma'am?" Instantly guessing the contents, I was overjoyed. My thoughtful Varanasi host, remembering my group's excitement at the *lal peda* shop, had arranged for a box of the red fudge to be delivered to the airport. So what if it arrived a little late and the plane was held up. We were talking about *lal peda* after all, and my host knew that no true devotee of this confection would deny it to another.

Indian sweets are rich, syrupy, and sticky, which is just the way Indians like them. They also represent good omens, hence both children and adults are encouraged to eat them. I remember giving my son *jalebis* and *gulab jamuns* when he was barely nine months old, and he ate them with great relish. Indians are passionate about their sweets and will go to great lengths to get them. I, for example, have

been known to make special trips to Agra, not only to see the wondrous Taj Mahal, but also to eat the city's famous candied winter-melon sweet, *petha*. Any Indian, when asked where the best milk-based sweets can be found, will point to West Bengal for the renowned *rasgulla* and *sandesh,* or to Rajasthan for the most delicious milk-fudge sweet imaginable—one so unbelievably rich that its name, *palang todh,* translates as "bed breaking." Gujaratis, on the other hand, have ingenious ways with vegetables, which they transform into mouthwatering *halwas* and *barfis* by cooking them with milk fudge, *usli ghee,* and sweet spices. Gujarat is also known for its *chenna* and *paneer,* cheeses that are used in many of the region's desserts.

Southern Indian sweets, made primarily with pounded rice flour, coconut, sesame, and jaggery, are mealy and a little rustic. The exception is *Mysore pak,* a foamy cake of

roasted chickpeas (garbanzo beans) bound with caramel flakes and *usli ghee.* This is the south's most glorious sweetmeat, and I grew up watching my mother make it. She used a giant tin-lined brass *karhai,* to allow ample room for the chickpea mixture to foam and froth. She stirred and stirred for over an hour until the mixture reached the right consistency, then quickly poured it into waiting *thalis* and, before it cooled completely, cut it into neat rectangles. When perfectly made, *Mysore pak* pieces are darker in the center than the outside and so light that they melt away the instant they touch the mouth.

There is no specific time for eating sweets in India. They are enjoyed whenever hunger pangs strike or the heat in the mouth from a spicy snack needs to be neutralized. Usually they are not accompanied by a beverage, except perhaps water, unless they are eaten with spicy hot snacks, when a beverage helps wash down the sweet-and-savory combination

Left: A tea stall caters to the Indian passion for beverages at all hours. **Below:** Traditional crafts, such as the bangles made by this Rajasthani woman, are the main source of income for many people. **Below bottom:** In India, tea is usually taken in glasses rather than in cups.

Above top: In the quiet of early morning, women sit by the holy pool at Amritsar's Golden Temple. **Above:** Of India's many varieties of rice, premium basmati is the most highly prized. **Right:** A camel cart winds its way through the streets of Bikaner, Rajasthan, with the city's Jain temple visible in the background.

smoothly. This union of sweet, snack, and beverage has given rise to Indian teatime, where everything from tea and coffee to milk coolers and yogurt drinks are enjoyed. *Chai,* the Indian-style tea laced with ginger, cardamom, or cinnamon, is perfect at the end of a spicy meal. Milk coolers and yogurt drinks also make fine nonalcoholic punch.

While Indian sweets tend to be heavy and rich, Indian desserts are generally mellow and creamy puddinglike preparations. They are specifically created to balance and temper the effect of spicy food on the system. After a highly seasoned meal, these delicate milk- and fruit-based desserts are the ideal way to calm and soothe the digestion. Most are easy to prepare and require minimal attention during cooking. They can also be assembled ahead of time, thus making entertaining easy.

The most popular dessert in India is rice pudding, which can be flavored with any number of ingredients, from coconut and cardamom to saffron and pistachios. Another dessert, one which I particularly like, is *sevian payasam,* made with Indian vermicelli noodles called *sevian,* which originated in Afghanistan.

During the years of British rule, India's only ice cream was *kulfi*. Introduced by the

Moghuls, it is more like a creamy sorbet than an ice cream. The Indians added their own flavorings such as cardamom, saffron, and rose water and juicy tropical fruits such as mango, banana, and coconut.

Goa has its own dessert specialties: *bibinca,* a coconut cake, and *kaju* ice cream, which uses cashew nuts, introduced by the Portuguese. Goans also cook the cashew fruit with sugar syrup and turn it into a thick, chunky jam that makes a wonderful topping for their ice cream, as does the local strawberry sauce.

I have fond memories of picking and eating strawberries the first thing in the morning at my grandfather's farm. They were small, delicate, and intensely fragrant. Today, strawberries are cultivated in many cooler regions of India. Thanks to modern distribution channels, these berries and many other fruits grown throughout the country are now available in big cities such as Delhi, Calcutta, Bangalore, Bombay, and Madras.

Those who are fond of bananas are in for a treat in southern India, where the fruits are found in abundance. Each of the four southern states has its own unique banana dessert or sweetmeat recipe, such as Karnataka's banana cream and Kerala's banana fritters. But it is the delicate *kelapura,* pancakes of banana and coconut milk that my grandmother made, that always stand out for me. She would mix the batter and mash the bananas by hand, lending the pancakes a unique texture. Then she cooked them on her century-old iron pan, which gave them an amazingly crisp exterior while leaving the inside soft and spongy.

Indian desserts, sweets, and beverages, although laced with sugar, are never cloyingly sweet. Instead, they are just sweet enough to lend harmony to the palate, the perfect end to a spicy Indian meal.

Left: At Calcutta's wholesale fruit market, oranges are auctioned. The oranges of Nagpur, in Madhya Pradesh, are famous throughout India. **Right top:** A colorful sign advertizes a juice stall. **Right bottom:** Bananas thrive in India's tropical coastal regions. Unripe bananas are deep-fried as fritters or used as a vegetable in stir-fries; the ripe fruit is eaten on its own, used in candies and desserts, or added to yogurt salads to temper the heat of spicy dishes. The leaves, too, are utilized; in the south, they serve as platters.

Maharashtra

Paneer Mithai

cardamom cheese cake

Paneer mithai was traditionally made as a barfi, or fudge, using the Indian chenna cheese. With the introduction of Western-style ovens during the British Raj, Indian cooks in cities such as Bombay and Calcutta began baking it like a cheesecake. Kewra extract comes from the leaves of the screwpine tree. If unavailable, use an equal amount of either rose or vanilla extract. Commercial breadcrumbs are unsuitable for this recipe because the bread is not trimmed and the crusts give the crumbs an uneven brown color.

12 green cardamom pods

2 lb (1 kg) ricotta cheese

2 cups (4 oz/125 g) fresh bread crumbs, made from about 8 slices of white bread, trimmed and processed in a food processor to produce soft, fluffy crumbs

⅔ cup (5 oz/155 g) sugar

7 tablespoons (3½ oz/105 g) unsalted butter, melted

½ teaspoon almond extract (essence)

½ teaspoon kewra extract (essence) (page 248)

½ cup (2 oz/60 g) sliced (flaked) almonds

Strawberry Sauce (optional; page 239)

❦ Preheat an oven to 325°F (165°C). Butter a 9-inch (23-cm) square baking pan.

❦ Pry open the cardamom pods, remove the seeds, and grind them to a powder. (This is best done using a mortar and pestle; you can also wrap the seeds in plastic wrap and crush them with a mallet or rolling pin.) You will need 1½ teaspoons ground cardamom. Discard the skins.

❦ In a large bowl, stir together the ricotta, bread crumbs, sugar, melted butter, cardamom, almond extract, and *kewra* extract. Spoon into the prepared pan. Smooth the top and sprinkle with the almonds.

❦ Bake until the top is golden, about 1¼ hours. Remove and let cool completely. Cut into 3-inch (7.5-cm) squares and serve with the Strawberry Sauce, if desired.

serves 6–9

Jammu and Kashmir

Kahwah

green tea

Uttaranchal, the cool and tranquil region to the south-east of Kashmir, is as well known for the green tea used in brewing the Kashmiri drink kahwah *as it is for its fragrant basmati rice. I first tasted this tea as a teenager and my uninitiated palate noticed nothing significant. A decade later, after many adventurous travels, I revisited* kahwah *and to my delight I could see why a Kashmiri would disdain a standard black tea with milk. The pine-like tea flavor with just a streak of saffron is so pleasing that it leaves an alluring and lasting impression.*

4–6 saffron threads, powdered

2 green cardamom pods, lightly bruised

2 cups (16 fl oz/500 ml) water

2 heaping teaspoonfuls loose green tea, preferably from Kashmir

❦ In a small pan, combine the saffron, cardamom, and water and bring to a boil over medium-high heat. Reduce the heat to low and simmer, uncovered, for 2 minutes. Add the tea, reduce the heat to very low, and simmer very gently for 2 minutes longer. Strain the tea into small (½ cup/4 fl oz/125 ml) cups, such as Kashmiri tea cups, and serve.

serves 4

During the festival of Diwali, sweets are sent to relatives, friends, neighbors, and colleagues to wish them good fortune.

Uttar Pradesh

Badaam Doodh

saffron milk cooler

This milk drink, infused with saffron and almonds, is a classic of the Hindu Brahmins. Almond and saffron are considered super brain foods. My private Sanskrit tutor Mr. Agnihotri used to say that if I wanted to pass the Sanskrit exam, I must drink this cooler. I don't know whether it was the pressure to make the grade or the sheer delight of its flavor, but badaam doodh *has since become a constant on my menu. Although Westerners are not accustomed to drinking milk warm, as Indians do, piping hot* badaam doodh *tastes just as lovely.*

2 tablespoons blanched almonds

¼ teaspoon saffron threads

¼ cup (2 fl oz/60 ml) boiling water

1¾ cups (14 fl oz/440 ml) milk

3–5 tablespoons (1½–2½ oz/45–75 g) sugar

4 ice cubes

2 fresh basil sprigs, preferably camphor or cinnamon basil

❧ In a mortar, blender, or coffee grinder reserved solely for spices, pound or process the almonds until finely powdered. Transfer to a small heatproof bowl. Reserving 6–8 whole saffron threads for garnish, crush the remaining threads with your fingers and add them to the almonds. Pour in the water and let the ingredients soak, covered, for 30 minutes.

❧ Pour half of the milk into a blender. Add the almond-saffron mixture and sugar and process until smooth. Add the remaining milk and the ice cubes and process until the ice cubes are crushed and the milk is frothy. Divide the milk between two tall glasses. Serve garnished with the basil sprigs and reserved saffron threads.

serves 2

Gujarat

Panna

mango cooler

To beat the summer heat, Indian cooks serve a wide variety of tasty and nutritious beverages. Panna is made with underripe mangoes, rich in potassium and iron, and is flavored with roasted cumin, jaggery, and black salt. The taste is sweet-sour and very pleasant.

1 unripe to medium-ripe mango, plus slices for garnish

1 mild green chile such as Anaheim, seeded and quartered lengthwise

2 cups (16 fl oz/500 ml) water

5 tablespoons (2½ oz/75 g) jaggery (page 248) or firmly packed light brown sugar

½ teaspoon cumin seeds, roasted and ground (page 246)

1 tablespoon fresh lemon juice (optional)

pinch of ground black salt (see sidebar, page 167; optional)

crushed ice

2 fresh mint sprigs

☙ Peel the mango and cut the flesh from the pit in large pieces. In a saucepan, combine the flesh, mango pit, chile, and water. Bring to a boil over medium-high heat, then reduce the heat to low, cover, and cook until the mango is very soft, about 20 minutes. Remove and discard the mango pit and the chile.

☙ Transfer the mango and cooking liquid to a blender or food processor. Add the sugar, cumin, lemon juice (if you are using a mildly sweet mango), and black salt (if using) and process until smooth. Strain the juice into a pitcher.

☙ Fill 2 tall glasses with crushed ice and pour the juice over the ice. Garnish with the mango slices and mint sprigs and serve.

serves 2

Punjab

Namkeen Lassi

minty yogurt drink

Lassi, a favorite beverage of India, is served any time of the day, alone to quench thirst or with a meal. It can be made with buttermilk as well as yogurt. Punjabis, known for their rich milk and milk products, flavor lassi with mint and roasted cumin.

2 cups (1 lb/500 g) low-fat or non-fat plain yogurt

8 fresh mint leaves, plus 2 sprigs

1 teaspoon fresh lime juice

¼ teaspoon cumin seeds, roasted and ground (page 246)

¼ teaspoon salt, or to taste

6–8 ice cubes

☙ In a blender, combine ⅔ cup (5 oz/155 g) of the yogurt with the mint leaves, lime juice, cumin, and salt. Process until the mint is finely minced. Add the remaining yogurt and the ice cubes and continue processing until the ice cubes are crushed and the mixture is chilled and frothy. Serve in tall glasses, garnished with the mint sprigs.

serves 2

Gold and Silver Leaf

Beginning in the sixteenth-century Moghul court, twenty-four-carat gold and sterling silver foils were used to garnish elaborate pilafs and roasts to symbolize wealth and power. Today, the foil, or *vark,* which is odorless and flavorless, is used primarily to decorate desserts and sweets at banquets, wedding feasts, and festivals. *Vark* is made by placing a thin piece of heated metal between layers of tissue paper and animal hide and pounding it until it is very thin. The sheets are about three by four inches (7.5 by 10 cm) and are sold in Indian grocery stores in packs of five to ten.

To apply *vark,* first ensure there is no draft, or before you know it, the fragile metal leaf will curl up and blow away. Gently remove one gold or silver sheet with the tissue paper attached on one side and place it directly on the food. Remove and discard the tissue. Store *vark* in an airtight container to prevent discoloration due to oxidization. It will keep indefinitely.

Bihar

Kheer

rice pudding

Kheer is the primary dessert of India. Home cooks generally prepare a simple rice-and-milk version; more elaborate renditions—with nuts, fruits, flower essences, and spice embellishments—are served in restaurants and at wedding feasts. Scented rice, such as Gobinda Bhog or basmati, is preferred, since it is the main flavor in the pudding. Indians like a rather runny consistency, and for the rice grains to be invisible, but the consistency and texture of this recipe have been adapted for the Western palate.

4 cups (32 fl oz / 1 l) milk

4 cups (32 fl oz / 1 l) light (single) cream

½ cup (3½ oz / 105 g) basmati rice, preferably small-grain Gobinda Bhog, or brown basmati rice, thoroughly rinsed

¾ cup (6 oz / 185 g) light-colored jaggery (page 248) or light brown sugar

4 green cardamom pods

½ teaspoon saffron threads, crushed

½ cup (3 oz / 90 g) raisins

¼ cup (1 oz / 30 g) sliced (flaked) almonds

6 pieces silver foil, each 2 inches (5 cm) square, (see sidebar, left; optional)

♛ In a large, shallow pan over high heat, bring the milk and cream to a boil, stirring frequently to prevent scorching. Add the rice, reduce the heat to medium-low, and cook, stirring occasionally, until the liquid is reduced to the consistency of custard and the rice is soft and creamy, about 50 minutes. Add the sugar and mix well.

♛ Pry open the cardamom pods, remove the seeds, and grind them to a powder. (This is best done using a mortar and pestle; you can also wrap the seeds in plastic wrap and crush them with a mallet or rolling pin). Discard the cardamom skins. Add the cardamom, saffron, raisins, and almonds to the cooked rice mixture and mix well. Transfer to a bowl, let cool, then cover and refrigerate until chilled.

♛ Spoon the pudding into small dessert bowls and garnish with silver foil, if desired.

serves 6

Andhra Pradesh

Sevian Payasam

creamy vermicelli pudding

In this recipe, noodles are first sautéed in usli ghee, *then cooked in reduced milk with cardamom and almonds, a technique distinct to regions influenced by Moghul cuisine. The dish takes its name from* sevian, *hair-thin wheat noodles introduced through Arab trade. This version from Hyderabad contains cashew nuts; pistachios are used in northern versions.* Sevian, *available in Indian grocery stores, is sold plain or roasted for a nuttier taste. Either type may be used here, although unroasted* sevian *will take longer to brown.*

1 cup (3.5 oz/105 g) broken vermicelli, preferably the thin Indian variety (2-inch/5-cm pieces)

3 tablespoons usli ghee *(page 247)* or butter

¼ cup (1½ oz/45 g) raw cashew nuts, roughly chopped

¼ cup (1 oz/30 g) sliced (flaked) almonds

¼ cup (1½ oz/45 g) golden raisins (sultanas)

4 green cardamom pods

4 cups (32 fl oz/1 l) milk

⅓ cup (3 oz/90 g) sugar

☙ In a large, shallow pan over medium-high heat, combine the vermicelli and 2 tablespoons of the *usli ghee* or butter. Cook, stirring constantly, until the vermicelli is golden brown, about 3 minutes. Transfer to a plate. Add the remaining 1 tablespoon *usli ghee* or butter to the pan along with the cashews, almonds, and golden raisins. Fry, stirring, until pale golden and puffed, about 1 minute. Transfer the nut mixture to another plate.

☙ Pry open the cardamom pods, remove the seeds, and grind them to a powder. (This is best done using a mortar and pestle; you can also wrap the seeds in plastic wrap and crush them with a mallet or rolling pin). Discard the skins.

☙ Wipe the pan clean and add the milk. Bring to a boil, stirring constantly, then reduce the heat to low and simmer, uncovered, until reduced by half. Add the vermicelli and cook, stirring, until very soft, about 3 minutes. Stir in the sugar, cardamom, and half of the nut–raisin mixture.

☙ Spoon into dessert bowls and garnish with the remaining nut–raisin mixture. Serve hot, at room temperature, or chilled.

serves 6

Punjab

Chai

spiced tea

Tea drinking, introduced by the British, is a national pastime. Teashops on every corner serve Indian-style sweet milky tea. Spices are often added for enhanced flavor and medicinal purposes. Orange pekoe is the premier tea from Darjeeling. Its name refers to the quality and grade of the tea; it is not orange flavored. Tea does not take well to reheating, so when drinking it as a hot beverage, make it just before serving.

2 cardamom pods

1-inch (2.5-cm) piece cinnamon stick

2 whole cloves

1 cup (8 fl oz/250 ml) water

1 cup (8 fl oz/250 ml) milk

1½ tablespoons sugar

2 heaping teaspoons loose orange pekoe tea leaves or 2 tea bags

ice, if serving cold

☙ Lightly crush the cardamom, cinnamon, and cloves in a mortar to release their fragrance. Alternatively, wrap the spices in plastic wrap and crush them with a mallet or rolling pin. (Do not powder the spices, as this will discolor the tea.)

☙ In a saucepan, combine the spices, water, and milk and bring to a boil over high heat. Reduce the heat to low and simmer, uncovered, until the spices release their flavor and aroma, about 2 minutes. Add the sugar and tea and continue simmering until the tea releases color, about 1 minute longer.

☙ To serve hot, strain the tea into cups and serve at once. For cold tea, strain and serve in wine glasses over ice.

serves 2

Spiced tea gently rounds out a meal of more robustly flavored dishes.

Gajjak

saffron sesame crunch

Making candies is a special skill, and no region is as well known for the craft as Gujarat. After centuries of assimilating waves of immigrants and of trade contact with far-off lands, Gujaratis have become adaptive and innovative. Gajjak is an Indian version of nut brittle in which any combination of nuts and spices can be used. Almonds, walnuts, pecans, macadamias, pine nuts, pistachios, and cashew nuts are particularly tasty and attractive. Cardamom is the most common flavoring, although I have also tasted gajjak flavored with ginger, clove, and cassia bud. A Persian influence can be seen here in the addition of rose water. Kewra extract and orange flower water can be substituted. Sunflower and sesame seeds are available at Middle Eastern and Indian grocery stores. Taste them to ensure they are fresh before you begin the recipe.

1 teaspoon unsalted butter

1½ cups (12 oz/375 g) sugar

1 cup (4 oz/125 g) sunflower seeds

½ cup (2½ oz/75 g) sesame seeds

1 teaspoon ground cardamom

½ teaspoon saffron threads

1 drop rose extract (essence) or ½ teaspoon rose water

✿ Use the butter to grease a rolling pin and a 10-inch (25-cm) square area on a large baking sheet. Set aside.

✿ In a saucepan over medium heat, melt the sugar, stirring constantly with a wooden spoon to avoid the formation of hot spots that will make the sugar burn and taste bitter. As soon as the sugar turns caramel colored, after about 10 minutes, add the sunflower seeds, sesame seeds, cardamom, saffron, and rose essence or rose water and mix quickly.

✿ Working swiftly, pour the contents onto the greased area of the baking sheet. Using the greased rolling pin, spread the mixture into as thin a sheet as possible, about 10 inches (25 cm) square.

✿ Let cool completely, then cut or break the brittle into pieces about 2 inches (5 cm) wide. Store the pieces in an airtight container, separating each layer with parchment (baking) paper, for up to 6 months.

makes about 1 lb (500 g)

Tamil Nadu and Kerala

Ingee Chai

madras ginger tea

Although ginger tea is one of the most popular herbal remedies of Ayurvedic medicine, the best reason to drink it is for the sheer joy of its taste. Flavoring beverages with spices and herbs is a very Indian touch, and no one does it better than the southern Indians. Ginger is one of the spices that has been growing in India since antiquity. Today several varieties are cultivated, each lending its distinct flavor to the tea made with it.

My aunt Minakshi in Madras once taught me the rules of brewing a perfect cup of ingee chai. She insists that the ginger must be chopped, because grating or grinding releases its hot and bitter flavors, which are undesirable in tea. It is also essential to cook the ginger, not merely steep it in the water. This process makes the tea richer tasting.

1-inch (2.5-cm) piece fresh ginger, peeled and finely chopped

2½ cups (20 fl oz/625 ml) water

2 heaping teaspoonfuls loose orange pekoe tea leaves or 2 tea bags

2 tablespoons jaggery (page 248) or brown sugar, or to taste

3 tablespoons milk

In a small saucepan, combine the ginger and water and bring to a boil over high heat. Reduce the heat to low and simmer, uncovered, for 3 minutes.

Add the tea and simmer for 1 minute longer. Stir in the sugar, remove from the heat, cover the pan, and let the tea and ginger steep for about 1 minute to mellow the flavors. Add the milk, strain into tumblers or cups, and serve at once.

serves 2

Tamil Nadu

Kesari

semolina halva with golden raisins

Halva is a sweetmeat made of various syrup-soaked ingredients. Crushed sesame seeds are commonly used in the Middle East; this Indian version has a base of semolina. It gets its name from its principal flavoring, saffron (or kesar in Sanskrit).

4 tablespoons usli ghee (page 247)

½ cup (3 oz/90 g) golden raisins (sultanas)

½ cup (2½ oz/75 g) chopped cashew nuts or blanched almonds

1 cup (5 oz/155 g) fine-grind semolina (farina)

6 green cardamom pods

2¾ cups (22 fl oz/680 ml) water

¾ cup (6 oz/185 g) sugar

½ teaspoon saffron threads, lightly crushed

In a large, shallow pan over medium–high heat, combine 2 tablespoons of the *usli ghee,* the raisins, and the cashews. Fry, stirring and tossing, until the nuts are golden, about 2 minutes. Transfer to a plate and set aside. Add the remaining *usli ghee* and the semolina to the pan and cook, stirring constantly, until the semolina is golden brown, about 4 minutes. Transfer to another plate and set aside.

Pry open the cardamom pods, remove the seeds, and grind them to a powder. (This is best done using a mortar and pestle; you can also wrap the seeds in plastic wrap and crush them with a mallet or rolling pin). Discard the skins.

Wipe the pan clean, add the water and sugar, and bring to a boil over medium–high heat, stirring often. Continue stirring until the sugar dissolves, then cook, without stirring, for 5 minutes more until the liquid thickens to a syrupy consistency. Stir in the saffron. Reduce the heat to low, add the semolina, and cook, stirring, until the mixture thickens to the consistency of oatmeal, about 2 minutes. Continue to cook, stirring, until the semolina is fully cooked and soft, about 5 minutes. Add the cardamom and fried nuts. Mix well, remove from the heat, and let cool.

When cool enough to handle, firmly pack small portions of the halva into small, ungreased molds, such as mini muffin pans or tart shells. When completely cool, unmold and serve, or cover and refrigerate for up to 5 days.

serves 8

Tea

Tea plants grow wild in the cool, wet climes of the northern Himalayas and are believed to date back to antiquity. It came as a surprise to me that Indians, who are generally associated with drinking black tea, also drink green tea—not just plain green tea, but aromatic varieties flavored with ingredients such as saffron, yak butter, *usli ghee,* mountain herbs, and salt.

Many families grow tea, just enough for their own consumption, in their backyard. At home we drank black tea with milk and sugar, a habit introduced to India in the eighteenth century, during the British Raj. The English are also credited with starting large-scale tea cultivation in Darjeeling and Assam, areas that are today considered to be the world's top producers of black tea. Among the most famous types is Darjeeling orange pekoe.

Thoroughly Indianized by the addition of aromatic spices such as cinnamon, cardamom, clove, and ginger, tea—called *chai* in Hindi—is the beverage of choice in northern India. Coffee is popular in southern India, roasted and ground freshly each day and served with milk.

Goa

Kaju Ice Cream

rum and cashew nut ice cream

Cashew nuts, introduced to Goa by the Portuguese in the fifteenth century, are a favorite Goan ingredient. This recipe will be slightly grainy and crystalline if not made with an ice-cream maker.

2 teaspoons usli ghee *(page 247) or walnut oil*

½ cup (3 oz/90 g) chopped cashew nuts

3 cups (24 fl oz/750 ml) light (single) cream

⅔ cup (5 oz/155 g) sugar

4 eggs, separated

1 teaspoon vanilla extract (essence)

¼ cup (2 fl oz/60 ml) Indian rum or good-quality Caribbean rum

Strawberry Sauce (following), optional

In a small frying pan over medium-high heat, warm the *usli ghee* or oil. When hot, add the cashews and fry, stirring constantly to ensure even browning, until light brown, about 4 minutes. Using a slotted spoon, transfer to paper towels to drain. Set aside.

In a large, heavy pan over medium-high heat, bring the cream and sugar to a boil, stirring constantly, then immediately remove from the heat.

In a bowl, lightly beat the egg yolks. Gradually whisk in 1 cup (8 fl oz/250 ml) of the hot cream until blended and smooth. Stir this mixture into the cream remaining in the pan. Cook over medium-low heat, stirring constantly, until the custard is thick enough to coat the back of a metal spoon, about 10 minutes. Remove from the heat.

In a large bowl, beat the egg whites until soft peaks form. Fold in the hot custard until the mixture is well blended. Stir in the vanilla and let the mixture cool completely.

The ice cream can be made in an ice-cream maker or food processor. If using an ice-cream maker, pour the cooled custard into the machine and freeze according to the manufacturer's instructions. Add the rum and the fried cashews halfway during the freezing, before the ice cream begins to harden and set.

If using a food processor, stir the rum into the cooled custard, then pour the mixture into ice-cube trays and place in the freezer until completely frozen, about 4 hours. Transfer the frozen cubes to zip-lock freezer bags and return them to the freezer. When ready to serve, transfer 8 frozen ice-cream cubes to a food processor and process quickly until the cubes are thoroughly crushed and creamy. Add some of the cashew nuts in the last 5 seconds of processing, to avoid them being completely pulverized. (Further mixing can be done while scooping the ice cream for serving.) Working swiftly, spoon the ice cream into dessert bowls. Repeat with the remaining cubes and cashews.

Scoop into dessert bowls and top with the strawberry sauce, if desired.

makes 2½ pints (40 fl oz/1.25 l); serves 8

Uttaranchal

Strawberry ka Sas

strawberry sauce

This recipe is from Mussoori, in the Himalayas. The British residents of this former hill resort introduced many wonderful fruits, among them the strawberry.

3 pints (24 oz/750 g) strawberries, stemmed and cut into 1-inch (2.5-cm) pieces

7 tablespoons (3½ oz/105 g) sugar

2 tablespoons cashew fenni *(see sidebar, page 124) or any fruit-flavored brandy*

1 tablespoon creme de Cassis or blackcurrant syrup

Place the strawberries in an enamel or other non-aluminum pan. Add the sugar, toss to combine, and let the berries sit for 15 minutes to draw out the juices.

Place the pan over medium heat and cook, stirring frequently, until the fruit is soft and the syrup is bubbling, about 6 minutes. Remove from the heat and stir in the *fenni* and cassis.

Pour into hot jars, let cool, then cover and refrigerate for up to 5 days.

makes 3½ cups (28 fl oz/875 ml); serves 8

Maharashtra

Aamphal

mango fool

This dessert comes from Bombay, home to the superb Alphonso mango. Its bright orange pulp is buttery smooth with a liquorlike aroma. The English believe that mango fool is an Indian interpretation of their classic pudding, but Indians think the name is a mispronunciation of manga phal. Manga *is the original Sanskrit name for mango, and* phal *means "fruit."*

4 cups (32 fl oz/1 l) milk

6 tablespoons (3 oz/60 g) custard powder (page 246)

½ cup (4 oz/125 g) sugar

1 teaspoon vanilla extract (essence)

1 cup (8 fl oz/250 ml) fresh mango purée, from Alphonso mangoes if possible, or canned purée

½ cup (4 fl oz/125 ml) heavy (double) cream, whipped to stiff peaks

¼ cup (1 oz/30 g) sliced pistachios

In a small bowl, combine ½ cup (4 fl oz/125 ml) of the milk with the custard powder. Mix with a fork until the custard powder is fully dissolved.

In a large, heavy pan over medium–high heat, bring the remaining 3½ cups (28 fl oz/875 ml) milk to a boil, stirring constantly. Remove from the heat.

Add 1 cup (8 fl oz/250 ml) of the hot milk to the custard powder solution and gradually whisk until blended and smooth. Return this mixture to the hot milk in the pan. Cook over medium–low heat, stirring constantly, until the custard is thick enough to coat the back of a metal spoon, about 10 minutes. Add the sugar and vanilla and cook for 1 minute longer.

Remove from the heat, stir in the mango purée, and let cool. Fold the whipped cream into the mango mixture and spoon into dessert glasses. Sprinkle with the pistachios, cover, and refrigerate. Serve well chilled.

serves 8

Tamil Nadu

Kelapura

banana coconut pancakes

Kelapura (kela *means "banana" and* pura *is "bread" or "pancake") are served all over southern India, where there is an abundance of banana and coconut palms. On such plantations, the pancakes are made only with rice flour and contain toddy, or fermented palm sap, which acts as a natural leavening agent.*

The original kelapura recipe evolved in the hands of creative Indian cooks. Any number of ingredients and flavorings can be added to the basic batter. Indians particularly like ripe jackfruit, mangoes, sapota, guava, and persimmon. You can also add nuts such as toasted cashews, pistachios, and pine nuts.

This recipe from Madras is extremely easy and quick to make. Purists in southern India will insist on cooking these pancakes in butter or coconut oil, but I prefer vegetable oil as it gives the pancakes a non-greasy texture when cold. If rice flour is unavailable, use an equal amount of cream of rice cereal and let the batter rest for fifteen minutes to soften the larger grains before making the pancakes.

½ cup (2½ oz/75 g) all-purpose (plain) flour

½ cup (2½ oz/75 g) rice flour

1¼ cups (10 fl oz/310 ml) coconut milk

½ cup (4 fl oz/125 ml) milk

⅓ cup (2½ oz/75 g) jaggery (page 248) or brown sugar

½ teaspoon baking powder

1 ripe banana, peeled and mashed

8 green cardamom pods

vegetable oil for frying

❀ In a medium bowl, combine the all-purpose flour, rice flour, coconut milk, milk, sugar, and baking powder. Beat with a whisk or electric mixer until a smooth, lump-free batter forms. Gently fold in the banana.

❀ Pry open the cardamom pods, remove the seeds, and grind them to a powder. (This is best done using a mortar and pestle; you can also wrap the seeds in plastic wrap and crush them with a mallet or rolling pin). Discard the skins. Add the ground cardamom to the batter and mix well.

❀ In a nonstick frying pan, pour in oil to a depth of ¼ inch (6 mm) and place over high heat. When hot, add a heaping tablespoonful of batter to the pan to form each pancake. (The number of pancakes you can cook at one time will depend upon the size of the pan. You can also vary their size to suit your preference.) Cook until the undersides are brown and the edges begin to crisp, about 2 minutes. Turn and cook until the second side is nicely browned, about 1 minute longer.

❀ If serving the pancakes immediately, keep them warm in a low oven while you cook the remaining batter in the same way, adding more oil as needed. If making the pancakes ahead of time, set aside, covered, until ready to serve. To reheat, place a nonstick frying pan over high heat. When hot, add the pancakes, one at a time, and warm them through for about 30 seconds. Alternatively, warm the pancakes, loosely wrapped in aluminum foil, in a preheated 375°F (190°C) oven for about 8 minutes.

serves 8

The Sweet Shop

Indian sweets, called *mithai*, are exquisitely flavored, shaped, and colored treats that are made with nuts, fruits, lentils, *usli ghee*, and sugar. No animal products such as suet, lard, or even eggs are used in them, and in spite of the fact that they use milk, they are acceptable to vegetarians. Milk, although an animal product, is consumed by vegetarian Hindus because it is acquired in an *ahimsa* (non-violent) way. It is considered the gift of the cow.

Since sweets are an important part of Indian religious, cultural, and social activities, you can always find a sweet shop in close proximity to temples, courthouses, and cinemas. These shops, called *halwai ki ducan*, display their confections attractively, enticing passersby. Rich, creamy boiled-down milk, called *khoya*, and cheese are used to make such specialties as *barfi* and *peda* (both types of fudge), *sandesh* (sweet cheese patties), *gulab jamun* (syrup-soaked milk dumplings), *rasgulla* (*kewra*-scented sweet cheese balls), and *laddoo* (sweet balls of various types).

But the sweet that makes an Indian's heart sing is *jalebi*, crisp-fried coils of sourdough bathed in a warm, sweet saffron syrup. Ghantewala, in the Chandni Chowk section of Old Delhi, has been famous for its *jalebi*s for over two hundred years.

Uttar Pradesh

Jalebi

crisp pastries in saffron syrup

Jalebis, *a syrupy, sticky dessert from north India, are best eaten freshly made, when the interplay of the crisp, hot exterior against the spongy, syrup-soaked inside is quite extraordinary. They can be prepared ahead then set aside, covered, at room temperature. Just before serving, warm them in an oven preheated to 425°F (220°C) for six minutes, or for thirty seconds at full power in a microwave oven.*

1 cup (8 oz/250 g) plain yogurt
½ cup (4 fl oz/125 ml) hot water
1 cup (5 oz/155 g) all-purpose (plain) flour
½ teaspoon baking powder, sifted
¼ teaspoon salt
1 cup (8 oz/250 g) sugar
1 cup (8 fl oz/250 ml) water
¼ teaspoon saffron threads, powdered
vegetable oil for deep-frying

❧ Place the yogurt in a bowl. With a fork, whip it while slowly adding the water. In a small bowl, combine the flour, baking powder, and salt and add to the yogurt mixture. Whisk to form a smooth, lump-free batter. Set aside while you make the syrup.

❧ In a small saucepan over medium heat, combine the sugar and water and cook, stirring, until the sugar dissolves, about 3 minutes. Increase the heat to medium-high and cook until the syrup is lightly sticky, about 3 minutes longer. Stir in the saffron and remove from the heat.

❧ In a wide saucepan, preferably nonstick, pour in vegetable oil to a depth of 2 inches (5 cm) and warm over medium-high heat to 375°F (190°C) on a deep-frying thermometer. Pour the batter into a squeeze bottle, such as a ketchup dispenser. When the oil is hot, squeeze a few spirals of batter, each about 3 inches (7.5 cm) in diameter, directly into the oil. Fry the pastries, turning once, until golden and crisp, about 1 minute. Using tongs, remove each pastry from the oil and immediately dip it in the warm syrup, immersing it fully, then transfer to a plate. Cook the remaining batter in the same way. Serve the pastries hot or at room temperature.

serves 4

GLOSSARY

The following entries cover basic recipes and key ingredients called for throughout this book. Indian ingredients may be obtained from Indian grocery stores, specialty-food stores, well-stocked supermarkets, and by mail order. For information on items not listed here, please refer to the index.

AJOWAN SEEDS

Ajowan seeds (also known as ajwain) come from the thymol plant, a close relative of caraway and cumin. Native to southern India, the plant also thrives in Egypt, Iran, Afghanistan, and Pakistan. The seeds resemble large celery seeds. They have a sharp taste and, when crushed, smell strongly of thyme. Ajowan has been used for centuries in India to flavor vegetable dishes, breads, pickles, and *pappadums*. It helps control digestive problems, so it is often added to starchy dishes and those containing legumes. If unavailable, thyme imparts a similar flavor.

ANISEEDS

The anise plant is a relative of dill, fennel, caraway, and cumin. Its seeds are used whole and ground in curries, pickles, and chutneys. Small, ribbed, and pale brown, they impart a licorice taste similar to, though milder than, that of fennel. Aniseeds and fennel seeds are used interchangeably in Indian recipes. They are also chewed after meals to aid digestion and freshen the breath.

ASAFETIDA

Asafetida, a resinous substance obtained from two species of the giant fennel, is best known for its foul smell. The odor is released when the spice is ground but mellows when it is cooked. Asafetida is always used in small amounts of ¼–½ teaspoon. It can be replaced with a little minced garlic—about 1 teaspoon, or to taste.

CARDAMOM

This tall, perennial shrub grows profusely on the Malabar coast of southern India. The fruits, or pods, must be harvested by hand, making this the costliest spice in the world after saffron. The most widely used of the two major types is green cardamom. It has pale green, three-sided, oval pods about ½ inch (12 mm) long, each of which contains up to 20 small, black seeds. When ground, the seeds give off an intense, camphorlike aroma, although the taste is sweet and mild. The whole pods are used in pilafs and curries and the ground seeds in sauces, spice blends, and desserts. White cardamom is simply green pods that have been bleached for aesthetic reasons; however, the bleaching process reduces the flavor somewhat, so it is preferable to buy green pods. The pods of black or brown cardamoms are larger, coarser, and somewhat stringy and contain larger gray-black seeds. Black cardamom has a less delicate flavor and texture than the green variety and is used mainly in chutneys and pickles. The loose and ground seeds of both varieties lose flavor quickly, so it is best to buy whole pods and remove and grind the seeds as they are needed.

CASSIA LEAVES

The leaves of the cassia tree, also known as Indian bay leaves, have a slightly clovelike aroma and flavor and are available dried from Indian grocers. Despite their alternative name, they are not related to European bay leaves (*Laurus nobilis*). If cassia leaves are unavailable, the same quantity of European bay leaves may be used, although they will give a somewhat different taste.

CASHEW NUTS

Cashew nuts come from a tropical tree up to 40 feet (12 m) in height. The trees produce fruits called cashew apples (though actually pear shaped), inside which the nut develops. When the fruits ripen, the nuts protrude from the end of them. The shells of the nuts contain an acidic, oily substance that can burn and blister the skin but is neutralized by heating. Cashews are a common ingredient in the cookery of southern India, complementing both sweet and savory dishes. They are used whole in curries or ground to a paste to thicken and enrich gravies. Because they have a high oil content that makes them prone to rancidity, it is best to buy small quantities and store them in a glass jar in the refrigerator.

CAYENNE PEPPER

Cayenne peppers are one variety of hot red pepper, *Capsicum frutescens*. They can be used fresh, but they are more usually ground to add heat and red color to a dish. Various grades are combined to make a powder of uniform color and consistent heat.

CHAPATI FLOUR

Chapati flour, or *atta,* is a fine-milled wholewheat flour used to make unleavened Indian breads such as *paratha* and chapati. If it is unavailable, any finely ground or stone-ground whole-wheat flour can be substituted. Many Indians ensure that they obtain the freshest flour possible by buying whole wheat, cleaning it themselves, then taking it to the nearest mill to be ground.

CHAT MASALA

In India, various saladlike snacks are known by the generic name *chat,* and *chat masala (masala* simply means "blend") is a tart and salty spice mixture commonly used in them. Every cook has a favorite recipe, but *chat masala* typically contains cumin seeds, red pepper, black pepper, black salt, coarse salt, asafetida, and mango powder; the last gives the blend its characteristic sharp, tart flavor.

CHEESE, INDIAN (CHENNA AND PANEER)

Fresh, homemade cheese is the main source of protein for India's millions of strict vegetarians (to whom milk is an acceptable food, as the animal is not harmed in its production). An acidic starter such as lemon juice is added to milk to separate it into curds and whey. The soft, crumbly, mild-flavored curds, known as *chenna,* resemble ricotta or feta and are used in many Indian desserts. (The whey is discarded or used as the starter for the next batch of cheese.) *Paneer* is simply *chenna* that has been compressed to expel more whey and give it a firmer texture. It is then cut into cubes and used in savory dishes. Indian cheese is easily made at home. Packaged *paneer* is also available from Indian grocers and will keep for 3 days after opening. It can be crumbled to make *chenna*. Farmer's cheese may also substitute for *chenna*. Tofu, although it has a different taste, may also replace *paneer*, or, when crumbled, *chenna*.

CHILES

Chiles are so ubiquitous in Indian food that it is easy to forget they are a comparatively recent addition to it, being introduced by the Portuguese from the Americas only 400 years ago. Since then, they have been so enthusiastically embraced that it is hard to imagine Indian food without them. There are five main species and hundreds of varieties. All chile fruits are green until they ripen, when they may turn yellow, orange, red, brown, purple, or almost black. The heat varies greatly between species, ranging from pleasantly mild to blisteringly hot. In general, the smaller the chile, the hotter it is. Capsaicin, the substance that gives chiles their heat, is concentrated around the seeds; removing the seeds will reduce the heat of the chile. Indians generally leave the seeds in unless they would affect the texture of a dish. In the recipes in this book, unless otherwise stated, the decision to seed or not is left up to the cook.

Some chile varieties contribute mainly heat; others also add their own distinctive flavor. Àrbol is the one most commonly used in India, but jalapeño, serrano, Anaheim, or any other variety may be used, of whatever heat level is preferred. Both fresh and dried chiles are used in Indian food. Dried chiles have a fruitier and sometimes smokier flavor than fresh. They are used whole or in pieces in curries, and ground in various spice blends.

CHUTNEY

Western-style chutneys, store-bought and often kept for months, bear little resemblance to Indian chutneys, which are traditionally freshly made for each meal. They may be raw or cooked combinations of vegetables, fruits, or herbs, and often also contain vinegar, sugar, salt, and spices. Their Hindi name, *chatni,* means "for licking." Served alongside curries and other savory preparations, they temper the heat of spicy dishes, add zest to mild ones, and provide extra nutrients. Chutneys made with fresh herbs are a good source of vitamins.

CILANTRO, FRESH

This lacy-leafed annual herb, also known as fresh coriander, has a fresh, assertive scent and clean, strong, citrusy flavor—an acquired taste for some. The leaves are used as an herb and a garnish; the stronger-scented stems and roots are used in relishes and spice pastes. Cilantro leaves should be added at the end of the cooking time, as their delicate flavor is destroyed by long cooking. The plant produces seeds (always known as coriander), which, whole or ground, feature prominently in Indian cooking.

The fresh herb and the seeds have completely different flavors and aromas; one cannot replace the other.

CINNAMON

The cinnamon tree, native to Sri Lanka, is related to the bay laurel and avocado. The paper-thin inner layer of the bark is laboriously hand-stripped from the trees in many layers that are then rolled into cylinders, known as quills, about ½ inch (12 mm) in diameter. The quills may be up to 3 feet (1 m) in length. The length commonly found in stores and called for in recipes, however, is about 3 inches (7.5 cm). When used in recipes, the quills are more commonly known as cinnamon sticks. Once harvested, the quills are dried; small or broken quills are ground to a powder.

Cinnamon has a warm, sweet flavor that marries well with both sweet and savory dishes. In India, cinnamon sticks are infused to make *chai,* or fried in oil or ghee as the first step for making Moghul pilafs. The ground spice is an essential ingredient in *garam masala*. Cassia, a close relative of cinnamon, has a coarser texture. Its flavor is similar, but stronger and more astringent, making it less suitable for sweet dishes. In many countries, including India, the two are often used interchangeably. What is labeled "cinnamon" in the United States and Europe is usually cassia.

CLOVES

The dried flower buds of a tropical evergreen tree that thrives only near the sea, cloves are reddish brown to dark brown and about ½ inch (12 mm) long. Their nail-like shape gives them their name, which comes from the Latin *clavus,* or "nail." They have a warm, strongly aromatic smell. On their own, their flavor is unpleasantly bitter and strong; however, it is tempered by cooking. Used in small amounts, cloves add warmth, depth, and sweetness. In India they are used to flavor pilafs and are an ingredient in *garam masala*.

COCONUT CREAM AND COCONUT MILK

Coconut cream and coconut milk are both derived from an infusion of grated coconut flesh in water or, less commonly, milk. (They are not to be confused with the clear juice inside the whole nut.) The first infusion yields coconut cream, a thick liquid with a high fat content that is sometimes used for frying spices. If the same batch of coconut is steeped again, the resulting liquid is called coconut milk; this is the liquid often called for in curries. A third steeping produces thin coconut milk. Freshly grated coconut gives the best results, but commercially packaged coconut can also be used. Canned coconut cream and milk are readily available and very convenient.

COCONUT OIL

Coconut oil is extracted from the dried kernel (copra) of the coconut and is high in saturated fats. In India's coastal regions, where coconut palms flourish, many foods are traditionally cooked in this rich-flavored oil.

CORIANDER SEEDS

The ripe fruits of the plant also known as fresh cilantro, fresh coriander or Chinese parsley, coriander seeds are pale brown, ribbed, ¼ inch (6-mm) spheres with a papery husk. They may be used whole or ground and have a tangy, citrusy flavor. Many Indian recipes use coriander seeds, both for their taste and also because the fiber in the ground husks soaks up moisture and helps to thicken curries and sauces. Coriander seeds are used in *garam masala*.

CUMIN AND BLACK CUMIN

A member of the parsley family, cumin is an annual plant reaching a height of about 2 feet (60 cm). The fruits, or seeds, resemble caraway seeds, being small, tapered at both ends, slightly curved, and finely ridged. They are used both whole and ground. The aroma and flavor of cumin are warm, earthy, pungent, and reminiscent of curry. Cumin is often roasted before use to intensify its flavor and should be used judiciously, as it can easily overpower other spices. The seeds of black cumin are similarly shaped but a darker brown, with a less earthy and more piney fragrance when crushed. (Black cumin is not to be confused with nigella seeds, which are often erroneously called black cumin.) Indian cooks use cumin extensively in curries, rice and vegetable dishes, breads, chutneys, and pickles. It is also an ingredient in the spice blend *panch phoron*.

TO ROAST CUMIN SEEDS, warm a small, dry frying pan over medium-high heat. When hot, add the seeds and cook, continually shaking the pan to prevent them from burning, until the seeds turn darker and give off a roasted aroma, 3–4 minutes or as long as specified in the recipe. Immediately transfer them to a small bowl so that they are not cooked further by residual heat.

CUSTARD POWDER

A mixture of cornstarch (cornflour), sugar, and artificial coloring and flavorings, custard powder is added to hot milk to make a custard sauce that may be eaten hot or cold or used as the basis for various puddings. A British product, it is available in stores specializing in British foods or in Indian or Asian grocery stores.

FENNEL SEEDS

The crescent-shaped seeds of the fennel plant are about ¼ inch (6 mm) long and greenish yellow (the greener the seed, the better the quality), with a mild anise scent and strong, spicy anise flavor. In Indian cooking, they are commonly roasted, giving them a distinctive sweetness. Fennel is used whole and ground in pickles, meat and vegetable dishes, and pilafs. After meals, Indians like to eat whole fennel seeds, sometimes sugar-coated, as breath fresheners and aids to digestion. Fennel seeds form part of the east Indian spice blend *panch phoron*. They are very similar in flavor to aniseeds, which may replace them.

GRAINS AND LEGUMES

Inexpensive, plentiful, nutritious, and versatile, grains and legumes provide a rich and vital source of protein, especially for India's vast population of vegetarians. Rice, the most important grain, is the staple in south India. Legumes—lentils, peas, and beans—are known generically in India as dal, the name also given to various soupy lentil stews. Throughout India, all meals include a legume component, such as a curry, side dish, pilaf, or pancake.

CHICKPEAS (GARBANZO BEANS) ~ These nutty-flavored, firm-textured peas, the seeds of *Cicer arietinum,* are an Indian staple. They grow vigorously in cold climates and are cultivated widely in India's cool, dry Indo-Gangetic plain. The pods are harvested in winter. Chickpeas are sometimes eaten fresh, when they are emerald green, but they are more commonly dried. Two types are found in India: white (also called yellow) and black (actually a reddish brown). Black chickpeas are less common and not used by all Indians. The white ones are the type usually stocked in Western supermarkets. Both types need to be soaked overnight before they are cooked. Even after lengthy cooking, they remain firm though tender; it is hard to overcook them. Chickpeas may be curried or added to salads; roasted, they are eaten out of hand as snacks, or ground into a fine flour (known as *besan*) to make breads, batters, pancakes, and to add to certain *masalas*. Hindus often eat chickpeas on Fridays, as this is considered auspicious.

GRAM BEANS, WHITE SPLIT ~ When black gram beans *(Phaseolus mungo)* are skinned and split, they are known as white gram beans, or *urad dal.* These chewy, nutty-tasting beans are used in two southern Indian specialities, *idlis* (steamed rice cakes) and *dosas* (rice and lentil pancakes), as well as in snack foods and dal.

LENTILS ~ These thin, lens-shaped seeds are the most commonly eaten legumes in India. Of the various colors, pink and yellow are the most widely used. Indian yellow lentils *(toovar dal)* are the hulled, split seeds of the plant *Cajanus cajan.* (The yellow lentils often sold in supermarkets are not the same variety; they will give a different result and a murky brown purée.) Pink lentils *(masar dal* or *masoor dal)* are the hulled, salmon-colored seeds of the plant *Lens culinaris.* They yield a creamy yellow puree when cooked. Red (Egyptian) lentils may be substituted. Pink and yellow lentils are often interchangeable in

FENUGREEK

Both the leaves and the seeds of funugreek are used in Indian cooking. They have different flavors and aromas, however, so are not interchangeable. The small, golden-brown, nuggety seeds have a maple-syruplike aroma and a bitter flavor, both of which are intensified by roasting. If the seeds are over-roasted, or added with too generous a hand, they can be unpleasantly bitter and overpower other flavors. The leaves, either fresh or dried, are used as in pickles, breads, and especially in vegetarian dishes.

GARLIC

Garlic is always used fresh in India, never dried. Along with fresh ginger and onion, it forms the basis of many classic Moghul sauces. However, garlic is taboo in the food of strict Hindu Brahmins and Jains, whose religious dietary laws proscribe its use. They substitute a small quantity of asafetida, which imparts an agreeable garlic-onion aroma and flavor.

GHEE

Ghee literally means fat. There are two types: *usli ghee* (clarified butter) and *vanaspati ghee* (vegetable shortening). A recipe that calls simply for ghee is understood to mean *usli ghee*. Indian clarified butter differs from the European equivalent in having been simmered until all the moisture is removed from the milk solids and the fat is amber colored. This gives *usli ghee* its unique nutty taste. Clarification also increases butter's storage life—still

an important consideration in many Indian homes that do not have refrigeration. *Usli ghee* may be made from cow's milk or, more commonly in India, from buffalo's milk, which has a higher fat content and gives a cleaner tasting, better colored result. *Vanaspati ghee* is a pale yellow, hydrogenated blend of various vegetable oils that is processed to look, smell, and taste very similar to *usli ghee*. Both types of ghee are readily available; *usli ghee* is also easily made at home.

TO MAKE USLI GHEE, heat ½ lb (250 g) butter in a pan over medium-low heat, uncovered, until it melts. Increase the heat to medium and simmer the butter, stirring often, until the clear fat separates from the milk solids, about 15 minutes. During this process a layer of foam will rise to the top of the butter and the butter will crackle as its milk solids lose moisture. When the milk solids lose all moisture, the fat as well as the milk residue will turn amber colored. When this occurs, remove the pan from the heat and let the residue settle on the bottom.

When cool enough to handle, pour the clear fat, which is the *usli ghee,* into a jar, ensuring that no residue gets in. Alternatively, strain it through two layers of cheesecloth (muslin). Discard the residue. *Usli ghee* may be refrigerated, covered, for up to 6 months or frozen for up to 12 months. Allow to thaw before use.
Makes ¾ cup / 6 fl oz / 180 ml

Indian recipes, although yellow ones take about twice as long to cook as the pink or red varieties.

MUNG BEANS ~ Also known as green gram beans, these are the seeds of the plant *Phaseolus aureus*. The beans develop inside pods and are threshed out after the pods are dried. Left whole and in their skins, they are known as green mung beans. Yellow mung beans are those that have been skinned and split; this is the form most commonly used in Indian cooking. The whole and split beans are quite different and not interchangeable. Green mung beans need soaking before they are cooked and are rather chewy; they are most popular in the northern and western regions. Yellow mung beans need no soaking, and are easily cooked and digested.

RICE ~ India grows over 1,000 types of rice, though most are unsuited to commercial cultivation. For southern Indians, rice is the staple food. In northern India, bread is the staple, but certain fine-grade basmatis are used for pilafs and *biryanis*. Rice is judged on various characteristics, including color, translucency, age, cooking quality, smell, and price. Different types produce different results, so choose an appropriate variety for the dish you are making. Pilafs and

plain steamed rice require a long-grain variety, such as basmati, that cooks into fluffy, separate grains.

SEMOLINA ~ Semolina is made by removing the germ from durum wheat, then coarsely milling the remainder into tiny pellets. It has a sandy, granular appearance and its color ranges from pale beige to a clear yellow, depending on the type of wheat used. When cooked, semolina has a porridge-like texture. Although rather bland tasting on its own, it readily absorbs other flavors, making it popular both in sweet dishes such as desserts and sweetmeats and in savory preparations such as pilafs. Fine-grind semolina is also known as farina, a hot breakfast cereal, or Cream of Wheat™, a trademarked breakfast cereal.

SPLIT PEAS, YELLOW ~ Known in India as *channa dal,* these are the hulled, split seeds of the black chickpea, *Cicer arietinum*. Yellow split peas look quite similar to yellow lentils, but are slightly larger. They should be plump and bright. Sometimes they are roasted before use; they can be purchased ready-roasted to be added whole to certain dishes or ground into flour. Indian split peas are not the same as the yellow split peas found in supermarkets, although these may be substituted.

GINGER

This versatile spice is the rhizome of the tropical plant *Zingiber officinale*. The rhizome grows in knobbly clumps called hands, with rough-looking beige skin and cream-colored, fibrous flesh. Fresh ginger (sometimes called, erroneously, ginger root) varies in taste and aroma, depending on which cultivar it comes from and at which stage it is harvested. In general, however, it smells pungent, sweet, and lemony, and its taste is tangy, spicy, and warm to hot. The texture of ginger is also affected by the stage at which the rhizome is harvested, older ginger being more fibrous. Ground ginger is the dried, powdered rhizome; it can be substituted for fresh ginger, although it tastes quite different, being sweet, warm, and woody. Crystallized or candied ginger cannot be substituted for fresh. In India, both fresh and ground ginger are used widely. As well as adding flavor and heat, fresh ginger acts as a thickener and a digestive; it also has a slight tenderizing effect on meat.

GOAT MEAT

In India, the most commonly eaten red meat is goat meat. The hardy goat can be raised more easily in hot, harsh climates than its close relative the sheep. The meat is mild and lean. Ordinary butchers usually do not stock goat meat, although they may be able to special order it. It is more often found in butcher shops in Indian, Italian, Middle Eastern, or Greek neighborhoods. Well-trimmed lamb or beef can be substituted.

JAGGERY

Jaggery—dehydrated sugarcane juice—is a by-product of sugar refining. Golden brown and with a maple-syrup-like flavor, it is used in Indian desserts and candies. Small amounts are also used in savory dishes to bring out the flavors of other ingredients. Brown sugar, palm sugar, maple syrup, or maple sugar may be substituted, although they do not accurately replicate jaggery's flavor.

KAFFIR LIME LEAVES

The small, shrubby kaffir lime tree grows throughout Southeast Asia. The skins of its knobbly fruits and its deliciously fragrant leaves are used in several of the region's cuisines, especially those of Thailand and Indonesia. Although less common in Indian cookery, they feature in some recipes, particularly Ayurvedic ones.

KARI LEAVES

These small, shiny, highly aromatic leaves come from the kari tree, native to southern India and Sri Lanka. Although sometimes called curry leaves, and often used in curries, they bear no relation to curry powder and are not interchangeable with it. Nor do they taste of curry. Rather, both their flavor and aroma are citrusy, as befits a member of the citrus family. Fresh and dried kari leaves are used extensively in savory dishes throughout southern India and are a characteristic flavor of the region. Kari leaves are available in Indian grocery stores. Fresh leaves have the best flavor, but dried are usually more easily found and may be substituted: Use double the quantity of dried leaves as for fresh. If unavailable, substitute a mixture of 2 teaspoons minced parsley and 1 teaspoon finely grated lemon zest for every 20 kari leaves.

KEWRA ESSENCE

Kewra essence is extracted from the male flowers of one of the 500 species of pandanus, or screwpine. It may be yellow or colorless and has an intense fragrance with notes of musk and jasmine. It is used in some meat, poultry, and rice dishes (particularly Moghul and festive Kashmiri ones) and in desserts, candies, and cold beverages. If unavailable, omit it or replace it with almond essence for a different but still pleasant flavor.

KOKUM

Kokum, which has no English name, is an evergreen tree native to south India. It yields small, purple, plumlike fruits that are described in ancient Sanskrit literature as resembling in color and texture the mouth of a beautiful woman. The rind, comprising about 50 percent of the whole fruit, is sun-dried until it is leathery and almost black. *Kokum* is used as a souring agent in a similar way to tamarind or mango powder, but with a milder effect. The pieces are added to curries, especially those containing fish; they impart a sour, slightly fruity taste. If it is unavailable, substitute ½ teaspoon fresh lemon juice for each piece of *kokum.*

MANGO

Mangoes belong to the same family as cashew and pistachio trees and are native to India, where they have been cultivated for thousands of years. Of the hundreds of varieties, the Alphonso is the most desired and therefore the most expensive. Mangoes are used green in curries and pickles, and ripe in summer puddings, chutneys, or by themselves.

TO CUBE A MANGO, cut the flesh in a single piece from either side of the pit. Crosshatch the flesh of each piece, being careful not to pierce the skin. Push the skin side so that the piece inverts and the cubes separate from each other, then cut them away from the skin.

MANGO POWDER

Made from unripe mangoes that have been peeled, dried, and ground to a pale gray-beige powder, mango powder has a strong aroma and sour tang. It is used as a souring agent, mainly in vegetarian cooking, and to tenderize meat. Lemon juice may be substituted.

MINT

The many varieties of mint all have a fresh, sweet smell and a mouth-freshening, sometimes peppery taste. The variety usually used for culinary purposes is spearmint; when dried, it is usually labeled simply as "mint." It is essential to North Indian cooking, where it finds its way into lamb dishes, breads, and snacks such as samosas and *chat.* When used in chutneys or *raita,* its freshness makes a welcome accompaniment to hot-and-spicy foods such as tandoori meats.

SPICE BLENDS

Spice blends, or *masalas*, are the heart of Indian food. Whether mild or hot, simple or complex, each blend provides the signature flavor of the dish for which it is created. A correctly blended mixture is one in which no single spice predominates; all should meld harmoniously, enhancing both each other and the other ingredients in the dish. To increase their flavor and aroma, most spices are roasted before being added to the *masala*. Grinding the mixture releases even more aroma. Many spices are roots, barks, and seeds, which are typically hard, woody, and/or fibrous substances and thus indigestible in their raw form. Cooking them solves this problem. They are usually fried in a small amount of ghee or oil as the first step in a recipe or to make a flavored oil that is added just before serving. Although many authentic spice blends are available commercially, it is easy to make your own. To maximize their shelf life, spice blends should always be stored in a sealed, airtight container in a cool, dry place. Do not keep stale spice blends; throw them out and start afresh.

CURRY POWDER

Curry powder is used mainly in the dishes of the south. Contrary to popular belief, it is not a single spice, but a mixture of spices. The Western-style curry powder that is stocked on supermarket shelves bears little similarity to the carefully blended, personalized mixtures that Indian cooks favor. The ingredients and their proportions vary between dishes, regions, and individual cooks, but the following is a typical blend.

3 tablespoons coriander seeds

2 teaspoons brown mustard seeds

2 teaspoons fenugreek seeds

2 teaspoons cumin seeds

1 teaspoon black peppercorns

6 whole cloves

8–12 dried red chiles, broken into pieces and seeds discarded

2 tablespoons roasted chickpeas (garbanzo beans)

2 tablespoons turmeric

In a dry frying pan over medium-high heat, combine the coriander, mustard, fenugreek, cumin, peppercorns, cloves, and chiles. Dry-fry the spices, shaking the pan constantly to prevent them from burning, until they are fragrant, about 5 minutes. Transfer to a small bowl, add the chickpeas and turmeric, and allow to cool. When completely cool, transfer to a mortar, blender, or coffee grinder reserved solely for spices and pound or process (in batches if necessary) until finely powdered. Use immediately, or store in a tightly sealed glass jar in a cool, dry place for up to 3 months.
Makes ½ cup (3½ oz / 105 g)

GARAM MASALA

This is the typical spice blend of northern India (indeed, garam masala simply means "spice blend"). It may be added during cooking or sprinkled over a dish just before serving. The more indigestible spices in this blend have already been roasted, which is why it can be sprinkled on at serving time, rather than cooked first in oil, as is the case with most other spices or spice blends.

2 tablespoons cumin seeds

2 tablespoons coriander seeds

2 tablespoons black peppercorns

1 tablespoon cardamom seeds

1 teaspoon whole cloves

3-inch cinnamon stick, broken into bits

1 teaspoon grated nutmeg

½ teaspoon saffron threads

In a dry frying pan over medium-high heat, combine the cumin, coriander, peppercorns, cardamom, cloves, and cinnamon stick. Dry-fry the spices, shaking the pan constantly to prevent them from burning, until they are smoking, fragrant, and turn several shades darker, about 6 minutes. Remove from the heat and stir in the nutmeg and saffron. Transfer to a bowl and allow to cool. When completely cool, transfer to a mortar, blender, or coffee grinder reserved solely for spices and pound or process (in batches if necessary) until finely powdered. Use immediately, or store in a tightly sealed glass jar in a cool, dry place for up to 3 months.
Makes ½ cup (3½ oz / 105 g)

PANCH PHORON

This is a blend of unroasted, whole spices that originated in Bengal and is now used mainly in eastern and northern India, where most seed spices are grown. Seed spices go well with carbohydrates, and *panch phoron* is often paired with potatoes. The name comes from the Hindi word for five, *panch,* and *phoron,* meaning "seeds." This five-spice blend should not be confused with Chinese five-spice powder.

1 tablespoon cumin seeds

1 tablespoon fennel seeds

1 tablespoon brown mustard seeds

1 tablespoon fenugreek seeds

1 tablespoon nigella seeds

In a glass jar, combine all the spices. Use immediately, or seal tightly and store in a cool, dry place for up to 1 year.
Makes ¼ cup (2 oz / 60 g)

MUSTARD SEEDS

Of the three types of mustard used as a spice, yellow mustard seeds have the mildest flavor. Black are the most pungent but are less easily obtained, as they cannot be mechanically harvested; they have largely been replaced by brown mustard, which is less delicate. Brown mustard seeds fall somewhere in between black and yellow in pungency; they can be substituted for black. Mustard seeds of any color have little aroma even when ground; it is only when they come into contact with a liquid that they give off their typical pungent, burning taste. When fried in oil as a preliminary step in the making of a curry, however, they develop a flavor that is nutty and piquant without being too hot. Mustard seeds are used in Indian pickles and in the spice blend *panch phoron.*

MUSTARD OIL

This strong-smelling, deep gold, viscous oil is widely used in eastern India and West Bengal. When used for frying, it is often heated to the smoking point, then allowed to cool a little to moderate its pungent smell.

NIGELLA SEEDS

Sometimes erroneously known as black cumin or onion seed (which it resembles but is not related to), nigella comes from an annual plant of the buttercup family. The tiny black seeds have little aroma and a sharp, metallic, peppery taste that tends to dry the throat. Nigella is used mostly in northern Indian cooking and in pickling. It has an affinity with carbohydrates, so is often used on nan bread and in dishes containing potatoes and other vegetables. It is also used in the spice blend *panch phoron.*

NUTMEG

The nutmeg tree is a tropical evergreen that produces both nutmeg (its seed) and the lesser-known mace (the seed covering). The fruit is sour and resembles a yellow nectarine. When ripe, it is split open and the mace and nutmeg are sun-dried separately. Once dried, the nutmeg has a thin outer shell and a hard inner kernel that is ground as a spice. Nutmeg has a high oil content; this enables it, unlike most other spices, to retain its strong, sweet, warm flavor very well even when ground. It is used mainly in Kashmiri and Moghul cooking.

PAPRIKA

Paprika is made from a range of finely ground, dried red bell peppers (capsicums). Spain and Hungary are the best-known producers of paprika, but India produces its own variety, which is grown in the valleys of Kashmir. Indian paprika is a brilliant red powder with a pungent scent but a mild, sweet taste. It features extensively in Kashmiri dishes, especially those containing meat, and is used mainly to add color. Hungarian or Spanish sweet paprika is a good substitute.

PEPPER

Pepper is the berry of the vine *Piper nigrum,* native to the equatorial forests of India and harvested in spring and summer. Black, white, green, and red peppercorns are the same berry, but picked at different stages of ripeness and processed in different ways. Green peppercorns are gathered while still unripe and are milder in flavor and less hot than ripe peppercorns. They are usually brined. Black peppercorns are simply green peppercorns that have been fermented for several days then dried. White peppercorns are obtained from berries that have been left on the vine until fully ripe, then soaked to loosen the skins, peeled, and the pale inner corns dried. Tree-ripened red peppercorns are seldom seen outside their country of origin. (The berries commonly called pink peppercorns do not come from the *Piper nigrum* plant and are not a true pepper at all but the berries of a South American tree.)

Black pepper is the most commonly used type in Indian recipes; it is used extensively in all regions and in all kinds of dishes. Until hot chiles were introduced to India late in the sixteenth century, pepper provided the heat for all Indian dishes. Ground pepper loses its pungency more quickly than other spices, so it is best to buy whole peppercorns and grind them as needed.

POMEGRANATE SEEDS

The deciduous pomegranate is native to Iran and may be either a large shrub or small tree. The red, apple-sized fruits have a leathery skin inside which a fibrous white membrane encases clusters of seeds. A juicy red pulp surrounds each seed; the seeds and pulp are the only edible parts of the fruit. Powdered, dried pomegranate seeds are used in Indian cooking as a souring agent, in much the same way as tamarind or mango powder. However, unlike mango powder, their flavor is fruity and sweet-sour rather than purely sour. There are three main varieties of pomegranate; the seeds of the sourer ones are preferred for drying. The seeds may be bought whole or ground in Indian grocery stores, where they may be labeled as *anardana.* If grinding the dried seeds yourself, use a mortar and pestle; their extreme stickiness will clog up a blender or coffee grinder. Store the dried seeds in an airtight container, as any humidity will make them even stickier. If unavailable, substitute 1 teaspoon of lemon juice for each teaspoon of pomegranate seeds.

POPPY SEEDS

Both white and black poppy seeds are available. The black seeds are usually used in Western dishes and the white in Indian, although they are quite similar in flavor and can be used interchangeably. Black poppy seeds are sometimes called blue, because of their slate-blue color. Both black and white poppy seeds come from the opium poppy, but have no narcotic effect; once the seeds have formed, all the plant's narcotic content is gone. Black poppy seeds are slightly larger than white, but both are tiny; one pound (500 g) of poppy seeds contains more than 750,000 seeds. Both types have a mild aroma and flavor; the flavor becomes stronger and nutty with roasting. Poppy seeds are used mostly in the cuisine of northern India. They are usually ground with other spices to serve as a thickener for meat, fish, and shellfish dishes.

ROSE ESSENCE AND ROSE WATER

Many classic Moghul dishes feature rose essence, which is extracted from small, intensely perfumed, deep-red roses grown for this purpose only. Rose essence may be used in its concentrated form or diluted to make rose water. Both preparations are used in Indian candies, desserts, and cold beverages.

SAFFRON

The world's most costly spice by weight, saffron comes from the perennial *Crocus sativus*. The crocus blossoms are hand-harvested, then the three stigmas from each flower are delicately removed, also by hand, and dried. Only when they are dried do they develop their intense, semisweet, woody aroma and pungent, earthy, slightly bitter flavor. Even more than for its flavor and aroma, however, saffron is valued for its brilliant orange-yellow color, which is characteristic of Spanish paellas and many Indian pilafs. (A natural dye in the stigmas is activated by water, which is why saffron is often infused in water, stock, or milk before being added to other ingredients.) Saffron should be used sparingly not only because of its cost, but also because increasing the quantity will not increase the aroma or flavor that it imparts.

SALT

Indispensable in every cuisine, salt has been prized since antiquity as both a preservative and a flavor enhancer. The different types of salt are mined from underground deposits or harvested from the sea. Common or cooking salt has been refined to remove impurities; it may be fine or coarse and sometimes has additives to make it flow freely. Table salt is a more refined version of common salt; it is finely ground and often iodized, a public health measure introduced in some countries in the 1920s to reduce the incidence of thyroid disorders. Coarse salt, also known as kosher salt, has a superior and less salty flavor than table salt. Sea salt has no additives, but has more minerals and flavor than table salt. Sea salts from different regions—such as the English Maldon sea salt and Fleur de sel from Brittany, France—possess subtle differences in flavor. Indian cooking employs many different varieties of salt, notably table, black, and coarse salt. Black salt is a characteristic ingredient of many northern Indian dishes.

SAMBAR POWDER

This hot spice mixture is used widely in the dishes of southern India. The ingredients and their proportions vary from one cook to another, but the essentials include red and black pepper, turmeric, fenugreek, coriander seeds, cumin seeds, and various types of legume.

SESAME OIL

Sesame seeds contain about 50 percent oil, which is extracted by cold pressing. Indian sesame oil is an important cooking fat in the south. Mild flavored and colorless, it cannot be replaced with Chinese or Japanese sesame oil, for which the seeds are roasted before pressing, intensifying the flavor and deepening the color.

TAMARIND

The fruits of the tamarind tree, native to India, bear seedpods containing dark brown seeds surrounded by an acidic pulp that is used as a souring agent in many Indian recipes. Tamarind is available commercially in two main forms. The block form comprises a sticky mass of compressed seeds and pulp. The required amount is taken from the block and soaked in hot water to extract the flavor; the resulting liquid is known as tamarind water. A concentrated form is available in jars and is very convenient.

TAMARIND WATER

1-inch (2.5-cm) ball tamarind pulp

1 cup (8 fl oz/250 ml) boiling water

❧ In a heatproof bowl, combine the pulp with the water and let stand until softened, about 30 minutes. Using your fingers, squeeze and press the tamarind to release as much pulp as possible into the water. Strain, discarding the fibrous residue.
Makes 1 cup (8 fl oz/250 ml)

STAR ANISE

The star-shaped fruits borne by a small evergreen tree of the magnolia family, star anise is picked unripe and dried. Despite the name, it is unrelated to anise. Both the flavor and aroma of star anise are sweet, strong, and licoricelike. The spice is not used widely in India, but it sometimes flavors pilafs and *biryanis*.

TURMERIC

This brilliant yellow spice comes from the rhizome of a tropical plant native to Southeast Asia. The knobbly rhizome has a buff-colored skin and resembles ginger, to which it is related. It can be used fresh, in which form it should always be peeled first. It is more commonly boiled, dried, and ground to produce a fine powder with an earthy smell and a sharp, lingering, slightly bitter flavor. Turmeric is widely grown and processed in India. It is the main ingredient in commercial curry powder and is used widely, mostly in southern India, to color and flavor vegetable, legume, meat, and poultry dishes. Turmeric has also been used for centuries as a dye, the various types giving different depths and tones of color.

YOGURT

Yogurt is an essential part of the Indian diet, especially that of vegetarians. Indian yogurt, generally made with buffalo's milk, is thicker, sweeter, and less tart than that made with cow's milk. Indian cooks use yogurt as a meat tenderizer, souring agent, thickener, and flavor enhancer. It turns up in almost every kind of food, from dumplings and curries to desserts and drinks. Most Indians make their own yogurt at home from fresh milk bought that morning. Indian yogurt is not commercially available in Western countries; any good brand of full-fat or low-fat plain yogurt may be substituted.

INDEX

Rasedar, 95

Rava dosa, 195

Religious laws and dietary restrictions, 75, 78, 111, 144

Religious festivals and customs 50, 59, 69, 72, 77, 80, 90, 154, 171, 183, 188, 195, 207, 230. *See also* Eating habits and styles

Rice, 180-181, 183, 188, 247. *See also* Pilaf
  lemon, with mustard seeds, 189
  plain basmati, 183

Rice flake pilaf with shallots, 213

Rice noodles with coconut, Madras stir-fried, 198

Rice pudding, 230

Richeiado, 124

Rose essence and rose water, 251

Roti, 196

Royal Lucknow kabobs, 34

Rum and cashew nut ice cream, 239

~ S ~

Saag gosht, 113

Sada chawal, 183

Saffron, 201, 251
  crisp pastries in saffron syrup, 242
  basmati pilaf, 201
  milk cooler, 228
  sesame crunch, 234

Sak, 159

Salad
  chicken *chat,* 107
  coconut and smoked chile yogurt, 157
  crispy noodle, with hot and sweet chutneys, 60
  lentil dumplings and yogurt, 167
  mango yogurt, 164
  mint-yogurt, 168
  peach, with mint and smoked cumin, 35
  tomato and yogurt, 150

Salad sandwich, egg, 114

Salt, 167, 251

Sambar, 88

Sambar powder, 251

Samosas, 33

Savory crackers with black pepper, 54

Savory pastries with vegetable stuffing, 33

Seafood, 76–7
  shrimp fry, masala, 69
  shrimp in spiced cream sauce, 106
  spice-rubbed grilled shrimp, 124
  spicy fish, 121

Semolina, 247
  crepes with bell peppers, 195
  halva with golden raisins, 237
  pilaf, 185

Sesame crunch, saffron, 234

Sesame oil, 251

Sev chatni, 192

Sevian payasam, 233

Shakkaravellikayangu bonda, 46–47

Shallots, rice flake pilaf with, 213

Shikampuri kabab, 99

Shrimp. *See* Seafood

Sindhi eggplant in sweet and sour tamarind sauce, 101

Sookha bomla nu cutless, 36

Sorpotel, 104–105

Soup
  buttermilk, with chickpea pearls, 65
  chilled fruity yogurt, 39
  cream of pumpkin, 49
  creamy lentil, with caramelized onion, 60
  curried chicken and vegetable, 43
  fragrant spinach, with cumin-scented potato croutons, 52
  kari leaf-scented tomato broth, 63
  sweet corn, with chile oil, 51

Spiced cashews, 67

Spicy scrambled eggs, 110

Spinach
  fragrant spinach soup with cumin-scented potato croutons, 52
  lamb with, 113
  Tanjore wilted, 151

Split pea
  fritters with cashew nuts, 65
  fritters in spicy sauce, 126
  nuggets, broccoli smothered with spicy, 98

Split peas, yellow, 247

Squash
  chutney, 199
  mung beans and squash with mustard seeds, 160

Star anise, 251

Strawberry ka sas, 239

Strawberry sauce, 239

Sweet corn soup with chile oil, 51

Sweets, Indian, 218–225, 242

~ T ~

Takkalipayam chatni, 214

Takkalipayam pachadi, 150

Tamarind, 129, 251

chutney, 185
water, 251

Tandoor cooking, 72, 75, 96
  tandoori chicken, 96–97
  tandoori grilled fish, 108
  tandoori mint bread, 209

Tandoori machi, 108

Tandoori murghi, 96–97

Tea, 237
  green, 227
  Madras ginger, 236
  spiced, 233

Tenga sevai, 198

Tethi kori, 88

Thali-style eating, 29

Tiffin, 69

Tomato
  broth, kari leaf-scented, 63
  chutney, hot and spicy, 214
  and yogurt salad, 150

Tori chatni, 199

Tori moong, 160

Turmeric, 251

~ U ~

Usili, 98

Usli ghee, 83, 247

~ V ~

Vanaspati ghee, 247

Vayakai bhajjia, 55

Vegetables, 77–78. *See also* by name of vegetable
  in cumin-scented tomato gravy, 95
  dried, 62
  savory pastries with vegetable stuffing, 33

Vermicelli pudding, creamy, 233

~ Y ~

Yam dumplings with roasted corn and cinnamon, 46–47

Yera varuval, 69

Yogurt, 83, 141, 251
  bread, puffy, 186
  drink, minty, 229
  Marvari okra in yogurt sauce, 102
  soup, chilled fruity, 39

Yogurt salad
  coconut and smoked chile, 157
  lentil dumplings and, 167
  mango, 164
  mint-, 168
  tomato and, 150

ACKNOWLEDGMENTS

Julie Sahni wishes to thank the following individuals and organizations for their assistance: I am deeply indebted to my mother, Padma Ranganathan, for nurturing my love of food and inspiring me to write this book. I also wish to thank Micki Trager, my assistant, for her help in its production; Arun Sinha, owner of Food of India, New York City, for his help with research; my editor, Janine Flew, for her enthusiasm and attention to detail; Sheena Coupe and Lynn Humphries of Weldon Owen for their encouragement and faith in the project. I also wish to extend my gratitude to Hazrat Ali; Asha Bhen; Veerappa Chettiyar; Victor D'Souza; Suchita Ghosh; Harbinder Kaur; Imayat Khan; Maya Parishad; Jaya Patel; Sunil Patel; Geeta Rajagopalan; Meenakshi Reddy; Begam Akhtar Rehman; Bimal Roy; Chandan Sen; Susheela Shetty; Rangeeta Uppal; the Government of India Spices Board; India Tourist Offices in New Delhi, Madras, Goa, Calcutta, Cochin, Hyderabad, Bombay, and Ahmadabad; the Rambagh Palace Hotel and Vilas Bhawan Hotel in Jaipur; the Maurya Hotel and Imperial Hotel in New Delhi; the Taj Coromandel Hotel in Madras; the Taj Hotel in Bombay; the Casino Hotel and Taj Malabar Hotel in Cochin; Michael Freeman, for his evocative scenic photography; the food photography team, Andre Martin, Sally Parker, Christine Shepherd, and Jacqueline Richards, for bringing my recipes so stunningly to life; and Marlene McLoughlin, for her exquisite illustrations.

Michael Freeman wishes to thank Subir Bhowmick, Chief Operating Officer and Sr. Vice-President, Luxury Division, The Taj Group of Hotels; and the staff at the Lake Palace Hotel in Udaipur, Rajasthan, for their hospitality and generous assistance.

Andre Martin wishes to thank Sally Parker for propping and styling; Jacqueline Richards for art direction; Lynn Humphries for her encouragement; and his wife, Nikki, and children, Benito, Pablo, and Isabella, for their patience and support.

Sally Parker wishes to thank Christine Shepherd for her excellence in the kitchen; and Bernard Heaphy, Dhruma Patel, and Kati Watson for their help in sourcing props.

Weldon Owen would like to thank Travel Spirit International; the Samode Palace Hotel, Jaipur, Rajasthan, for kindly allowing the use of the photograph on page 178; Jatinder Taneja of indiaheritagehotels.com; Sarah Anderson, Michael Hann, Marney Richardson, and Bronwyn Sweeney (editorial assistance); Nancy Sibtain (index and proofreading); Hannah Rahill; Donita Boles; Gaye Allen; and Chris Hemesath.

OXMOOR HOUSE INC.

Oxmoor House books are distributed by Sunset Books,
80 Willow Road, Menlo Park, CA 94025
Telephone: 650-321-3600 Fax: 650-324-1532

Vice President/General Manager: Rich Smeby
Director of Special Sales: Gary Wright

Oxmoor House and Sunset Books are divisions of
Southern Progress Corporation

WILLIAMS-SONOMA INC.
Founder and Vice-Chairman: Chuck Williams
Book Buyer: Cecilia Michaelis

WELDON OWEN PTY LTD.
Chief Executive Officer: John Owen
President: Terry Newell
Chief Operating Officer: Larry Partington
Publisher: Sheena Coupe
Associate Publisher: Lynn Humphries
Art Director: Sue Burk
Project Editor: Janine Flew
Design Concept: Kari Ontko, India Ink
Design: Jacqueline Richards, PinchMe Design
Editorial Coordinator: Tracey Gibson
Consulting Editor: Sharon Silva
Production Managers: Helen Creeke, Gilly Biven, Chris Hemesath
Production Coordinator: Kylie Lawson
Calligraphy: Jane Dill
Vice President International Sales: Stuart Laurence

THE SAVORING SERIES
conceived and produced by Weldon Owen Inc.
814 Montgomery Street, San Francisco, CA 94133
Telephone: 415-291-0100, Fax: 415-291-8841

In collaboration with Williams-Sonoma Inc.
3250 Van Ness Avenue, San Francisco, CA 94109

Savoring® is a registered trademark of Weldon Owen Inc.

p 2: Chicken Malai Kabob and Lamb with Spinach (recipes page 113). **pp 4–5:** A couple finds an escape from India's characteristic crowds in a recess of Agra's famous Taj Mahal. **pp 6–7:** In the mountainous northeastern state of Assam lies Darjeeling, where tea plantations flourish due to the cool air and abundant rainfall. **pp 8–9:** A vendor in Old Delhi's Naya Bazaar displays the spices and legumes that form the cornerstones of Indian cuisine. **pp 12–13:** A *sadhu*, or holy man, sits by his dwelling on a hill above the Tamil Nadu town of Tiruvannamalai; in the distance is the Arunachaleshvara temple.

A WELDON OWEN PRODUCTION
Copyright © 2001 Weldon Owen Inc.

First printed 2001
10 9 8 7 6 5 4 3 2

Library of Congress
Cataloging-in-Publication Data

Sahni, Julie.
Savoring India : recipes and reflections on Indian cooking /
recipes and text Julie Sahni ; general editor, Chuck Williams ; recipe
photography, Andre Martin ; food stylist, Sally Parker ; illustrations,
Marlene McLoughlin
p. cm.
Includes index.
ISBN 0-7370-2050-4
1. Cookery, India. I. Williams, Chuck. II. Title.
TX724.5.I4 S33 2001
641.5954—dc21   2001027506

Separations by Colourscan Overseas Co. Pte. Ltd.
Printed in Singapore by Tien Wah Press (Pte.) Ltd.